Charles A. Higgins

New Guide to the Pacific Coast

Santa Fé Route

Charles A. Higgins

New Guide to the Pacific Coast
Santa Fé Route

ISBN/EAN: 9783337147815

Printed in Europe, USA, Canada, Australia, Japan

Cover: Foto ©Lupo / pixelio.de

More available books at **www.hansebooks.com**

GREAT CABLE INCLINE ON MOUNT LOWE RAILROAD, CALIFORNIA.
(See page 207.)

NEW GUIDE

TO THE

PACIFIC COAST

Santa Fé Route.

—

CALIFORNIA,

ARIZONA, NEW MEXICO, COLORADO, KANSAS, MISSOURI, IOWA, AND ILLINOIS.

By C. A. HIGGINS.

CHICAGO AND NEW YORK:
RAND, McNALLY & COMPANY.
1894.

CONTENTS.

	PAGE
PREFACE, - - - - - -	7
ILLINOIS, - - - - - -	10
IOWA, - - - - - -	14
MISSOURI, - - - - - -	14
KANSAS, - - - - - -	18
COLORADO, - - - - - -	38
NEW MEXICO, - - - - -	64
ARIZONA, - - - - - -	108
CALIFORNIA, - - - - -	158
VOCABULARY, - - - - -	262

PREFACE.

THIS Guidebook embraces a journey from Chicago to the Pacific Coast by way of the Santa Fé Route, and covers a similar journey from St. Louis as well, since after the first few hundred miles, namely, beyond Burrton, Kan., the route is the same from both cities. It aims to furnish general information regarding the regions traversed, and specific data concerning particular points of interest by the way. Doubtless more has been included than would suffice to answer the general inquiries of any one tourist, but he must offer much who would bring something to many, and what one reader may consider good matter to skip another may regard as pertinent and profitable. To facilitate both, so far as practicable, the text has been systematically arranged under definitive headings. Extended description of special objects of interest has been restricted to such as can not be seen, or can not be appreciated, except by stopping over and making a side-excursion away from the thoroughfare.

The United States Census for 1890 is authority for the population of towns and cities given herein, unless otherwise stated. Since the date of that census, it is hardly necessary to add, the number of inhabitants of many of those communities has materially increased.

The attention of the reader is invited to the index of this volume, and for the pronunciation and signification of unfamiliar names he is referred to the appended vocabulary.

CHICAGO TO KANSAS CITY.

ILLINOIS, IOWA, AND MISSOURI.

IT IS customary for through trains from Chicago to the Pacific Coast to leave that city at night. Description of a State which the traveler is assumed to be in the act of quitting, or of its immediate neighbor on the west, which will have been crossed and left far behind before the dawn of another day, should be confined to narrow limits, and in the nature of the case a brief and somewhat general mention will suffice for the features of the entire region east of Kansas; for while Illinois, Iowa, and Missouri are indeed western, the West lies farther on, and the active curiosity of the tourist is usually concentrated upon that section of the country which is beyond the Missouri River. Although there still is room and to spare in these three States, they no longer wear a marked romantic aspect to the traveler. The Indian has long since abandoned their plains and river-valleys, the large game has fled, and the era of the pioneer has given place to that of general agriculture, manufacture, and trade. Have many years gone by since a song was current glorifying a dimly apprehended region somewhere far toward the sunset, "Where the mighty Missouri rolls down to the sea"? Did we not sing that as school-children, we whose heads are not yet quite gray, not yet conspicuously unthatched; picturing an adventurous land at the end of

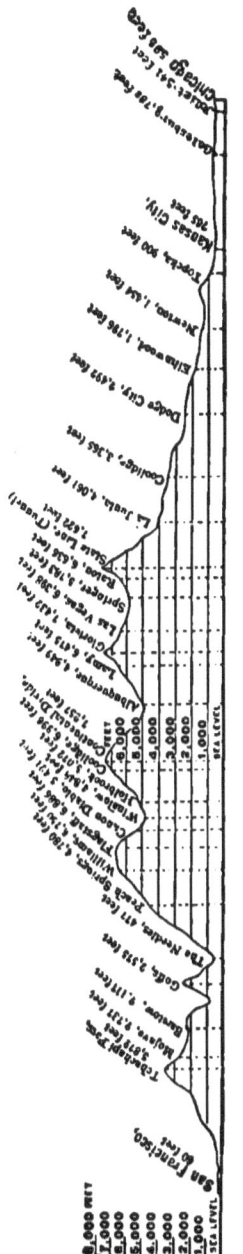

the westernmost ray of the Star of Empire, beyond which lay the mystery of a vast untrodden wild? The Missouri! If we see it at all we must be up betimes to-morrow, for its channel lies almost at the threshold of our journey; it is in the very heart of the United States. And across and beyond it our way lies on and on, over still wider prairies, over mountain passes, over deserts in the sky, and down again to where the blue waves of the Pacific beat upon sunny sands, where the violet and poppy smother the hillsides, and the olive and fig and orange grow.

In the prospect of such an array of varied and interesting scenes as marks a journey to the Pacific Coast, therefore, only an enumeration of a few landmarks and mileposts will be attempted until, the first night having passed, there is something to see and inquire about.

ILLINOIS.

Chicago.— Los Angeles, 2,265 miles; San Diego, 2,348 miles; San Francisco (via Albuquerque), 2,577 miles. Altitude, 579 feet above sea level. Population (in the year 1891), 1,438,010. Terminus of the following railroads: Atchison,

Topeka & SantaFé; Baltimore & Ohio; Chicago & Erie; Chicago & Alton; Chicago & Eastern Illinois; Chicago & Grand Trunk; Chicago & Northern Pacific; Chicago & North-Western; Chicago, Burlington & Quincy; Cleveland, Cincinnati, Chicago & St. Louis; Chicago, Milwaukee & St. Paul; Chicago, Rock Island & Pacific; Chicago & West Michigan; Chicago Great Western; Illinois Central; Lake Shore & Michigan Southern; Louisville, New Albany & Chicago; Michigan Central; Milwaukee, Lake Shore & Western; New York, Lake Erie & Western; Northern Pacific; Pennsylvania lines (Pan-handle, and Pittsburg, Fort Wayne & Chicago); Wabash, and the Wisconsin Central Line.

The terminal passenger station of the Santa Fé Route in Chicago is situated at the intersection of Dearborn and Polk streets, and is familiarly known both as Dearborn Station and as Polk Street Station. Here also the trains of the Chicago & Grand Trunk Railway; the Chicago & Erie Railroad; the Chicago & Eastern Illinois Railroad; the Chicago & Western Indiana Railroad; the Louisville, New Albany & Chicago Railway (Monon Route); and the Wabash Railroad, arrive and depart.

The many other depots that furnish terminal facilities are spacious and substantial. The 1,400 hotels in the city easily accommodate 200,000 people, their charges varied to suit every class of traveler.

The first building on the present site of Chicago was erected in the year 1779 by a negro named Jean Baptiste Point de Saible. The first white inhabitant was John Kinzie, an Indian trader, who became possessor of this man's hut in 1804. In the year 1825 Chicago was a hamlet, consisting of fourteen cabins. It was incorporated as a town in 1833, with a population of 150. The first paper was issued November 26, 1833. In 1837 the population had increased to 4,170. The year previous the first railroad — the Galena & Chicago Union — entered the town. From that time the city rapidly grew until the fire of

1871 swept away the greater part, and destroyed property valued at $196,000,000. It soon started afresh on its course of progress, which has gone on uninterruptedly until the present day, except for the check caused by the second fire in 1874. Perhaps the feature that most strikes the visitor is the great number of immense and lofty business blocks. One of them, the Masonic Temple, twenty-one stories high, is one of the largest office buildings in the world. It stands at the corner of State and Randolph streets. The city covers an area of 184 square miles, 1,793 acres of which are public park. The assessment for tax purposes is $250,000,000, which is about one-fifth of the real value. It will surprise many to know that Chicago is the greatest port in America. In the year 1891 vessels to the number of 9,803 entered the harbor, making it the third port, if not the second, in the world — Liverpool, and possibly London, taking precedence of it.

After quitting the environs of the World's Fair city several small towns are passed before any point of particular prominence is reached.

INTERMEDIATE STATIONS: McCook, Gary, Willow Springs, Byrneville, Tedens, Lemont, Romeo, Lockport.

Joliet.—Chicago, 41 miles; Los Angeles, 2,224 miles; San Diego, 2,307 miles; San Francisco, 2,536 miles. Altitude, 553 feet. Population, 23,264. Junction with Chicago, Rock Island & Pacific Railway, Chicago & Alton Railroad, and Elgin, Joliet & Eastern Railway (Belt Line).

A very important manufacturing city on the Desplaines River. The State penitentiary stands on the left of the railroad track, and on the right are the rolling mills of the Illinois Steel Company and the wire works of the Consolidated Steel & Wire Company.

INTERMEDIATE STATIONS: Patterson, Millsdale, Drummond, Blodgett, Knappa (at the crossing of the Kankakee River), Lorenzo, Coal City, Mazon, Verona, Kinsman, Ransom, Kernan.

Streator.—Chicago, 94 miles; Los Angeles, 2,171 miles; San Diego, 2,254 miles; San Francisco, 2,483 miles. Altitude, 640 feet. Population, 14,414. Junction with the Wabash Railroad, Chicago & Alton Railroad, and Chicago, Burlington & Quincy Railroad.

A manufacturing and coal-mining city situated on the Vermilion River.

INTERMEDIATE STATION : Reading.

Ancona.—Chicago, 100 miles; Los Angeles, 2,165 miles; San Diego, 2,248 miles; San Francisco, 2,477 miles. Altitude, 645 feet.

Diverging point of the line of the Santa Fé Route to Pekin, Ill., and to Peoria by a connection with the Toledo, Peoria & Western Railway at Eureka.

INTERMEDIATE STATIONS: Leeds, Caton, Toluca, La Rose, Wilburn.

Chillicothe.—Chicago, 134 miles; Los Angeles, 2,131 miles; San Diego, 2,214 miles; San Francisco, 2,443 miles. Altitude, 530 feet. Population, 1,632. Junction with Chicago, Rock Island & Pacific Railway.

Located on the Illinois River. A heavy grain-shipping point, and headquarters of the Chicago-Kansas City Division of the Santa Fé Route.

INTERMEDIATE STATIONS: Edelstein, Princeville, Monica, Laura, Williamsfield, Dahinda, Appleton, Knox.

Galesburg.—Chicago, 182 miles; Los Angeles, 2,083 miles; San Diego, 2,166 miles; San Francisco, 2,395 miles. Altitude, 771 feet. Population, 15,264. Junction with Chicago, Burlington & Quincy Railroad, and the Fulton County Narrow Gauge Railway.

A manufacturing city. Also a center of importation of European draft horses.

INTERMEDIATE STATIONS: Surrey, Cameron, Nemo,

Ormonde, Ponemah, Smithshire, Media, Stronghurst, Decorra, Lomax, Dallas, Pontoosuc.

Niota.—Chicago, 235 miles. Altitude, 539 feet.

On the banks of the Mississippi River.

Mississippi River Bridge.—Chicago, 236 miles. 3,240 feet long, and 32 feet above low-water mark.

IOWA.

Ft. Madison.—Chicago, 237 miles; Los Angeles, 2,028 miles; San Diego, 2,111 miles; San Francisco, 2,340 miles. Altitude, 537 feet. Population, 7,901. Junction with Chicago, Burlington & Quincy Railroad and Chicago, Ft. Madison & Des Moines Railway.

An important Mississippi River port.

From Ft. Madison the route crosses the southeastern corner of the State of Iowa from the Mississippi River to the Des Moines River, a distance of twenty miles.

INTERMEDIATE STATIONS: Ft. Madison Shops, Macuta, New Boston, Argyle.

MISSOURI.

INTERMEDIATE STATIONS: Dumas, Revere.

Medill.—Chicago, 268 miles. Altitude, 719 feet. Junction with the Keokuk & Western Railroad, one mile east of Medill Station.

INTERMEDIATE STATIONS: Cama, Wyaconda, Gorin, Rutledge, Baring, Kenwood.

Hurdland.—Chicago, 315 miles. Altitude, 842 feet. Population, 248. Junction with the Quincy, Omaha & Kansas City Railway.

INTERMEDIATE STATION: Gibbs.

La Plata.—Chicago, 317 miles. Altitude, 929 feet. Population, 1,169. Junction with the Wabash Railroad.

INTERMEDIATE STATIONS: Oliver, Elmer, Ethel, Hart.

Bucklin.—Chicago, 346 miles. Altitude, 932 feet. Population, 711. Junction with Hannibal & St. Joseph Railroad.

Marceline.—Chicago, 352 miles; Los Angeles, 1,913 miles; San Diego, 1,996 miles; San Francisco, 2,225 miles. Altitude, 873 feet. Population, 1,977. Junction with Chicago, Burlington & Kansas City Railway.

INTERMEDIATE STATIONS: Rothville, Mendon, Dean Lake, Bosworth, Newcomb, Carrollton, Palemon, Norborne, Nimrod, Hardin.

Lexington Junction.—Chicago, 416 miles; Los Angeles, 1,849 miles; San Diego, 1,932 miles; San Francisco, 2,161 miles. Altitude, 709 feet. Junction with Wabash Railroad. Diverging point of the line of the Santa Fé Route to St. Joseph, Mo., and Atchison, Kan.

INTERMEDIATE STATIONS: Camden, Floyd.

Missouri River Bridge.—Chicago, 429 miles. 7,552 feet long, including approaches, and 92 feet above low-water mark.

INTERMEDIATE STATIONS: Sibley, Atherton, Courtney, Wayne, Sheffield, Fifteenth Street (Kansas City), Grand Avenue (Kansas City).

Kansas City (Union Depot).—Chicago, 458 miles; Los Angeles, 1,807 miles; San Diego, 1,890 miles; San Francisco, 2,119 miles. Altitude, 765 feet. Population, 171,032. Junction with Chicago, Rock Island & Pacific Railway; Hannibal & St. Joseph Railroad; Burlington & Missouri River Railroad; Kansas City, St. Joseph & Council Bluffs Railroad; Wabash, St. Louis & Pacific Railway; Chicago & Alton Railroad; Missouri Pacific Railway; Kansas City, Fort Scott & Memphis Railroad; Union Pacific Railway; Chicago, Milwaukee & St. Paul Railway; Chicago Great Western Railway; Kansas City, Wyandotte & North-Western Railroad; Kansas City, Pittsburg & Gulf Railroad; Kansas City, Osceola & Southern Railway.

16 NEW GUIDE TO THE PACIFIC COAST.

UNION DEPOT, KANSAS CITY.

The city is located on the south bank of the Missouri River. It is a city of hills and bluffs, not particularly intelligible nor attractive in the few inadequate glimpses possible from the train; but that is commonly true of cities. The residence portion, as well as most of the business district except that which naturally clusters closely around railroad terminals, lies above and on the right. The steeply inclined bridge over the track, just beyond the Union Depot, over which cable cars are passing, leads to the main part of the city.

It was at first a landing-place for river steamboats, and was known as Westport Landing. The first stock of goods was thus landed in 1834. In the course of the next half a dozen years a few frame houses were erected, but so late as 1853 the inhabitants numbered only 478. The arbitrary laws of commerce, however, had decreed that at this point a great city should arise, and in 1870 the population had increased to 32,286. In 1885, 128,474 people dwelt here, and the commercial activity of the city had become something extraordinary. It offers to the traveler from older communities a striking example of the rapidity of Western progress. It is second only to Chicago in pork-packing and beef-canning and in the number of live-stock handled in its stock-yards. Ore-smelting and numerous manufactures are also carried on upon a large scale. It is a transcontinental gateway, and the natural trade center for much of Missouri, Kansas, Arkansas, Texas, and Colorado, and for Oklahoma, New Mexico, and Arizona; the distribution of its wares and the absorption of much of the products of the regions named being rendered easy by water-carriage and by the many railroads that center here.

It is really composed of two cities — Kansas City, Mo., and Kansas City, Kan., the population of each being, respectively, 132,716 and 38,316.

KANSAS.

HISTORICAL.—The name is Indian, and was borne by the particular people whom the first settlers of Kansas found in possession of the country. The French fur traders — *voyageurs* — had stations here nearly a century and a half before it was actually settled, and to their pronunciation of the word Kansas has been ascribed the origin of the word Kaw, long applied both to that particular tribe of Indians and to the river upon whose banks they dwelt. Coronado indelibly stamped his name as discoverer upon a very large part of the West. His extraordinary expedition from Mexico in 1540 extended as far as the northern boundary of this State, which he appears to have traversed in a northeasterly direction. His advent into this particular region was barren of result. He came, saw, and went away. In 1719 a second Spanish invasion came from New Mexico to occupy the country in advance of the French, who were actively exploring the Missouri River, but the Spaniards, with the exception of a priest, were massacred by the Indians. A large tract of central North America thereupon fell to France. It stretched from the Gulf of Mexico north to British America, and from the Mississippi River west to a line which serves now for the eastern boundary of Texas, thence along the north bank of the Arkansas River to central Colorado, and from there irregularly northwest to a point near the upper western corner of Montana. This was the province of Louisiana, whose entire purchase by the United States was completed by the treaty of April 30, 1819. The little southwestern corner of Kansas below the Arkansas River was subsequently acquired from Mexico, in the final solution of the Texas struggle. In 1823 a trading route was established between Booneville (now Franklin), on the Missouri River, and Santa Fé, in New Mexico. Nine years afterward Independence, near Kansas City, became the point of outfitting and departure for western freighters. The story of the Santa Fé Trail is one of the most romantic and tragic chapters in the history of the West. The Indians promised it freedom from molestation, in a council meeting with United States Commissioners, but the old trail marks a line of blood across many hundred miles of plain. Ambuscade and butchery, with all the fearful details of savage warfare, were a daily occurrence. Fort Leavenworth was established to protect the traders, and escorts of mounted soldiers accompanied the wagon trains. This trade with Santa Fé and the Southwest became in time so great as to employ thousands of men and wagons. The trail led along the Arkansas River, over the Raton Pass from Colorado to New Mexico, thence through Wagon Mound and Las Vegas to the New Mexican capital. The course of the Santa Fé Route is almost identical with the old trail throughout. The military post at Fort Leavenworth was established in 1827, and there, in 1850, the first real settlement of Kansas began. In ten years Kansas numbered a hundred thousand inhabitants, and in 1861 was admitted to the Union.

The greater part of Kansas was originally included in the extensive Territory of Missouri, that portion of the Louisiana province purchased from the French in 1803. A portion of that Territory became the State of Missouri in 1821, after long opposition on the part of the antislavery States, by virtue of the Missouri Compromise, a compact which resulted in the passage of an act forever forbidding slavery in all that part of the Louisiana purchase north of 36° 30', except within the comparatively small bounds of the newly admitted State of Missouri. In

1854 that act was repealed, and each new commonwealth arising in the formerly exempted Territory was left free to settle the question for itself. In Kansas the struggle of the two great sectional ideas for supremacy was a bitter contention, and here the armies of North and South first encountered. John Brown first became famous in connection with this Kansas war, and the State won the sobriquet of "Bleeding Kansas." Property was destroyed and many lives were lost, until in 1859 the question at stake was settled by the adoption of a constitution forbidding slavery. In the immediately ensuing War of the Rebellion the State suffered further, and not until the close of ten years' strife did these men who had so actively contended for opposing principles find uninterrupted opportunity to develop the resources of the State. The building of railroads was wisely encouraged by immense grants of land in alternate parcels contiguous to several proposed lines, conditioned upon actual construction within a specified period. Eastern capital promptly seized the proffered opportunity, the sale and settlement of the acquired lands was undertaken by the recipient corporations through numerous agencies both at home and abroad, and in consequence immigrants poured into the State by thousands, from the Middle and Eastern States and from foreign countries. In 1870 the population had increased to 364,369. In 1880 it was 996,096. The United States census of 1890 gives 1,427,096.

Kansas boasts a smaller percentage of illiteracy and crime than any other community of which such statistics are kept. There are 3,800 churches and 9,000 schools within its borders.

DESCRIPTIVE.—Kansas comprises an area of 82,080 square miles in the center of the Union. In length it is 408 miles, and in breadth 208 miles, having the form of a parallelogram, symmetrical in outline, save where the Missouri River cuts a slice from the northeastern corner.

THE KAW VALLEY PEOPLE OF 1855.

It is an inclined plane, with undulating surface, rising easily from an altitude of about 750 feet upon the east to nearly 3,500 feet at the western bound. Although a prairie country, it is neither flat nor monotonous, but rolls in gentle billows, forming a pleasing pastoral landscape that becomes exceedingly beautiful in early summer. It has the breadth of ocean to the eye, nevertheless, and a charm that outlasts the novelty of first acquaintance. It can not boast a mountain, nor much timber, save that which has been planted since its settlement. It is carpeted with nutritious grasses, and the intervals are green with orchards, gardens, and growing grain.

Progressing westward the amount of rainfall and the number of small streams decrease, until in the extreme western counties a condition of aridity is reached that, over large areas, thus far has proved hostile to agriculture, except in the moister valleys, or where the waters of the Arkansas can be diverted by means of irrigating ditches, although in many localities artesian wells provide a good supply of water. Many prairie-dog towns will be seen by the traveler in that region.

The rock formations that underlie Kansas have yielded great numbers of fossils of the most uncouth and gigantic prehistoric animals, many specimens of which are exhibited in the National Museum at Washington. When Kansas was the shore of a vast sea it was inhabited by monsters whose existence would be scouted did not the imperishable rock preserve their skeletons.

It is a land of pretty towns, developing with astonishing rapidity year by year. In each of them the church and school-house are prominent objects, and the public saloon is conspicuous by utter absence. These energetic old fellows, who settled the question of slavery for themselves before the Civil War began, established prohibition in Kansas long before they took up the Farmers' Alliance or formed the Populist party. They have a remarkable faculty of putting theories into practice.

CLIMATE.—The average annual rainfall varies greatly, according to locality. The record at Fort Leavenworth for fifty-seven years gives a yearly average of thirty-three inches; twenty-three years at Lawrence averaged thirty-four inches; twelve years at Topeka, thirty-two inches; thirty-five years at Manhattan and Fort Riley, thirty inches; fourteen years at Dodge City, twenty-one inches; five years at Fort Wallace, thirteen inches. The rain comes principally in the early summer months, and in some years, following a period of extreme dryness in July or August, excessive heat is experienced, accompanied by hot winds, sometimes of a high velocity. These hot winds were formerly believed to originate on the "staked plains" of Texas and New Mexico, as they most commonly came from the southwest, but are now known to be caused, as in Nebraska and the Dakotas, by the passage of ordinary winds over the heated surface of the dry, unbroken plains of the State. The increasing area of cultivation has already very greatly reduced the frequency and severity of the hot winds, which acquired an unpleasant notoriety in the days of the buffalo and the caravan.

The mean annual temperature varies from 52° to 57°, according to locality, that of the extreme western portion being a few degrees lower than that of the eastern, by reason of a higher altitude. The climate of Kansas is heathful, and commonly very agreeable. Even when in midsummer the sun becomes torrid and the air oppressive through the day, with nightfall a delicious breeze blows over the prairie, and after the hottest day the Kansan sleeps in comfort. The winters are commonly mild. For persons who have weak lungs it is a desirable dwelling place, and several points in the western part, where the altitude is less pronounced than in Colorado or northern New Mexico, are utilized by sensitive patients journeying to those regions for recuperation as temporary stopping places where to accomplish a gradual adjustment to greater elevations and more rarefied air.

INDUSTRIAL.— Kansas is most familiarly known to the world as an agricultural and grazing State. In the ten years from 1882 to 1891, inclusive, it produced the astonishing total of 1,561,972,631 bushels of corn and 284,085,374 bushels of wheat. The average yield per acre for the entire period of ten years was 27.88 bushels of corn and 15.14 bushels of wheat, the highest average for any single year being 40.1 for the former and 22.6 for the latter. In 1892 the yield of corn was 138,658,621 bushels, and of wheat 74,538,906 bushels. The State includes many other important agricultural products, a few items in addition to the two great cereals being as follows: Oats, 43,722,484 bushels; barley, 3,842,954 bushels; rye, 4,042,613 bushels; buckwheat, 62,808 bushels; flax, 1,245,555 bushels; hemp, 32,900 pounds; cotton, 145,300 pounds; potatoes, 4,557,504 bushels; tobacco, 222,600 pounds; castor beans, 81,987 bushels; broomcorn, 34,016,950 pounds; and 800,000 pounds of sugar was manufactured from sorghum. Vast quantities of apples, pears, peaches, cherries, and plums are annually raised, and there are numerous vineyards. Of livestock there are in round numbers 805,000 horses, 79,000 mules and asses, 631,000 milch cows, 240,000 sheep, 1,605,000 swine, and 1,708,000 other cattle.

A large aggregate capital is invested in manufactures, chiefly flour, meats, lard, sugar, and salt.

Mines of coal and lead and stone-quarries are worked extensively.

PRINCIPAL POINTS OF INTEREST.

INTERMEDIATE STATIONS: Argentine, Turner, Morris, Holliday, Choteau, Wilder, Cedar Junction, De Soto, Weaver, Eudora

Lawrence.— Chicago, 499 miles; Los Angeles, 1,766 miles; San Diego, 1,849 miles; San Francisco, 2,078 miles. Junction with Union

A KANSAS STATE UNIVERSITY BUILDING.

Pacific Railway, and Atchison, Topeka & Santa Fé lines from southern points in Eastern Kansas. Altitude, 837 feet. Population, 9,997.

A city of New England appearance and character, situated on the Kansas River. Site of the Haskell Indian

School, which is comprised in fifteen buildings, and of the State University, whose seven structures crown Mount Oread, west of the city, and are visible at a distance of many miles. The dam across the river furnishes excellent water power for a number of manufactories — of flour, paper, wire, and nails, whose yearly product reaches an aggregate value of nearly a million and a half dollars. Lawrence was settled in 1854, and was the center and capital of the Free State side of the Kansas struggle, and the headquarters of John Brown during that trying period. It was burned on August 21, 1863, by the rebel guerrilla, Quantrell, who, with three or four hundred followers, surprised the town at daybreak. In the space of four hours, upon that occasion, 143 men were shot dead in the streets and some thirty desperately wounded, and the value of the property pillaged or sacrificed to the torch was in the neighborhood of $2,000,000.

INTERMEDIATE STATION: Lake View.

Lecompton.— Chicago, 509 miles; Los Angeles, 1,756 miles; San Diego, 1,839 miles; San Francisco, 2,068 miles. Altitude, 861 feet. Population, 450.

Named after Lecompte, a leader of the Pro-Slavery party. This was the ancient capital under that organization. The "Lecompton Constitution," intended for a Pro-Slavery Kansas, was signed here. The foundations of the present Lane University were originally laid for the projected capitol of a slave State. Many men of the opposition party were forcibly incarcerated for their principles in the Lecompton jail, whose ruins are still visible. The old legislative hall also still exists. The interest of Lecompton is reminiscent, and attaches to the early history of Kansas, when strife was violent between the two political parties.

INTERMEDIATE STATIONS: Glendale, Grover, Spencer, Tecumseh.

Topeka.—Chicago, 525 miles; Los Angeles, 1,740 miles; San Diego, 1,823 miles; San Francisco, 2,052 miles. Dining station. Junction with Chicago, Rock Island & Pacific Railway; Union Pacific Railway; Missouri, Kansas & Texas Railway; and Atchison, Topeka & Santa Fé lines to Leavenworth and Atchison, Kan., and St. Joseph, Mo. Altitude, 901 feet. Population, 31,007.

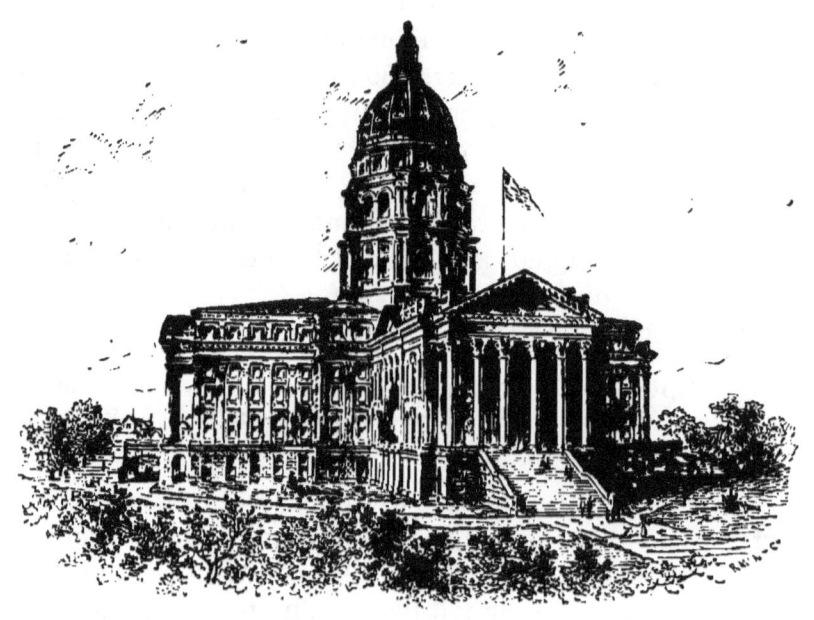

KANSAS STATE CAPITOL.

Very little that is characteristic of the capital of Kansas can be seen from the railroad station. It is a most attractive city, with broad business streets and sightly residence districts profusely shaded with ornamental trees. Situated on the Kansas River, its chief industries are flour-milling, manufacturing, and labor in connection with railroad service. The general offices and shops of the Atchison, Topeka & Santa Fé Railroad are located here, over 2,700 men being employed in the city by that company, and upward of $150,000 being disbursed monthly in wages. There are six flour mills, with an aggregate output of 2,850 barrels per day, and seven grain elevators, with a total capacity of 835,000 bushels, besides stock-yards and packing houses.

The capitol is imposing, and in it is stored the magnificent ornithological collection of the late Prof. N. S. Goss. Topeka contains the State, city, Washburn, and Bethany libraries, aggregating 100,000 volumes, the State Insane Asylum and State Reform School, Washburn and Bethany colleges, and twenty-three public schools. It possesses the largest system of electric street-car lines in the country.

West of Topeka are extensively-worked coal mines, notably those of Osage City, twenty-nine miles distant. Some 750 miners are there employed, and the yearly output is 145,000 tons.

INTERMEDIATE STATIONS: Pauline, Wakarusa, Carbondale, Scranton, Burlingame, Peterton, Osage City, Barclay, Reading, Lang, Emporia Junction.

Emporia.—Chicago, 586 miles; Los Angeles, 1,679 miles; San Diego, 1,762 miles; San Francisco, 1,991 miles. Junction with Atchison, Topeka & Santa Fé branch line to Southern Kansas points. Emporia Junction, one mile east, is point of crossing of Missouri, Kansas & Texas Railway, and junction for through fast freight line of the Atchison, Topeka & Santa Fé Railroad from Kansas City, by way of Olathe, Ottawa, and Quenemo. Altitude, 1,149 feet. Population, 7,551.

Placed at the joining of Cottonwood and Neosho valleys, Emporia is the center of an exceedingly rich agricultural region. The State Normal School is visible upon the main street from the train in passing. It has about

1,200 students. There is also a Presbyterian college. Twenty miles beyond, at Strong City, is the point of departure of Atchison, Topeka & Santa Fé trains northwestward to Abilene, Salina, Minneapolis, and Concordia, Kan., and Superior, Neb. Emporia enjoys the reputation of being the wealthiest city in Kansas per capita.

INTERMEDIATE STATIONS: Sterry, Plymouth, Bennett, Saffordville, Ellinor, Strong City, Evans, Elmdale, Clements, Cedar Grove.

Florence.—Chicago, 631 miles; Los Angeles, 1,634 miles; San Diego, 1,717 miles; San Francisco, 1,946 miles. Dining station. Junction with proprietary lines southward through El Dorado, Augusta, and Winfield, and westward through Marion, McPherson, and Lyons to Ellinwood. Altitude, 1,277 feet. Population, 1,229.

INTERMEDIATE STATIONS: Horners, Peabody, Braddock, Doyle, Walton.

Newton.—Chicago, 659 miles; Los Angeles, 1,606 miles; San Diego, 1,689 miles; San Francisco, 1,918 miles. Dining station. Junction with St. Louis, Ft. Scott & Wichita Railroad, and diverging point of Santa Fé line through Wichita, Arkansas City, and Oklahoma to Galveston and other Texas cities. Altitude, 1,455 feet. Population, 5,605.

By way of contrast this is remembered as perhaps the most abandoned community to be found in the States twenty years ago, when it was a border town, the western terminus of the railroad, and the extreme verge of Kansas settlement. Poker and monte, carousal, and the practice of every conceivable form of vice and violence were the principal industries. The hanging of eleven men occurred in a single night. It was then a slab-and-canvas settlement. It is now an orderly, pretty city of churches, schools, and happy homes, surrounded by productive farms.

It is a division point of the railroad.

INTERMEDIATE STATIONS: Mission, Halstead, Paxton.

Burrton.—Chicago, 678 miles; St. Louis, 538 miles; Los Angeles, 1,587 miles; San Diego, 1,670 miles; San Francisco, 1,899 miles. Junction with St. Louis & San Francisco Railway (Santa Fé Route). Altitude, 1,465 feet.

Connecting point of trains to and from St. Louis, direct through southwestern Missouri and southeastern Kansas, and junction with the St. Louis & San Francisco line to Ellsworth.

This is largely a Mennonite farming community, about 800 of that sect being settled in the neighborhood. The Mennonites are a denomination combining some of the characteristic principles of the Baptists and the Quakers. The main distinctive doctrines consist of non-resistance, abstinence from oaths, and the baptism only of adults upon profession of faith. Menno Simons, a Hollander who lived from 1496 to 1561, was the organizer, although not the founder, of the sect. It increased rapidly in Holland, Switzerland, and Germany, and was the object of bitter persecutions. Many members removed to Russia, where they were promised exemption from military service. Not a few also emigrated to America, some being among the original Dutch settlers of New York. But the first Mennonite settlement in this country was at Germantown, Penn., in 1683. Afterward branch colonies were established in Tiffin, Ohio, Somerville, Ill., and Mountain Lake, Minn., and when the prairies of the West were still further opened up by the extension of railroads, they scattered even more widely, preserving their distinctive communities. In 1871 the exemption under which they had existed in Russia was revoked, and they were given until 1880 to leave the country or abandon their peculiar tenets as to bearing arms.

Most of the Mennonites in Kansas came directly from Russia, in consequence of that decree, as purchasers and settlers of lands placed on the market by the Atchison, Topeka & Santa Fé Railroad Company. About 10,000 located on and near this line, between Peabody and Pawnee Rock, from Marion to Barton County. They are a thrifty and worthy people, self-maintaining in all vicissitudes. In the general catastrophe of the grasshopper plague of Kansas, in 1873–74, the Mennonite colonies in other parts of the country contributed money by thousands of dollars to their impoverished brethren, which sufficed for their needs, and has since been paid back, dollar for dollar, with interest added. All are prosperous, and not a few have become wealthy.

INTERMEDIATE STATION: Kent.

Hutchinson.— Chicago, 693 miles; St. Louis, 553 miles; Los Angeles, 1,572 miles; San Diego, 1,655 miles; San Francisco, 1,884 miles. Dining station. Junction with Chicago, Rock Island & Pacific Railway; Missouri Pacific Railway; Hutchinson & Southern Railroad; and Santa Fé line through Ellinwood, Great Bend, and Larned to Kinsley. Altitude, 1,541 feet. Population, 8,682.

One of the prettiest and most vigorous towns in the State; settled in 1872. Stock-yards, packing houses, flour mills, grain elevators, sugar, lard, and salt works, furniture and ice manufactories, numerous wholesale mercantile houses, and half a dozen banking houses are examples of its commercial activity. It has a State Reformatory, a business college, and a conservatory of music.

The enormous deposits of rock salt that underlie vast regions in Kansas at a depth of several hundred feet are here laid under tribute by forcing water into the subterranean beds, afterward pumping the resultant brine to the surface and evaporating it, first in open-air tanks and then by boiling to the point of crystallization. The method of obtaining the brine is simple, though ingenious. A hole is drilled, as for an artesian well, until the deposit is struck. A small pipe is then inserted to the bottom, and over that a larger and shorter one. The water is forced downward through the space between the two, and the brine solution, whose specific gravity is much greater than that of pure water, seeks the lowest level in the flooded cavity. The upward pumping is then done

STREET SCENE, HUTCHINSON, KAN.

through the smaller and longer tube, which reaches to the briniest depth. Six hundred men are employed in these salt works alone, and the full capacity is stated to be 5,000 barrels of pure white table salt per day.

It is after a stretch of level prairie, over the latter portion of which the railroad runs in an absolutely straight line for thirty miles, that you come to Hutchinson. The Arkansas River is encountered and crossed at this point.

Henceforward the course of that river is closely followed, except for two cut-offs (from the present crossing through Kinsley to Dodge City), for nearly 350 miles, namely, to La Junta, in Colorado, and many of the trains do not make these cut-offs. Silent, sandy, and unattractive, the Arkansas is really a great and beneficent river. It rises in Tennessee Pass, above Leadville, in Colorado, issues between the Park and Saguache ranges into the idyllic valley of Buena Vista, plunges through many miles of profound gorges, and reappears to wander over 500 miles of plain before reaching Hutchinson, receiving the tribute of upward of fifty considerable streams on its way. It continues on through Kansas, Oklahoma, Indian Territory, and Arkansas to find its outlet in the Mississippi, its extraordinarily fertile valley sustaining an agricultural population that numbers hundreds of thousands.

Formerly these plains, for a width of two or three hundred miles, were crossed from south to north by innumerable paths cut deep into the sod. They marked the annual migration of countless millions of bison from Texas to Manitoba and back, feeding in the wake of the seasons. The plow has obliterated most of these trails upon the plain, but buffalo wallows are still occasionally discernible in sunken spots, and portions of the old trails are easily discoverable among the adjacent hills.

INTERMEDIATE STATIONS (via Great Bend): Fruit Valley, Nickerson, Sterling, Alden, Raymond, Clarendon, Ellinwood, Dartmouth, Great Bend, Dundee, Pawnee Rock, Larned, Hamburg, Garfield, Nettleton.

INTERMEDIATE STATIONS (via Kinsley cut-off): Sherman, Partridge, Abbyville, Plevna, Sylvia, Zenith, Stafford, St. John, Dillwyn, Macksville, Belpre, Lewis.

Kinsley.—Chicago, 791 miles; St. Louis, 651 miles; Los Angeles,

1,474 miles; San Diego, 1,557 miles; San Francisco, 1,786 miles. Altitude, 2,179 feet. Population, 771. Dining station.

A second crossing of the Arkansas River.

INTERMEDIATE STATIONS: Offerle, Bellefont, Speareville, Wright.

Dodge City.— Chicago, 827 miles; St. Louis, 687 miles; Los Angeles, 1,438 miles; San Diego, 1,521 miles; San Francisco, 1,750 miles. Dining station. Junction with Dodge City, Montezuma & Trinidad Railway, and Chicago, Rock Island & Pacific Railway. Altitude, 2,493 feet. Population, 1,763.

This is the location of the old Fort Dodge Military Reservation, where now is the State Soldiers' Home, with about 300 inmates.

Dodge City acquired some celebrity, not many years back, as a rendezvous for cowboys, whose particular pleasure, when nothing more exciting engaged their attention in idle hours, was to make a characteristic demonstration when the overland trains passed. And the life of the city was a wild and reckless one. But phases in the West change rapidly, and all that is now a matter of reminiscence. It possesses electric lights, water-works, and a flour mill, and is a receiving and distributing point for the surrounding agricultural and grazing country.

Here the time changes one hour.

The adoption of arbitrary standards of time grew out of the difficulties of adjusting business operations, particularly the complicated details of arranging railroad train schedules to the differences of local solar time. For the purpose of simplification, four divisions are recognized in the United States, namely, Eastern, Central, Mountain, and Pacific, in which respectively the solar time on the 75th, 90th, 105th, and 120th degrees of west longitude is used. The difference of 15 degrees longitude between the consecutive standards is one-twenty-fourth of the earth's circumference, and the difference in time is consequently exactly one hour. Railroads commonly adhere to one of these standards, but in not a few cities both standard and local time are in use, and clocks have an additional minute-hand in order that both may be indicated. The actual working boundaries between these

OLD-TIME CAMPING FREIGHTER.

standards, however, far from conforming to meridian lines, are extremely irregular, as will be seen in the following:

Actual dividing points, in practice, between Central and Mountain Sections — Dodge City, Ellis, Phillipsburg, and Oakley, Kan.; El Paso and Texline, Texas; Holyoke and Hoisington, Colo.; Long Pine, North Platte, and McCook, Neb.; Mandan and Minot, N. D.

Between Mountain and Pacific Sections — Barstow and

Mojave, Cal.; Deming, N. M.; Hope and Troy, Idaho; Ogden, Utah.; Huntington, Ore.

Convenience in railroad operation is the controlling cause of this irregularity. El Paso, Texas, for example, is the focal point of four ponderous railroad systems, each basing on a different standard of time. In that city, as a consequence, four standards are in use — Central Time by the city and the Atlantic System of the Southern Pacific Company; Mountain Time by the Atchison, Topeka & Santa Fé Railroad Company; Pacific Time by the Pacific System of the Southern Pacific Company; and City of Mexico Time by the Mexican Central Railway Company.

As the earth revolves toward the east, it follows that the east is farther advanced in time than the west, and consequently a traveler journeying westward from New York or Boston will, if he does not correct his watch in transit, find it just three hours fast after crossing the eastern boundary of the Pacific Division.

INTERMEDIATE STATIONS: Howell, Cimarron, Ingalls, Charleston, Pierceville, Mansfield.

Garden City.—Chicago, 877 miles; St. Louis, 737 miles; Los Angeles, 1,388 miles; San Diego, 1,471 miles; San Francisco, 1,700 miles. Altitude, 2,844 feet. Population, 1,490.

An experimental grass and forage station, for investigating the agricultural problems presented by the dry plains of western Kansas, is located here. Mr. J. A. Sewall, superintendent of the station, is authority for the following information concerning its work.

It has been in operation since 1889, having been established by the United States Department of Agriculture and maintained out of the botanical investigation fund. Seeds of grasses and forage plants, and of grains grown in arid countries, have been brought here from all parts of the world for a test of their practicability under the conditions that prevail. The total yearly rainfall of the region being exceedingly small, the inquiry is directed to the discovery of the adaptability of particular species and advantageous methods of cultivation without irrigation. Two hundred and forty acres are under cultivation, and about one hundred botanical varieties are under test in areas varying from a single square rod to forty acres. As a species

A WESTERN KANSAS IRRIGATION DITCH.

gives evidence of being grown successfully, it is given additional space. The ground is plowed not less than one foot deep, and the surface finely pulverized with a harrow containing 1,600 short, small teeth. The deep plowing holds all the rain that falls, and pulverizing minimizes the evaporation. By such a method of cultivation, without any irrigation whatever, and with a total rainfall of only five inches from seed-time to harvest, excellent crops of hay, forage, and special varieties of corn, wheat, oats, and rye are raised yearly, to wit: Jerusalem corn, 30 bushels per acre, weight, 58 pounds per bushel; winter rye, 26 bushels, weight, 58 pounds; Poland wheat, 20½ bushels, weight, 60 pounds; Algerian wheat, 24½ bushels, weight, 64 pounds; oats, 70 bushels, weight, 37 pounds; white barley, 36 bushels, weight, 48 pounds; black barley, 23½ bushels, weight, 66 pounds. Over ninety tons of seeds have been gratuitously distributed from the station to farmers in the Southwest, and are reported to have been cultivated with gratifying success.

The significance of such work as this of the experimental station will be appreciated by the traveler who has seen the enormous tracts of similar land in our Western country that up to the present time have lain barren on account of small rainfall and difficulties in the way of irrigation.

At Garden City, also, grain is handled in elevators to the value of nearly $150,000 yearly, and there is a flour mill in operation whose daily capacity is 150 barrels.

INTERMEDIATE STATIONS: Sherlock, Deerfield, Lakin, Hartland, Lantry, Kendall, Mayline, Syracuse, Medway.

Coolidge.— Chicago, 943 miles; St. Louis, 803 miles; Los Angeles, 1,322 miles; San Diego, 1,405 miles; San Francisco, 1,634 miles. Altitude, 3,365 feet. Dining station.

COLORADO.

HISTORICAL.— Part of the region now comprised in Colorado was included in the original Louisiana Territory, and the remainder was contained in New Mexico. In making up the present State portions of New Mexico, Utah, Nebraska, and Kansas were taken. The first American explorer was Lieut. Zebulon M. Pike, who came here in 1806 and gave his name to the great mountain peak whose summit he vainly attempted to reach. Maj. S. H. Long came this way in 1820 and similarly perpetuated his name in a peak a little higher than Pike's. About twenty years later Charles Bent established a fort and trading post on the Arkansas River, near the present railroad junction La Junta, and in 1844 John C. Fremont made his first explorations of this part of the country. In 1858 gold was discovered on the South Platte River, near Denver, and Pike's Peak became a landmark for thousands of fortune seekers who ventured across the plains.

The northern limit of Spanish settlement was the Arkansas River, which served as a partial boundary between Spanish and French territory in the early partition of the country.

The Ute Indians, now almost wholly banished to Utah, were the ruling aborigines, although, in the southeastern part, Apaches and other tribes roamed.

DESCRIPTIVE.— Colorado is 380 miles long, from east to west, by 280 miles wide, and contains 103,925 square miles. Topographically it is divided into the plains, the foot-hills, and the ranges of the Rocky Mountains. The plains occupy about one-third of the area of the entire State, rising rather steeply from an altitude of 3,500 feet at the Kansas boundary to nearly 6,000 feet at the edge of the foot-hills. They are treeless, save along the water-courses and where trees have been planted since settlement. The foot-hills extend north and south at an altitude of from 6,500 to 8,000 feet, and are generally covered with timber and are rich in mineral. The Rocky Mountains are an intricate, many-branched chain, but are separable into three prominent divisions, Front, Park, and Saguache ranges, in which nearly 200 individual peaks rise above an altitude of 13,000 feet, and about one-fifth as many, not all of which are named, above 14,000. The highest point in Colorado is Mount Elbert (14,436 feet). Pike's (14,147 feet), Long's (14,271 feet), and Gray's (14,341 feet) are the best known peaks of the Front Range. Lincoln (14,297 feet) and Quandary (14,266 feet) are the highest peaks of the Park Range. The Saguache is perhaps the most notable range of the chain, being a rugged mass of granite about 13,000 feet high, nearly 20 miles broad, and more than 75 miles long. Harvard (14,403 feet), Yale (14,204 feet), Princeton (14,202 feet), Mount Massive (14,424 feet), and Mount Ouray (14,043 feet) are a few of its prominent pinnacles. This range is the backbone of the Continental Divide, and is crossed by two world-famous railroad passes, Hagerman Pass on the Colorado Midland Railroad, which reaches a height of 11,528 feet on the side of Mount Massive, and Marshall Pass on the Denver & Rio Grande Railroad, which climbs Mount Ouray to a height of 10,852 feet. The three ranges named extend from north to south, and between them lie North, Middle, and South Parks. The Saguache Range is prolonged southward by the Sangre de Cristo Range, which in turn is extended by the Culebra Range, and west of the last two lies the largest of the Colorado parks, San Luis, whose area is 9,400 square miles. There are many other parks of smaller size, and all are beautiful mountain-walled basins of great fertility, well-watered and timbered.

Here the Arkansas, Platte, and Grand rivers and the Rio Grande del Norte take rise, besides innumerable tributaries to these and other streams. In this titanic land the water-courses are an unnavigable series of rapids and falls, which, in the lapse of ages, have worn deep, imposing gorges in their beds of rock.

Colorado is the equal of any part of the United States

in grandeur of scenery, save only the Grand Cañon of the Colorado River in Arizona, Yosemite Valley in California, and Yellowstone Park in Wyoming. It is the most popular summer resort in the West, thousands every year turning to it from east, south, and north upon the approach of the warm season. The climate is healthful and restorative, and the air is dry, pure, and cool, by reason of the great elevation of the region. It has numerous mineral

A COLORADO BEGINNING.

springs which are beneficially used for a beverage, as at Manitou, or for bathing, as in the great pool at Glenwood Springs.

Our route lies south of the great Colorado resorts, leading across the southeastern portion of the State, over rather desolate plains, which at length give place to the beauties of mountain scenery.

CLIMATE.—Altitude, pure, dry, and bracing air, predominance of sunny weather, a short, mild winter, and cool nights after the warmest days of summer, make the climate of Colorado exceedingly agreeable and healthful. On the summits of the ranges winter is a severe season, with deep snows, ice, and piercing winds; but while such extreme temperature rules aloft, the towns in the valleys and on the plains are generally favored with spring-like weather, the snow-fall there being usually light and remaining on the ground only a few days.

In the lower altitudes the direct rays of the sun are hot in midsummer, but the heat lasts only through the middle of the day, and the summer climate can be properly termed a cool one. Sunstroke is unknown.

For the benefit of such as are interested in the formal statistics of climate, the following tables are given. They are taken from the records of the Signal Service at Denver, and cover a period of nineteen years:

TOTAL PRECIPITATION IN INCHES.

	Jan.	Feb.	Mar.	Apr.	May.	June.	July.	Aug.	Sept.	Oct.	Nov.	Dec.
1872	0.55	0.22	1.71	2.09	3.74	2.07	2.69	1.75	1.57	0.68	0.69	0.29
1873	0.13	0.24	0.22	2.43	0.75	2.24	2.00	1.41	0.89	0.73	0.16	0.61
1874	0.84	0.53	0.49	1.70	2.43	1.21	3.35	0.68	1.34	0.64	0.08	0.17
1875	0.38	0.60	0.39	2.24	1.94	0.43	4.32	1.97	2.89	0.22	1.28	0.59
1876	0.21	0.11	1.80	1.22	8.57	1.10	1.16	2.03	0.60	0.12	1.50	1.70
1877	1.90	0.40	1.40	2.77	2.30	1.93	0.33	1.30	0.38	2.15	0.73	0.79
1878	0.10	0.48	1.82	0.05	2.90	2.78	1.38	2.25	1.23	0.80	0.67	1.05
1879	0.40	0.39	1.00	2.62	3.36	0.32	0.64	1.38	0.02	0.19	0.21	0.33
1880	0.38	0.32	0.21	0.31	1.11	1.22	1.38	1.46	0.89	1.37	0.83	0.10
1881	0.49	1.22	0.87	0.50	2.21	0.09	2.50	2.33	0.57	0.32	1.68	0.00
1882	0.57	0.20	0.20	1.47	2.98	4.96	0.66	1.20	0.06	0.75	0.71	0.73
1883	2.35	0.45	0.21	3.10	4.30	0.85	2.27	0.75	1.08	1.49	0.32	2.32
1884	0.22	0.86	0.93	3.93	4.61	1.47	0.65	1.71	0.13	1.21	0.19	0.76
1885	0.41	0.75	0.97	4.94	2.13	0.66	1.33	1.18	1.22	0.73	0.55	1.08
1886	0.62	0.72	2.36	2.79	0.09	2.26	0.50	1.62	0.98	0.33	1.93	0.87
1887	0.67	0.30	0.23	2.16	1.13	0.53	2.49	2.68	0.97	0.97	0.22	0.14
1888	0.11	0.37	1.15	1.71	2.66	0.29	0.41	1.51	0.11	0.77	0.33	0.09
1889	0.50	0.70	0.40	1.34	3.44	1.88	2.94	0.33	0.28	2.11	0.53	0.30
1890	0.18	0.46	0.35	2.50	2.01	Tr'ce	0.79	1.89	0.17	0.64	0.30	0.04

NEW GUIDE TO THE PACIFIC COAST. 43

MONTHLY MEAN RELATIVE HUMIDITY.

	Jan.	Feb.	Mar.	Apr.	May.	June.	July.	Aug.	Sept.	Oct.	Nov.	Dec.
1872	63	56	61	48	56	51	54	52	51	42	47	54
1873	45	44	29	53	52	41	45	49	43	50	42	59
1874	51	61	59	54	42	43	42	45	44	54	42	56
1875	56	47	49	47	40	29	55	47	52	32	57	45
1876	42	40	52	39	45	38	40	45	43	34	47	52
1877	62	63	48	54	46	39	34	37	38	52	52	55
1878	54	48	43	34	50	51	40	51	45	30	43	53
1879	54	58	46	60	41	40	47	43	35	33	50	60
1880	41	51	42	39	38	39	49	48	46	57	66	64
1881	60	58	57	48	55	35	47	54	44	49	60	51
1882	57	48	40	49	59	58	47	43	39	47	51	44
1883	56	64	53	57	57	53	50	49	48	56	46	61
1884	54	57	56	57	58	53	43	53	41	49	47	63
1885	57	64	57	62	59	51	54	57	54	55	56	57
1886	67	52	65	67	31	55	48	56	53	50	61	53
1887	54	51	43	47	47	44	53	55	60	56	53	52
1888	54	53	55	41	56	38	45	51	46	51	62	50
1889	66	56	49	50	56	52	50	50	44	53	68	56
1890	58	55	43	48	52	22	44	50	40	40	43	36

MAXIMUM TEMPERATURE.

	Jan.	Feb.	Mar.	Apr.	May.	June.	July.	Aug.	Sept.	Oct.	Nov.	Dec.
1872	56.0	......	......	80.0	91.0	92.0	95.0	95.0	88.0	85.0	66.0	59.0
1873	62.0	60.0	75.0	81.0	84.0	99.0	99.0	96.0	90.0	86.0	71.0	59.0
1874	62.0	60.0	62.0	83.0	92.0	98.5	102.3	96.5	92.0	83.2	72.0	71.0
1875	56.0	64.0	73.0	80.0	87.0	97.0	95.0	96.0	91.0	84.0	75.0	66.0
1876	59.0	66.0	70.0	82.0	85.0	97.0	101.0	100.0	90.0	85.0	76.0	68.0
1877	58.0	60.0	75.0	72.0	85.0	95.0	99.0	99.0	92.0	85.0	67.0	64.0
1878	55.0	61.0	76.0	80.0	87.0	93.0	100.0	105.0	93.0	83.0	73.0	62.0
1879	61.0	72.0	81.0	76.0	90.0	95.0	98.0	95.0	89.0	84.0	76.0	66.0
1880	63.0	59.0	73.0	77.0	89.0	96.0	95.0	93.0	89.0	79.0	61.0	61.0
1881	63.0	60.5	69.0	80.0	83.8	95.0	99.0	95.8	88.0	81.7	66.0	67.0
1882	67.0	61.0	71.0	76.0	78.0	88.2	91.3	94.0	89.0	76.0	65.0	64.0
1883	61.0	56.0	70.0	73.0	79.2	91.0	95.5	91.0	87.7	75.2	73.2	62.0
1884	59.0	61.3	61.1	70.3	80.5	90.2	96.5	92.2	87.8	80.3	69.8	68.2
1885	64.0	60.4	68.3	71.2	86.0	86.2	97.3	92.8	89.6	80.1	75.0	74.1
1886	62.8	71.0	68.0	74.6	89.9	92.7	96.3	94.3	85.7	77.0	63.0	64.8
1887	66.9	70.9	74.7	82.5	89.4	95.9	92.1	94.6	87.6	85.1	73.7	66.6
1888	76.0	70.5	70.0	80.6	80.5	97.7	100.3	92.4	90.0	79.8	70.2	67.5
1889	56.0	61.0	70.0	78.0	83.0	92.0	100.0	98.0	94.0	85.0	60.0	66.0
1890	78.0	77.0	71.0	77.0	88.0	94.0	97.0	98.0	87.0	75.1	74.0	75.0

AVERAGE TEMPERATURE.

	Jan.	Feb.	Mar.	Apr.	May.	June.	July.	Aug.	Sept.	Oct.	Nov.	Dec.
1872	24	33	36	45	57	66	68	69	60	50	34	28
1873	30	31	44	38	53	68	71	70	60	46	41	23
1874	32	26	36	43	61	69	75	77	59	53	42	30
1875	17	32	33	44	59	69	68	69	61	54	38	38
1876	28	38	35	49	56	66	74	70	62	55	38	28
1877	25	35	43	44	56	64	73	70	62	46	35	33
1878	27	36	46	49	54	63	73	72	58	50	42	23
1879	24	36	46	50	61	68	74	69	62	52	38	29
1880	36	28	34	47	57	67	70	69	61	48	22	30
1881	26	30	38	52	59	71	75	73	60	50	36	39
1882	30	38	43	47	52	65	71	72	63	50	37	35
1883	28	22	44	46	54	65	71	71	62	47	43	32
1884	32	30	39	44	54	67	74	68	65	46	42	25
1885	29	32	38	46	53	64	70	68	62	49	43	36
1886	21	39	34	44	61	65	74	71	60	52	33	37
1887	31	32	46	49	60	69	69	68	63	48	40	29
1888	27	29	33	53	53	68	71	65	61	48	34	34
1889	27	30	43	51	56	64	72	73	60	52	32	40
1890	28	34	41	48	58	68	75	69	68	50	40	22

MINIMUM TEMPERATURE.

	Jan.	Feb.	Mar.	Apr.	May.	June.	July.	Aug.	Sept.	Oct.	Nov.	Dec.
1872	—22.0	— 4.0	.0	19.0	27.0	43.0	45.0	.....	.....	.....	.....	— .8
1873	—17.0	30.0	11.0	10.0	27.0	42.0	42.0	50.0	28.0	1.0	1.0	— 5.0
1874	— 7.0	—11.0	12.0	14.0	29.0	40.0	51.0	51.2	34.6	13.2	8.0	— 5.0
1875	—29.0	— 3.0	1.0	9.0	35.0	38.0	53.0	50.0	32.0	27.0	5.0	— 3.0
1876	2.0	7.0	3.0	4.0	32.0	38.0	43.0	44.0	32.0	24.0	3.0	—25.0
1877	—15.0	16.0	0.0	12.0	32.0	39.0	48.0	47.0	37.0	22.0	—18.0	— 5.0
1878	—12.0	15.0	21.0	25.0	32.0	43.0	54.0	54.0	34.0	10.0	11.0	—12.0
1879	—10.0	— 3.0	17.0	28.0	37.0	43.0	52.0	50.0	38.0	20.0	11.0	—17.0
1880	— 6.0	— 8.0	—10.0	80.0	32.0	39.0	54.0	50.0	35.0	26.0	—13.5	—11.0
1881	—12.0	—20.0	8.0	180.0	34.6	48.9	57.0	53.1	37.0	28.0	10.5	18.0
1882	1.2	10.5	10.0	21.0	34.0	43.0	49.0	47.0	38.8	27.3	— 4.0	— 2.0
1883	—20.0	—22.0	18.0	22.0	31.5	37.0	52.0	50.0	40.5	25.0	23.4	2.0
1884	— 2.0	—15.0	10.9	22.5	28.0	48.0	52.0	51.0	40.0	26.0	13.2	— 8.0
1885	—10.9	0.2	5.4	17.6	27.1	41.0	50.3	46.4	42.5	21.9	11.2	— 5.6
1886	—18.9	2.9	—10.7	20.5	35.5	46.8	55.5	48.5	29.0	22.6	6.0	1.4
1887	—17.6	— 2.6	13.2	20.5	30.9	43.7	50.0	46.9	35.0	7.8	—14.2	—13.6
1888	—20.3	15.5	— 1.5	30.0	31.5	41.0	51.4	49.2	38.0	26.0	11.5	7.2
1889	3.5	— 7.0	18.0	29.0	32.0	37.0	50.0	46.0	30.0	25.0	3.0	4.0
1890	— 7.5	— 8.0	5.0	19.5	31.8	37.0	54.0	48.0	34.0	25.1	17.0	13.8

Dash (—) denotes below zero.

WEATHER.

	Clear	Fair	Cloudy	.01 in.		Clear	Fair	Cloudy	.01 in.		Clear	Fair	Cloudy	.01 in.		Clear	Fair	Cloudy	.01 in.
JAN.					**APRIL.**					**JULY.**					**OCT.**				
1872	13	14	4	4	1872	9	12	9	9	1872	12	14	5	8	1872	22	6	3	2
1873	11	13	7	4	1873	7	14	9	8	1873	13	5	3	9	1873	16	12	3	4
1874	12	13	6	3	1874	10	13	7	10	1874	10	14	7	12	1874	14	12	5	10
1875	10	15	6	7	1875	10	14	6	8	1875	3	17	11	16	1875	14	11	6	3
1876	23	7	1	2	1876	12	14	4	6	1876	15	13	3	8	1876	10	16	5	2
1877	16	12	3	7	1877	11	6	13	10	1877	16	12	3	3	1877	12	8	11	10
1878	21	9	1	1	1878	20	13	7	1	1878	11	17	3	12	1878	25	3	3	1
1879	4	8	2	4	1879	10	14	6	12	1879	11	17	3	7	1879	22	5	4	2
1880	19	10	2	5	1880	14	11	5	4	1880	12	15	4	5	1880	12	12	7	8
1881	9	15	7	7	1881	10	15	5	6	1881	15	14	2	9	1881	16	9	6	3
1882	20	10	1	6	1882	12	13	5	10	1882	18	12	1	7	1882	18	11	2	6
1883	15	11	5	7	1883	8	9	13	13	1883	15	10	6	12	1883	13	13	5	7
1884	18	11	2	5	1884	6	19	5	13	1884	8	21	2	12	1884	12	15	4	4
1885	15	11	5	1	1885	7	13	10	13	1885	9	19	3	15	1885	16	14	1	5
1886	14	15	2	8	1886	5	12	13	16	1886	16	11	4	5	1886	16	13	2	4
1887	12	19	0	8	1887	8	14	8	10	1887	10	17	4	9	1887	13	14	4	9
1888	21	7	3	4	1888	14	12	4	5	1888	7	22	2	11	1888	7	20	4	4
1889	14	11	6	8	1889	4	16	10	10	1889	6	19	6	10	1889	9	16	6	7
1890	16	11	4	4	1890	8	13	9	9	1890	1	21	9	8	1890	17	12	2	5
FEB.					**MAY.**					**AUGUST.**					**NOV.**				
1872	7	19	3	6	1872	7	13	11	16	1872	8	15	8	11	1872	14	13	3	5
1873	12	13	3	3	1873	7	13	11	18	1873	10	18	3	4	1873	15	12	3	3
1874	11	10	7	5	1874	8	16	7	9	1874	7	15	9	11	1874	16	10	4	5
1875	12	12	4	3	1875	8	18	5	11	1875	7	15	9	15	1875	9	13	8	7
1876	17	12	0	5	1876	9	15	7	10	1876	13	12	6	9	1876	15	9	6	7
1877	15	7	6	4	1877	8	17	6	9	1877	9	20	2	7	1877	10	15	5	5
1878	11	10	7	6	1878	7	16	8	20	1878	13	10	8	12	1878	14	10	6	4
1879	10	16	2	2	1879	20	8	3	2	1879	14	11	6	5	1879	18	10	2	6
1880	14	12	3	6	1880	12	16	3	7	1880	15	13	3	10	1880	10	13	7	10
1881	8	13	7	7	1881	6	20	5	10	1881	12	16	3	16	1881	19	6	5	11
1882	17	10	1	3	1882	7	14	10	13	1882	20	8	3	8	1882	23	6	1	4
1883	22	6	0	2	1883	7	14	10	11	1883	16	15	0	5	1883	18	12	0	3
1884	16	11	2	8	1884	9	13	9	17	1884	9	19	3	13	1884	20	9	1	2
1885	11	15	2	9	1885	6	15	10	17	1885	12	14	5	16	1885	15	7	8	5
1886	11	12	5	4	1886	16	15	0	4	1886	11	18	2	10	1886	15	11	4	6
1887	18	9	1	5	1887	12	15	4	5	1887	11	16	4	9	1887	17	9	4	2
1888	13	9	7	5	1888	7	15	9	16	1888	7	19	5	8	1888	9	15	6	6
1889	4	9	15	6	1889	1	18	12	12	1889	6	21	4	6	1889	13	11	6	6
1890	8	12	6	7	1890	5	19	7	12	1890	9	12	10	10	1890	20	6	4	2
MARCH.					**JUNE.**					**SEPT.**					**DEC.**				
1872	9	11	11	10	1872	11	12	7	9	1872	21	6	3	7	1872	11	11	9	4
1873	16	10	5	4	1873	15	10	5	7	1873	16	11	3	4	1873	15	11	5	5
1874	7	17	7	8	1874	14	13	3	9	1874	18	7	5	8	1874	16	14	1	3
1875	15	11	5	6	1875	13	14	3	4	1875	9	9	12	13	1875	16	16	0	2
1876	12	9	10	11	1876	15	10	5	9	1876	12	13	5	6	1876	18	10	3	8
1877	12	10	9	8	1877	16	10	4	5	1877	19	7	4	5	1877	18	8	5	4
1878	9	12	10	8	1878	11	14	5	14	1878	18	7	5	6	1878	13	16	2	8
1879	15	11	5	5	1879	15	15	0	3	1879	25	5	0	1	1879	10	19	2	5
1880	17	12	2	3	1880	14	15	1	7	1880	13	11	6	2	1880	16	14	1	2
1881	9	14	8	8	1881	11	17	2	1	1881	23	4	3	3	1881	20	11	0	0
1882	21	7	3	2	1882	8	18	4	15	1882	23	6	1	3	1882	15	15	1	8
1883	18	9	4	4	1883	21	5	4	8	1883	17	10	3	9	1883	17	10	4	9
1884	13	15	3	7	1884	5	21	4	9	1884	18	12	0	3	1884	7	19	4	3
1885	14	14	3	8	1885	12	14	4	9	1885	14	13	3	9	1885	16	12	3	5
1886	11	16	4	11	1886	9	18	3	11	1886	18	11	1	4	1886	16	15	0	6
1887	10	18	3	4	1887	10	17	3	6	1887	12	15	3	9	1887	17	11	3	5
1888	13	10	8	11	1888	15	15	0	5	1888	23	6	1	3	1888	16	12	3	4
1889	3	25	3	4	1889	5	22	3	12	1889	9	18	3	6	1889	8	18	5	3
1890	6	16	9	4	1890	9	21	0	0	1890	8	19	3	4	1890	17	10	4	2

INDUSTRIAL.—Mining in Colorado began with the discovery of gold in 1858, but it has grown to be the second silver-producing State, the principal smelters being located at Denver and Pueblo. The extent of its iron mines is very great. It has 40,000 square miles of coal fields, in whose mines nearly 6,000 men are employed. Its annual coal product is 2,500,000 tons, in which both anthracite and bituminous are included. Petroleum wells have been in operation here for ten years past. Variegated

A COLORADO RANCH.

marbles and sandstone, granite, and gypsum are largely quarried.

In spite of the large output of metals, the value of the yearly agricultural and horticultural product is even greater. Alfalfa, wheat, barley, oats, corn, potatoes, apples, peaches, grapes, and berries are extensively raised. Colorado fruit is of the very best quality, and fruit-raising in suitable localities is one of the most profitable of legitimate industries.

The annual export of wool reaches 10,000,000 pounds,

and there are about 1,500,000 cattle. The winter climate is peculiarly favorable to the raising of stock and sheep, as feed is always to be had on the ranges, and the animals rarely suffer from severity of the weather.

PRINCIPAL POINTS OF INTEREST.

INTERMEDIATE STATIONS: Holleys, Byron, Granada, Koen, Carlton, Morse, Lamar, Prowers, Caddoa, Hilton.

Las Animas.—Chicago, 1,010 miles; St. Louis, 870 miles; Los Angeles, 1,255 miles; San Diego, 1,338 miles; San Francisco, 1,567 miles. Altitude, 3,871 feet. Population, 611.

An old Mexican town, at the confluence of the Las Animas (or Purgatory) River with the Arkansas. This tributary in its course flows through a lengthy and profound cañon, in which, according to legend, an entire company of Spanish soldiers perished in the days of the early exploration. On this account, if the legend is true, or perhaps merely exercising their poetic faculty, the Spaniards called this stream Rio de las Animas Perdidas, the River of Lost Souls. The *voyageurs* translated the name into the French word *Purgatoire*, which, in the vernacular, has been subjected to the pronunciation "Picketwire." This is worthy of note as an example of the manner in which names may lose their original form by translation, and may be subsequently corrupted into something quite meaningless until the clew is discovered. Las Animas, it will be observed, is a contraction of the original name of the river, and its signification, The Souls, would be perplexing without the explanation above given.

INTERMEDIATE STATION: Robinson.

La Junta.—Chicago, 1,029 miles; St. Louis, 889 miles; Los

Angeles, 1,236 miles; San Diego, 1,319 miles; San Francisco, 1,548 miles. Altitude, 4,061 feet. Population, 1,439. Dining station.

Diverging point of the Santa Fé line to Pueblo, Cañon City, Colorado Springs, and Denver, and through Colorado Springs to the principal Colorado resorts, and via Salt Lake City and Ogden to San Francisco.

A short distance west from La Junta, on the north side of the Arkansas, is the site of Bent's Fort, which was established in the "forties." Of this memento of the old wild life of the frontier, James W. Steele writes as follows:

> The occupants of Bent's Fort were hunters by predilection. They loved the wilderness, and never returned to civilization. They were fur-hunters and Indian traders, and Indian fighters at the same time. They kept no records; they did not care. The American history they were making never got into any books. They were intolerant and savage-tempered men, desperadoes on a pinch, every one. Their ranks were recruited by fugitives from justice. Life was held very cheap. At Bent's Fort a sod wall, thick and high, inclosed about an acre. There never was a more terrible acre of ground. It was full of the most reckless men ever gathered in one spot. The man Bent was the recognized head of them, and was afterward the first American Governor of New Mexico. The commercial idea was probably predominant, for everything was kept for sale there. The place was in the midst of a great buffalo range, and around it Apache, Cheyenne, Comanche, and Pawnee gathered and hunted and fought. They used, when lacking a quarrel among themselves, to attack the fort. They charged the wall on horseback. They never captured it, but if one should visit those ruins now he might be sure that he was standing upon ground that had been repeatedly soaked with human blood.

The following graphic picture of that early time is from the pen of Mr. Frank Wilkeson:

> As emigration increased on the Arkansas trail, Bent's Fort became an important place. United States troops, marching to the Southeastern Territories, camped there, and frequently secured

guides from the post. Thousands of dollars' worth of goods were sold annually. Enterprising young men bought goods at Bent's and loaded them onto their pack animals. Then they rode north, south, west, in search of Indian camps, which they entered and there traded with savage customers. The peddlers of the plains traded only for the more valuable furs. They penetrated into the remote recesses of the Rocky Mountains. They crossed that mighty snow-capped range and drummed up trade in then unnamed valleys where unknown Indians lived. These men acquired trading routes along certain trails and jealously defended them against all intruders. They recklessly entered all the Indian villages they discovered. In time, if they were not shot or burned, they became widely known among the Indians, and were welcomed and trusted. They supplied the warriors with powder and lead and percussion caps. They also dealt in traps, bright-colored cloth, beads, knives, axes, fish-hooks, buttons, and brass wire. Many of these traders married Indian women, and from these unions sprang the half-breeds — dangerous men in whom the courage of their fathers was supplemented by the crafty treachery of their mothers. Some of the white traders, especially in the Rocky Mountain region, adopted the dress and habits of the Indians, and frequently became men of consequence in the tribes.

Other men, lured from the bloody frontier by hope of profitable barter or love of adventure, or who sincerely desired to put a greater distance between themselves and pursuing sheriffs, loaded wagons with goods and drove westward to the buffalo range, expecting to meet wandering tribes of Indians. They were careless whether they met Sioux, Cheyennes, Crows, or Blackfeet. These men generally traveled in groups of three or four, each driving a team of horses, behind which rolled a heavily-loaded wagon. To-day they traded with Sioux; to-morrow they met Comanche braves; the next day painted and blanketed Cheyenne warriors crowded around their wagons and exchanged furs for powder, balls, blankets, and hardware. Or, to-day they fought, and to-morrow their corpses lay blackening in the sun, and glossy ravens perched on their scalpless heads and plucked their eyes, and foul buzzards stalked around them and prairie wolves tore them to pieces. Their goods were scattered throughout the villages, and their scalps, suspended from sticks thrust in the ground at the entrance of lodges, waved in the wind, and little Indian children spat on them as they played.

THE COLORADO RESORTS.—Many California tourists whose plan does not include a return by way of Ogden and central Colorado, make, either going or returning, a side excursion from La Junta to the famous resorts of Colorado. For the benefit of such the following brief account of the most noted is included:

Pueblo.—64 miles west from La Junta. Chicago, 1,093 miles; St. Louis, 953 miles. Altitude, 4,656 feet. Population, 24,558.

Sometimes called "The Pittsburg of the West." It is in the midst of a large tract of country particularly favorable for the culture of fruits, vegetables, and cereals, and adjoins a rich mineral-bearing region. Its site was formerly a Mexican village, to which fact its Spanish name happens to be due. It is a metropolitan city, with handsome public buildings, and business blocks of stone and brick, and costly residences. Its industries include Bessemer steel works; ore-stamping, smelting, and refining works; foundries, car and machine shops, and flour mills. Its climate, like that of all the Colorado resorts hereinafter mentioned, is mild in winter and very agreeable and healthful in summer.

A famous attraction at Pueblo is the Mineral Palace, erected in 1891. This is a costly and handsome structure of modernized Egyptian architecture, 224 feet long and 134 feet wide, and capable of containing 4,000 persons. The ceiling is 90 feet high, and consists of 28 domes, supported by gilded columns, around whose bases are arranged plate-glass cabinets filled with rich mineral specimens. The Mineral Palace is open to visitors every day in the year.

Colorado Springs.—43 miles north of Pueblo. Chicago, 1,136 miles; St. Louis, 996 miles. Altitude, 6,000 feet. Population, 11,140.

The name is fanciful. It is a town without a spring, but

pure, cold mountain water is supplied in abundance. It stands on the plain closely bordered by the Rockies, Pike's Peak very near at hand and conspicuously towering above the neighboring summits.

Four or five miles distant, and easily reached by a charming ride on the electric cars, lies Broadmoor Casino,

HELEN HUNT JACKSON'S GRAVE.

an elaborately beautiful structure by the side of a miniature lake. Here the tourist visitors to Colorado Springs throng for band music and dancing. Just beyond the Casino is Cheyenne Cañon, the location of Seven Falls, and formerly of Helen Hunt Jackson's grave. The authoress particularly loved this locality, and had a log-cabin home above the head of the falls, which still stands and attracts many of her admirers.

A visit to Cheyenne Cañon is a good preliminary to the more stupendous mountain scenery of Colorado. Carriages or burros are procurable at the end of the electric-car terminus, or the trip can be easily made afoot, as the distance is not great. Seven Falls is a name applied to a brilliant waterfall that tumbles through a rock gorge in a series of seven leaps, by the side of which a long stairway extends to the very top, where is an upper valley or basin of great beauty, surrounded by timbered mountain slopes. Every day in summer the entire cañon is dotted with excursionists, driving, riding or walking to the foot of the falls, climbing the stairway to wander still farther into the woodland, or urging slow but sure-footed burros along the intricate trail that leads by a roundabout way past the falls. There are huge isolated cliffs, domes, and pillars of rock warm with color; and the contrasting tones of evergreen and deciduous trees, and bright hues of wild flowers, and the diversity of landscape, which includes level stretches of shaded wood-road, smooth, fir-clad slopes, tremendous heights and gorges, a clattering mountain stream and roaring cascades, combine to make this a well-loved spot and one often returned to.

There are good hotels at Colorado Springs, and many attractive boarding places, and there are more summer homes of people who are nominally residents of the North, East, and South, than anywhere else in Colorado. It is considered to possess the most salubrious climate of any city in the State, where healthfulness is, however, generally the rule. There are no factories, and no other noisy or disagreeable business activities to detract from the quiet charm of the place.

Colorado Springs is connected with Manitou by electric and steam railroads.

Manitou.—Six miles west of Colorado Springs. Chicago, 1,142 miles; St. Louis, 1,002 miles. Altitude, 6,442 feet. Population, 1,439.

An Indian name, meaning Great Spirit. Manitou lies at the bottom of Ute Pass, at the point where the profound mountain-notch opens out into the plain. It is at the very foot of Pike's Peak, and the scenic environment is surpassingly beautiful. A broad avenue, eighty feet in width, runs through the village, and on either side are ranged villas, cottages, and a large number of hotels. The Soda Springs are in the heart of the settlement, in the center of a pretty little park. The Iron Springs are situated a few minutes' walk distant. Aside from the natural loveliness and exhilarating air of this resort, there are very many objects of special interest, a few of which will be enumerated:

PIKE'S PEAK.—There are two popular methods of ascending the Peak, one by way of the Cog-wheel Railroad, over which trains are regularly run in summer from Manitou, the other by carriage or on horseback from Cascade, half a dozen miles beyond Manitou. The railroad station of the Manitou & Pike's Peak Railway is in Engelman's Glen, near the Iron Springs. The railway itself is a few feet short of nine miles in length, and reaches the topmost pinnacle, stopping at the side of the old Signal Service Station, which has been made over into an inn. The Peak is 14,147 feet above sea level, and is 7,525 feet above the starting point in Manitou. A railway that permits the safe ascent and descent of such a tremendous incline, which, in spite of the circuitous path is in some places one foot in four, must be constructed very strongly, and the locomotives themselves must be perfectly adapted to the work. Perhaps it never occurred to the unprofessional reader that nine miles of heavy track slanting up a mountain side at a steep pitch might be subjected to the peril of sliding bodily downward by reason of its enormous weight. But the builders of this railway thought of that, and anchored the track to the mountain bed rock at nearly one hundred and fifty points. The road is of standard gauge (4 feet 8½ inches), with the ordinary T rails, and in the middle are twin rack-rails, made of the best Bessemer steel, upon the teeth of which the six separate cog-wheels of the locomotive take bearing. The cog-wheels also have a corrugated surface upon which both steam and hand brakes are used to check speed in the descent. The locomotives are constructed for strength rather than speed, and are placed below the coaches in order that an accident may not possibly happen in consequence of the breaking of a coupler, although the cars themselves are equipped with powerful brakes.

Shady Springs, Gog and Magog, Grand Pass, Echo Falls and Echo Rocks, Hanging Rock, Artists' Glen, Sheltered Falls, Minnehaha Falls, Devil's Slide, Pinnacle Rocks, and Grand View Rock are some of the features by the way below the Half-way House; beyond are Hell Gate, Ruxton Park, Sheep Rock, Lion's Gulch, and a particularly steep incline, and then comes the timber line, 11,625 feet above the sea. The rest of the peak is wind-swept ledge, bowlder, and gravel. Windy Point and the Saddle follow, from which last-named point a noble view of Manitou is had. A further ride of nearly a mile and a half brings one to the summit. Forty minutes' stop is made before the train returns, but of course the visitor is not compelled to descend on that train. One may even remain over night at the inn.

Although there are many mountains in Colorado a

little higher than Pike's Peak, this is high enough for most travelers, and those with a weak heart or feeble lungs will do well not to attempt the ascent, for the rarefaction of the air at such an altitude is very pronounced, and the most able-bodied person, unless he is accustomed to mountain-heights, will find himself short of breath and disinclined to attempt any violent exertion. The view, as is the case with all lofty peaks, is sometimes obscured by clouds, haze, or flurries of snow or rain; but the trip will invariably repay the genuine lover of mountains. The round trip, including the forty minutes' stop on the summit, consumes four and one-half hours.

The carriage-road, from Cascade, is double the length of the railway, namely, about eighteen miles, and the fatigues of the ascent by carriage or on horseback are naturally greater, but for those who do not count such a cost too closely, the carriage-road offers much more of enjoyment than the brief railroad trip permits.

GARDEN OF THE GODS.— This is a park of several hundred acres, through which are scattered myriad upright forms of rock, indiscriminately grand or grotesque, as if they had been sculptured by nature in the most whimsical moods, shifting incontinently from austere to frivolous. Many are clear caricatures, irresistibly suggesting the object travestied, and although perhaps the one who named the Garden may not have had this idea in mind, it is a peculiarly fitting appellation for a spot where there are so many signs of supermundane laughter. You might take it to be an original playground of the little gods, where they hewed out crude designs, as children make creations of mud, while now and then an older hand condescended to show them how the thing ought to be done.

The Eastern Gateway is a splendid natural portal, two august isolated masses of red sandstone towering on either side of a narrow but sufficient driveway to a height of 330 feet. Balanced Rock stands toward the western extremity of the Garden, a ponderous bowlder resting upon a pivotal base. The levity of the character of the smaller figures may be inferred from such names as Punch, Judy and the Baby, Kissing Camels, Irish Washerwoman, Ant Eater, Hedgehog, Toad, Turtle, Flying Dutchman, and Grandfather's Hat; and there are scores of like sort.

The critical visitor may perhaps feel that many of the fancied resemblances have been forced, but there is no question of the grandeur and motley interest of the scene, and the individual names are an accumulation of years, for many thousands visit the Garden of the Gods every season, and enjoy scrutinizing every contour in search of face and form.

GLEN EYRIE.— This is a private estate, the property of General Palmer, but except on the first day of the week it is freely open to visitors. It is nearly three times as large as the Garden of the Gods, and contains Queen Cañon, which is seven miles long. Neighboring the garden, it has much of the same character, and its attractiveness is enhanced by landscape gardening, which is maintained at great cost to the owner.

GRAND CAVERNS AND CAVE OF THE WINDS.— One and a half miles from the center of the village, separated on the surface by a high ridge, and not feasibly connected in the interior, although it is supposed that intercommunicating passages exist. The way to Grand Caverns is along Ute Pass, by the Fountain que Bouille and past Rainbow Falls, to a lofty eminence that overlooks the entire basin. . The Cave of the Winds is reached by way of Williams Cañon, a narrow gorge with magnificent rock walls. To these, as to the other attractions, there are admirable carriage-roads.

The two cave-groups named are similar in character, although the "rooms" in the first named are the larger. The ceilings are high, in some instances fifty or sixty feet, except in the narrow corridors between the principal compartments, although through those one may walk erect; and the floors are smooth and quite dry. The ceilings and walls are hung with remarkable stalactites and innumerable stalagmite forms. Some of the compartments are good-sized amphitheaters, with natural galleries, and each one has its name, appropriately descriptive or suggested by fancied adaptability to the uses of man. There is in Grand Caverns a natural xylophone of stalactites, called by the guides "The Grand Organ," upon which simple melodies are played with a fullness of tone and approximate correctness of pitch that are surprising. Heard in that gloomy under-world, which lanterns and magnesium lights illuminate only enough to half disclose the brilliancy of natural adornment against a background of midnight shadows, some of the deep notes struck upon those ponderous stalactites will linger long in memory. The route over which the visitor to Grand Caverns and the Cave of the Winds is conducted by the guide is in each case about three-quarters of a mile long, and an hour is easily consumed in the most cursory examination of these really wonderful grottoes.

Cascade Cañon.—Altitude, 7,241 feet, 6 miles west of Manitou; **Ute Park,** 7,511 feet, 8 miles; **Green Mountain Falls,** 7,734 feet, 9 miles; **Woodland Park,** 8,484 feet, 14 miles; and **Manitou Park,** 8,500 feet, 20 miles west of Manitou,

complete the series of resorts on the Ute Pass. The main line of the Colorado Midland Railroad (Sante Fé Route) runs from Colorado Springs directly through every one, except Manitou Park, which is six miles distant from Woodland Park, and is reached from that station by a four-in-hand stage-coach of the Concord type. In the Colorado tourist season, which covers the period from June to September, inclusive, these localities are thronged with visitors. There are very many first-class hotels, most of which are marvels of beauty and luxury, and tents and cottages are also plentifully availed of.

CRIPPLE CREEK.— This mining camp is conveniently visited from Manitou, via Divide, a station on the west, the entire distance being forty miles. The way leads through the uplifting scenery of the Ute Pass resorts already mentioned, and from Divide southward its character does not deteriorate. The Midland Terminal Railway, recently constructed, is now in operation from Divide to a point eight miles distant from Cripple Creek, and will shortly be completed through.

UTE PASS.

In the summer of 1891 the site of Cripple Creek was a

lonely ranch, and in a few months thereafter nearly 15,000 people had gathered there in consequence of the discovery of gold. A number of very valuable mines are understood to have been developed, and there are many claims of excellent promise. The claims are both placer and lode. The ledge lies underground, near the surface. It is necessary to uncover the rock before it can be examined to discover whether or not it contains "mineral," and the pretty slopes of Cripple Creek are liberally heaped with the debris of such excavations. Out of the original desperately scrambling mob of gold-seekers several thousand have remained, and the town has subsided into legitimate, sober work; but it is still very ragged and exceedingly picturesque, and the trip is a very entertaining one.

There is an excellent hotel, constructed at a great deal of expense and maintained in first-class style, which is a fact sufficiently unique in a young mining camp to merit specific mention. The trip is entirely practicable for ladies and children.

The name of the camp is derived from the stream that flows through the region, which in turn is indebted to some small accident which happened to a prospector or ranchman in former days.

The leisurely traveler, desirous of seeing the best of Colorado, should continue on through Granite Cañon, a rock gorge thirty-five miles west of Manitou, through whose notch the railroad runs by the side of a fork of the Platte River; through Buena Vista, ninety-six miles west of Manitou, an exquisitely located city some 8,000 feet above sea level, in the valley of the Arkansas, at the feet of Mounts Princeton, Harvard, and Yale, which are known as the College Peaks; through Leadville, the greatest mining camp in the world, 130 miles west of Manitou, at an altitude of 10,103 feet; over the Hagerman Pass, where the railroad crosses the Continental Divide at an altitude of 11,528 feet, by a tunnel through Mount Massive; down the Pacific Slope, through Red Rock Cañon, and past the grandly beautiful Seven Castles of red sandstone; and past Aspen Junction to Glenwood Springs.

Glenwood Springs.—Two hundred and sixteen miles west of Manitou. Chicago, 1,358 miles; St. Louis, 1,218 miles. Altitude, 5,800 feet. Population, 1,170.

One of the most attractive of mountain resorts. A conjunction of mountain, cañon, and valley, clear mountain rivers and hot mineral springs, supplemented by a magnificent hotel and bath-house. The swimming pool is 700 feet long, 110 feet wide, and from 3½ to 5½ feet deep, fed by a hot spring and tempered to a comfortable degree of warmth by a fountain of cold water in the center. In winter and summer alike people bathe in this vast out-of-door pool, and find the practice beneficial to health. Special trains, facetiously called "laundry trains," are run from Aspen, and other near cities and villages, one day in every week, to accommodate the multitude of bathers. There are also natural caves in the mountain-side, where the hot vapor from the springs accumulates by way of subterranean conduits, and these have been fitted up for the radical treatment of stubborn diseases.

The analysis of the waters of Yama Spring at Glenwood is as follows:

Chloride of sodium	1089.8307 grains.
Chloride of magnesium	13.0994 "
Bromide of sodium	0.5635 "
Iodide of sodium	Trace.
Fluoride of calcium	Trace.
Sulphate of potassa	24.0434 "
" " lime	82.3861 "

Bicarbonate of lithia	0.2209 grains.
" " magnesia	13.5532 "
" " lime	24.3727 "
" " iron	Trace.
Phosphate of soda	Trace.
Biborate " "	Trace.
Alumina	Trace.
Silica	1.9712 "
Organic matter	Trace.
Totals	1250.0411 grains.
Temperature	124.2° Fahr.
Carbonic acid, copiously discharged from the springs	Undetermined.
Sulphuretted hydrogen, discharged in perceptible quantity from the springs	Undetermined.

The vicinity of Glenwood Springs also affords good trout fishing, and bear, elk, and deer shooting. Trappers' Lake is reached by trail from this point.

Denver.—Seventy-three miles north of Colorado Springs. Chicago, 1,209 miles; St. Louis, 1,069 miles. Altitude, 5,190 feet. Population, 106,713.

Named after ex-Gov. James W. Denver of Kansas. This magnificent queen city of the plains has been created in thirty-five years, for in 1858 gold was first washed out from the sands of the South Platte by Caucasians, and from a mining-camp that arose after the gold discovery Denver has developed. Mining was the first impulse, and that and the treatment of ores has steadily contributed to the growth of the city to this day, three of the largest and most complete smelting and refining works in the world being established here, their yearly output amounting to nearly twenty-five millions of dollars in value. But Denver is also surrounded by a vast area of rich, arable lands, which produce wheat, oats, barley, and other grains, and roots and vegetables. It has acquired immense cattle and sheep interests, and furnishes a market for the apples, pears, peaches, plums, grapes, and smaller fruits and berries which are grown in the Colorado valleys. It is an important junction point for many concentering railroads, has large manufacturing interests, and is regarded as the trade-center for 400,000 people. Its residences, business blocks, and public buildings afford numerous examples of architectural beauty; the streets are broad, generally level, and frequently shaded, and there is an almost perfect system of electric and cable street railroads. And behind all this lie the attractions of superb climate and scenery.

We return to our point of digression at La Junta.

In this vicinity Pike's Peak is visible for some time upon the northwest, at a distance of about ninety miles, and the beautiful Spanish peaks, twin-mountains at the end of a spur of the Culebra Range, northwest from Trinidad, soon come into view, alternately disappearing and recurring until the summit of Raton Pass has been reached.

INTERMEDIATE STATIONS: Benton, Timpas, Ayer, Iron Springs, Delhi, Thatcher, Tyrone, Earl, Hoehne's.

Trinidad.—Chicago, 1,111 miles; St. Louis, 971 miles; Los Angeles, 1,154 miles; San Diego, 1,237 miles; San Francisco, 1,466 miles. Altitude, 5,982 feet. Population, 5,533. Junction with Union Pacific Railway and Denver & Rio Grande Railroad.

The mining of coal and the manufacture of coke, iron, lumber, mineral paint, lime, plaster of paris, and fire-brick are the principal industries of Trinidad, although flour and beer are also produced, and it is the largest wool and hide shipping point in Colorado. It has water-works, gas, and electric lights. St. Raphael's Hospital, St. Joseph Academy, and the Tillotson University are located here.

The city is beautifully environed by mountain scenery.

The conspicuous flat-top peak on the range beyond is known as Fisher's Peak. On the right a ruddy cliff rises to a height of a few hundred feet. Upon its top a party of pioneers was besieged by Indians in the early days, and one of the survivors, named Simpson, chose to be buried there many years after, when his time came to die. A rude monument surmounts Simpson's Rest, which may be seen from the train at the station.

The tunnel at the summit of Raton Pass is fifteen miles beyond Trinidad, at an altitude more than sixteen hundred feet greater. The difficulties of the ascent of the pass appear in the last few miles, but here the approach may be said to begin.

Raton Pass.—Altitude (at the tunnel), 7,622 feet.

There are three stations along the ascent beyond Trinidad, at intervals of five miles. Starkville is a coal-mining and coke-manufacturing point, and the remaining two, Morley and Wooten, are small and commercially unimportant settlements. The entire ascent affords a series of exhilarating views, best enjoyed from the rear platform of the train. The track follows the old Santa Fé trail, which is one of the most ancient of recognizable human pathways to be found on the continent. Wooten was named for an old-timer, "Uncle Dick" Wooten, whose partially-burnt and wholly abandoned house on the right of the track is a relic of the days of the six-horse Concord stage-coach, caravans of emigrants, and long wagon trains loaded with valuable goods and escorted by mounted soldiers to repel the attacks of Indians. Wooten kept the trail over the pass in repair, and collected toll from those who used it. But it was a frequented road centuries before Wooten was born, before the Spanish Invasion, and doubtless before the discovery of America;

for the practicable passes of the Rockies are comparatively few in number, and one at all aware of the great antiquity of human life in the Southwest will vainly grope backward for a time in the past when this must not have been a thoroughfare for aboriginal peoples.

The scenery is not of the tremendous type, but frequently wide in scope and full of incident. The road is tortuous, and the pace slow, two heavy locomotives being required to haul the train. The last broad view, before entering the final cut that forms the immediate approach to the tunnel, is a farewell glimpse of the Spanish peaks, seen directly over the Wooten house, rising from the far horizon of the plains below.

When the railroad was first built, it climbed over the top of the mountain, by means of a many-angled "switchback" which began near this point. The Raton Tunnel is 2,011 feet in length, and lies in New Mexico. A boundary post will be noticed some fifty feet short of the entrance.

From the other end of the tunnel the descent of the pass is a comparatively short matter, and the city of Raton is quickly reached.

NEW MEXICO.

HISTORICAL.—The oldest existing civilization in the United States is here. Whether or not Cabeza de Vaca passed this way in 1536, after being wrecked with the Narvaez expedition on the Florida reefs, it is certain that Marcos de Nizza saw this country three years later, and that, in 1540, Coronado came with his soldiers for conquest. This same Coronado was a tireless explorer himself, shirking none of the hardships of such enterprise, but intrusting numerous side expeditions to the command of chosen subordinates. He and his proxies discovered nearly everything except that which they sought, namely, gold. They tramped north and east as far as the Missouri River, they pushed to the northwest until they were stopped by the Grand Cañon of the Colorado River, and they braved the terrors of the desert on the west until they came to the shores of that river on the border of Southern California. They hoped to find what Cortez had found among the Aztecs, some hundreds of leagues to the south — precious metal wrought into ornamental shapes, all ready for the hand of the conqueror; but in all the native villages of New Mexico no fragment of gold has ever been found. Here, at least, the aborigine seems to have regarded it with disdain, provided he had ever regarded it at all. They did find, as Cortez had found, a resident people of temperate, frugal, and industrious habit, civilized in a way. These were the Pueblos, an Indian people who tilled the soil and dwelt in large communal houses made of stones and sun-dried mud, several stories in height, and in some instances containing a thousand compartments. The Spanish word *pueblo* means a village or a people, and these natives, as well as their curious habitations, have ever since been generally known by the name casually applied by their discoverers, although among themselves they are Moquis, Zuñis, Quéres, Tiguas, etc.

How long the Pueblos had dwelt in New Mexico prior to Spanish occupation is as much a matter of mystery to us of to-day as it was to Coronado, three and a half centuries ago. Their origin, even their kinship, has baffled research. History disowns them. They are essentially unlike the roving Indians of the plains, and it is denied that they are Aztecs. They possess a tradition of having come from the north, fighting inch by inch against the southward invasion of a fierce foe, until at last they came to these plateaus and built permanent fortress homes. This tradition, if authentic, offers explanation of the mysterious cliff dwellings which, like swallows' nests, mark the faces of cañon walls for hundreds of miles in southern

PUEBLO WOMEN.

Utah and Colorado and northern Arizona and New Mexico. In any event, when the Spaniards came the Pueblos had local ruins which themselves were the subject of traditions centuries old.

The soldier and the priest marched side by side in the old days of Spanish conquest, and simultaneously with the occupation of New Mexico mission churches of the Jesuit and San Franciscan orders arose. Colonists from Mexico followed in the wake of the soldiery, and the first white settlement was made at San Gabriel, on the Chama River, in 1598. Seven years later the present city of Santa Fé was founded. Upon its site a native capital is reputed to have been already in existence, and the visitor to Santa Fé is shown the house where Coronado is believed to have lodged in 1540. The Pueblos at first welcomed the Spaniards in the effusive manner of world-ignorant aborigines, but they ultimately grew discontented with Castilian oppression, and after a few small outbreaks united under the leadership of Po-Pe, in 1680, and drove every Spaniard whom they did not kill out of the Territory, burning and sacking the missions and destroying every reminder of the white men. After a struggle of twelve years to regain the lost province, the Spaniards reconquered under leadership of General Diego de Vargas. The colonization of New Mexico was then once more begun, and its development continued without serious interruption.

Early in our century Santa Fé became commercially significant, and was connected by wagon route with the Missouri River, and also with Los Angeles, in California. In 1837, after Mexico had become independent of Spain, this Territory revolted against unjust methods of government and taxation, but failed to achieve independence. It was occupied in 1847 by General Kearney and the Army of the West, for the United States, to which that portion west of the Rio Grande was ceded a year later. The eastern portion came by the Texas cession of 1850. Congress subsequently, at different times, rearranged its bounds and extent, which formerly embraced Arizona and a portion of Nevada and Colorado.

Several engagements between Federal and Confederate forces, during the Civil War, took place within the Territory, and up to a comparatively recent date the soldiers of the frontier army were kept busy pursuing Apaches with varying success.

DESCRIPTIVE.— The Territory has an average breadth of 335 miles, and its length from north to south is, upon the east 345, and upon the west 390 miles. Its area of 122,444 square miles is larger than that of Great Britain and Ireland. It is composed of vast upland plains of exceeding fertility, where rainfall is sufficient or irrigation is practiced, broken by innumerable alluvial valleys, and of mesas, foothills, spurs, and, finally, the lofty ranges of the Rocky Mountain chain, many of whose peaks attain an altitude of more than 12,000 feet. The Raton Range, trending eastward, is crossed by the pass. The Sangre de Cristo, Taos, and Costillo ranges lie contiguous or adjacent to our route. The Oscuro, San Andreas, and Organ mountains are farther to the south. The mean altitude of the entire Territory is nearly 6,000 feet above sea level, and that of the northern plains themselves is fully as great, the lower portions of New Mexico lying upon the south.

From the Raton Tunnel to the bottom of the pass the distance is nearly ten miles. Then the Great Plains begin to open before the view. The route makes southwestwardly toward the middle of the Territory, at Watrous entering the fair green expanse, sixty-odd miles square, to which the Spaniards gave the name Las Vegas, *The Meadows*, near whose side, midway, stands the old city of the same name.

Then come occasional Mexican villages scattered by the way, quaint communities of adobe huts, the white cross of the humble sanctuary infallibly discernible. These give a novel interest to the ride, as fragments of the purely picturesque. There is something oriental about every Mexican house. It is either built around a square or is a modification of that architectural plan. It is always of adobe—bricks of clay mixed with chopped straw and dried in the sun. The floor is of earth, and the roof as well. If for want of repair the hut wears the appearance of a hovel, the fault is not of the structure. It is the house of the country, and, as a rule, is extremely tidy. Adobe is really the best material for walls in a climate like this. It resists heat in summer and cold in winter.

The Mexicans are courteous, kindly, hospitable, and intelligent for their circumstances. Some of their strain represent the most active and prosperous residents of New Mexico, but not such as you see in these wayside villages. These are the reverse of enterprising. You may chance to see them hauling wood in ancient carts with cumbrous wooden wheels. They prefer to till the soil by precisely the same methods practiced by their great-grandfathers before them. Even the primitive plow, consisting of a forked limb and dragged through its perfunctory ceremony of tickling the ground by a thong attached to the horns of an ox, may happen to meet your eye. Although the modern methods of a more progressive race are fast taking root about them, the Mexicans are still numerically in the ascendant, and stubbornly cling to the old life of the Spanish peasant, as poor, as happy, and as quaint, here and now, as ever it was at home.

NEW MEXICO OVEN.

After these comes another mountain pass, that of the Glorieta, a lovely ride through park slopes to a commanding height, then a downward whirl on the brink of alluring gorges that are green with pine and fir and rosy with color of rock and earth. Glorieta Pass is on the westward sweep of the railroad from a little beyond Las Vegas to the banks of the Rio Grande del Norte, below Santa Fé.

Reaching the Great River of the North, its course is followed for many miles. This is a Nile valley, every year inundated by the mighty stream that is swollen by melting of mountain snows all the way back to its source in Colorado. When the flood comes in spring nothing can stand in its path. The sand-laden volume gnaws and undermines and rolls huge bowlders away like balls in its rush. The earth, too, is of a character easy to wash, a finely pulverized adobe. Among the notches of the hills waterspouts and the shed of heavy rains cut deep *arroyos* into the seemingly bottomless soil. You will observe many places where heavy rocks are heaped in between rows of sturdy piles, the only adequate protection against this formidable excavating force, which, in this territory and along this very railroad, has, in times past, repeatedly undone labor representing a cost of many hundred thousand dollars.

Immediately upon passing Albuquerque, having crossed the Rio Grande, a type of country is encountered different from any previously seen. The land of desert and volcano is fairly entered. It should not prove dreary, nor even monotonous, for in addition to its unaccustomed natural and human interest it is full of vivid color. Black and white illustrations do not convey the whole charm of the western country. You could as adequately represent the beauties of a brilliant water-color sketch by a steel engraving. The sky of Italy is not more intense than this marvelous flaming arch of blue. Sand and rock are warm with tints of red and brown or cinder black. Mesa and mountain on the horizon wear the hue of indigo in shadow. The after-shine of a sunset is yellow fire. There is no "atmosphere." You can not judge, with even approximate correctness, the distance of a fairly remote object. Two miles or ten miles distant are the same to the eye, as if the laws of optics had been unaccountably modified to increase the powers of vision.

The most famous of the inhabited pueblos of New Mexico lie adjacent to the road through this region, two of them, Isleta and Laguna, close beside the track. Acoma, the most poetic habitation in the world, is a dozen miles to the south, and Zuñi is likewise to one side, farther on. All are easily accessible to a Caucasian, and will richly compensate the delay involved in visiting them.

Ancient rivers of lava here parallel the way for long distances. The flow oozed from fissures in the plain, as

PUEBLO OF LAGUNA, NEW MEXICO.

well as from the towering craters whose slopes sweep upward to ragged rims against the sky.

Shortly before reaching the Arizona line the Continental Divide is crossed, and the rivers begin to flow toward the west and the sunset sea.

CLIMATE.—It is no exaggeration to say that here the sun shines nearly every day. There is a fairly well-defined rainy season, extending from the middle of June to the middle of September, but the aggregate annual precipitation averages only 13.61 inches. The showery afternoons of that period are usually preceded by bright mornings, and during the remainder of the year the sky is unspotted by a cloud for weeks at a time. But it is not a land of distressful heat, as one might infer. It has a summer climate whose equability of comfort has no superior in the Union. To understand this it is necessary to bear in mind the important factors of pronounced altitude and low humidity. Altitude is everywhere a proportional equivalent for latitude, and the climatic effect of the altitude of New Mexico is to give it the same temperature that would prevail at sea level just seven degrees farther north — upon the New England coast, for example, other conditions remaining unchanged. Low humidity, however, operates as an element of still further amelioration. Humidity is the amount of invisible moisture in the air, as distinguished from rain and fog. The percentage

YOUTH, SUNSHINE, AND LEISURE.

of humidity here is exceedingly low, that of Santa Fé, whose altitude is 7,019 feet, being 48.8 per cent, and that of lower and more arid regions diminishing to 29 per cent. For comparison in this interesting particular the humidity of the following localities outside of New Mexico is given: Boston, 69 per cent; New York, 72 per cent; Buffalo, 73 per cent; Detroit, 71 per cent; New Orleans, 79 per cent; San Diego, 71 per cent; Los Angeles, 68 per cent; San Francisco, 76 per cent; Olympia, 79 per cent. The effect of humidity is to accentuate bodily sensibility to heat and cold, the common discomforts of summer and winter being due to this quite as much as to the degree of temperature registered by the thermometer. This is strikingly illustrated in New Mexico. The direct rays of the sun in midsummer are really fervent, but their effect

PRIMITIVE INDUSTRY.

is not cumulative, and, by reason of the low percentage of humidity, is literally not to be feared. Violent exercise in the sun is not attended by noticeable perspiration, nor by any added discomfort, save only that which may be due to unwonted altitude. The shade is invariably cool. The case has no parallel in the Middle, Eastern, or South Atlantic States. It follows that nights are cold in winter, and in summer entirely free from oppressiveness. Residents of New Mexico wear the same variety of clothing the year round, and always sleep under blankets, although there are but few days when persons in delicate health may not freely venture abroad. The following weather statistics of Santa Fé may be taken as approximately representative of the northern half of the Territory at high altitude. The lower altitude and latitude of the southern half would naturally result in somewhat higher temperatures:

U. S. DEPARTMENT OF AGRICULTURE — WEATHER BUREAU.
OFFICE OF THE STATE WEATHER SERVICE, SANTA FÉ, N. M.
Summary of Weather for Ten Years, 1882 to 1891, inclusive.

MONTHS.	Mean Temperature.	Mean Maximum Temperature.	Mean Minimum Temperature.	Mean Relative Humidity.	Monthly Rainfall.	Average Hourly Velocity of Wind.	Average No. Days with .01 of an inch or more of rain or snow.	No. Clear Days.	No. Partly Cloudy Days.	No. Cloudy days.
January	27.4	37.5	17.2	60.8	0.55	6.7	7	17	10	4
February	33.8	44.1	23.6	57.0	0.83	7.5	6	12	10	5
March	41.7	51.8	29.6	48.3	0.66	7.6	7	14	12	5
April	47.6	59.6	35.6	42.7	0.88	8.3	6	12	13	5
May	55.9	68.3	43.5	39.4	1.03	7.8	6	13	14	4
June	64.8	77.5	52.2	36.0	0.83	7.0	6	14	12	2
July	70.0	81.9	58.0	46.4	1.58	6.6	12	24	16	4
August	67.6	79.2	56.1	49.2	2.18	6.2	12	11	17	3
September	61.0	72.5	49.5	50.4	1.57	5.9	8	17	10	4
October	50.9	62.4	39.4	45.6	0.81	6.4	3	22	7	2
November	38.6	49.1	28.2	50.9	0.76	6.7	5	18	8	3
December	32.4	41.8	22.9	59.2	1.03	6.6	7	19	9	6
Sums	590.7	728.6	455.1	585.9	12.71	83.3	85	193	138	48
Means	49.2	60.5	38.0	48.8	1.06	6.9	7.1	16.1	11.5	4.0

I certify that the above is a correct summary of the records of this station for the years stated.

H. A. HERSEY,
Observer Weather Bureau.

By virtue of the climatic conditions thus briefly noted, New Mexico has won wide recognition in recent years as a sanitarium for sufferers from catarrhal and pulmonary affections. It is the center of a region of similar character which extends northward into western Kansas and central Colorado, westward through upper Arizona, and southward into Mexico, with many gradations of adaptability to different stages and complications of disease. Numerous sanitariums have been established in the Territory at different altitudes, and in environments especially suited to the requirements of particular classes of consumptive patients, who are scattered all the way from Colorado to Mexico. Many of the present active business men of New Mexico came here years ago with no better hope than to experience a speedy euthanasia, which is a word by which physicians disguise a painless but inevitable death. It appears to be an indubitable fact that in climate lies the only hope of the consumptive, and that here, provided he does not too long delay his coming, the progress of the fell disease may be effectually arrested, and in many cases the disease itself practically cured.

INDUSTRIAL.—Old as it is in the historical sense, New Mexico is very youthful so far as concerns development of its resources. In spite of its totally inadequate rainfall, the agricultural possibilities of its plains are very great, and the valley of the Rio Grande alone should in time become one of the most fruitful valleys in the world. The primary difficulty has been the necessity of irrigation. Enough water runs to waste in the season of flooded streams to water the whole Territory many times over, but capital is required to utilize it except in a relatively insignificant way. The small farms of the Mexicans are located convenient to natural water supply, and individual enterprise has created a large number of other small farms, which are exceedingly profitable, but the large areas have lain unused, except for grazing, save where conjoint capital has supplied the need, and these cases have been few in comparison with the extent of the opportunity. From time to time new enterprises are inaugurated for the construction of dams to check and store the water of the streams and to ditch the neighboring lands, and their number will undoubtedly increase year by year, for the reward is great. Another embarrassment operating to the retardation of agriculture has been that the most available land was principally held in large tracts under the old Spanish grant system, which got itself into such a state of confusion that what Americans and American law consider good titles could not be given to purchasers. The land court appointed by Congress will shortly relieve this embarrassment. The court is now engaged in the work of adjudicating disputed titles. Besides the lands included in the doubtful grants there are some sixty millions of Government lands unhampered by grant or adverse claim of any kind, but the limit of available water supply and topographical considerations probably will permit only a fraction of this ever to be cultivated. Hand in hand with the scantiness of its rainfall goes a very small number of water courses of magnitude in New Mexico. When these shall have been fully economized it is regarded as unlikely that more than two million acres will be practically irrigable. But 2,000,000 acres of such soil as this under cultivation will mean a great deal in establishing this vast territory upon an ample foundation. At present it consumes more produce than it raises, and the business of farming is attended with unusual profit as a consequence. All the vegetables, grains, and fruits of the north temperate zone, omitting only the citrous varieties (oranges, lemons, and the like), and such as are peculiar to regions that neighbor the tropics, are grown in perfection. Insect and parasitic pests are said to be unknown.

New Mexico is rich in gold, silver, copper, iron, lead, zinc, anthracite and bituminous coal, and in garnets, agates, amethysts, and turquoise. The annual product of gold has reached $500,000, of silver $3,300,000, and of coal 675,000 tons. The vast areas of pine and cedar timber in the mountains lie almost untouched. Two million horned cattle, 2,500,000 sheep and goats, and 200,000 horses and mules are owned in the Territory.

Phenomenally rich in resource, it offers extraordinary opportunities to capital and individual settlers.

IRRIGATION.— Old as is the practice of irrigation, and common as it is throughout the West, a few words under that head will not come amiss to the average traveler to whom arid regions are new.

The idea is apparently as old as history. At least it was known to the ancient Egyptians, to whom it may have been suggested naturally by the beneficent periodical inundations of the Nile, as doubtless to other nations in a like manner, for where prior to such inundation it was impossible to profitably till the parched earth abundant crops followed the overflow. It was practiced by the prehistoric peoples of New Mexico and Arizona, as evidenced by existing ruins of irrigating systems, and the Spaniards were wise of it and applied their knowledge generally in colonizing America.

In the simplest form it consists in flooding the entire surface of the ground with water at frequent intervals, thus artificially making substitution for rain. But the common method of irrigating crops is to let the water into collateral trenches, which are dug sufficiently near together to permit the flowing water to "seep" through the intervening space of earth. In orchards a shallow serpentine furrow, winding along a row of trees, passing one upon the right and another upon the left, is a sufficient conduit. An irrigating ditch is termed in Spanish an *accquia*, and the main ditch, by which the entire volume is conveyed from point to point for distribution, is the *accquia madre*, or parent ditch. In some localities the volume is transmitted through enormous flumes, supported on trestle work to conquer topographical difficulties. Again it is sometimes conveyed through pipes, along the upper side of a tract, with cocks at frequent intervals, and the farmer turns the cock and directs the rivulet as he may choose, with a few strokes of spade or hoe.

The turbid waters of New Mexico do more than moisten; their burden of sediment is a distinct fertilizer, like that of the Nile flood. Sandy and apparently worthless tracts are thus converted into most prolific gardens.

Irrigation makes agriculture an almost exact science, stripped of the hazard of drought or flood, from which the Eastern farmer is never quite secure until his harvest is garnered. Successful agriculture requires a suitable soil, abundant sunshine, and neither too much nor too little water. Often the first two conditions are present, but the third is wanting. Farming by irrigation in the West combines all three. It matters not whether it is in western Kansas, or Colorado, or New Mexico, or Arizona, or California; it is a logical business, and as certain as anything can be in this world. When the crops are thirsty the farmer here does not scan the horizon anxiously for sight of a cloud; he turns on the water. And when that thirst is slaked he is not consumed with the apprehension that the fields will be drowned by superabundance of rain; he turns it off.

The cost of irrigation per acre is ordinarily rated at $2.50 per annum. One dollar and fifty cents of this sum is the charge made for delivering the water by the company or community that supplies it and keeps the canal in repair, and the remaining $1.00 is the value of the labor involved in actually applying the water to the land.

PRINCIPAL POINTS OF INTEREST.

INTERMEDIATE STATIONS: Lynn, Hillside.

Raton.—Chicago, 1,134 miles; St. Louis, 994 miles; Los Angeles, 1,131 miles; San Diego, 1,214 miles; San Francisco, 1,443 miles. Dining station. Altitude, 6,637 feet. Population, 1,255.

This town, which is almost exactly midway between Chicago and Los Angeles, is an important center of the cattle industry, and is located on the line of those inexhaustible coal deposits which extend unbroken through this region for 250 miles. Blossburg, a coal-mining town of nearly as many inhabitants as Raton, lies only a short distance west, a branch railroad connecting it with Dillon, three miles below. Raton is the site of extensive railroad machine shops, and the headquarters of the Maxwell Land Grant Company.

THE MAXWELL GRANT.—What is seen of northernmost New Mexico belongs to this great land grant. For sixty miles your route runs through it, namely, from Starkville on the Colorado side of the Raton Pass, to Springer. Before New Mexico was ceded to the United States two agents of the American Fur Company, Carlos Beaubien and Guadalupe Miranda, obtained the grant, consisting of 1,714,765 acres. Precisely what equivalent was rendered does not appear, but the old Spanish rulers had a large-handed way of dealing out parcels of the earth to their favorites, and certainly the land was worth comparatively little at the time. Lucien B. Maxwell, a companion guide with Kit Carson on Fremont's expeditions, married the daughter of Beaubien, and ultimately acquired the entire property by inheritance and by purchase, thus becoming the largest individual land-owner in the United States The Spanish title to the grant was subsequently confirmed by this Government and patent issued. The ownership afterward took the form of a corporation, of which Dutch capitalists now have control. It is a little empire in itself, its principal settlements and activities being some distance removed from the railroad upon the west. Within its limits there are Mexican villages and prosperous farms owned by Dutch and English ranchmen. It embraces mines of coal, the surface croppings providing the Mexicans with an easily collected fuel, and of gold, silver, and iron, gold placer fields, deposits of fire-clay and cement, quarries of building-stone, and forests of timber. It

A NEW MEXICAN MATRON.

has a telephone system of 120 miles. There are single ranches of twenty or thirty thousand acres each, and many modest farms of small acreage occupied by settlers. Its agricultural products may be taken as typical of northern New Mexico. Corn is the poorest average crop among the grains. Wheat, oats, and barley yield very heavily, and the kernels are of extraordinary weight; 35, 45, and 60 bushels per acre respectively are the average crops of these grains; 400 bushels of potatoes are raised to the acre; onions weighing 4 pounds, and cabbages 45 pounds, are common. Thousands of barrels of the best quality of apples, and large quantities of cherries, plums, peaches, pears, strawberries, currants, gooseberries, raspberries, and blackberries are regularly shipped. Alfalfa is the principal hay crop. The grazing lands sustain innumerable sheep and vast herds of cattle. Irrigation is practiced, the water being taken chiefly from the head of the Cimarron and Vermejo rivers.

Among the foot-hills and their cañons are cinnamon bear and mountain lions, and clear streams thronged with trout; and in the broad and beautiful parks on the mesas above are white-tail and mule deer, grouse, and wild turkeys. The ranchmen and their Mexican employes are usually enthusiastic hunters, and are particularly fond of riding to hounds on the hot trail of the bear.

INTERMEDIATE STATIONS: Dillon, Otero, Hebron, Dorsey.

Maxwell City.— Chicago, 1,160 miles; St. Louis, 1,020 miles; Los Angeles, 1,105 miles; San Diego, 1,188 miles; San Francisco, 1,417 miles. Altitude, 5,900 feet.

Created for the convenience of the business of the Maxwell Grant. The intersecting water course is the Vermejo.

The old Mexican town of Cimarron, on the Cimarron River, lies at a distance of twenty miles on the west, this side the mountains, which are farther distant than they appear to the eye. Until a few years ago Cimarron was a rendezvous of cowboys and fugitive desperadoes, and the scene of numerous deeds of violence. One of its conspicuous landmarks is the burial-ground of men who died with their boots on, some in personal altercation, some by murder, some by verdict of outraged citizens acting on behalf of law and order. But that epoch has forever gone by for all the Southwest. The railroad was a species of Augean broom, sweeping ever along in its westward advance the most turbulent of lawless spirits, who found upon the border a greater toleration of their unrestraint than elsewhere. Their era was short. What has become of them as a class it would be hard to say. Such burial-grounds as that above mentioned accounts for some few; the rest have disappeared.

INTERMEDIATE STATION: Dover.

Springer.— Chicago, 1,174 miles; St. Louis, 1,034 miles; Los Angeles, 1,091 miles; San Diego, 1,174 miles; San Francisco, 1,403 miles. Altitude, 5,783 feet. Population, 600.

Another Maxwell Grant town, exactly midway between Chicago and San Diego. A large irrigating system, with many miles of ditch in operation, exists upon the east, of which glimpses may be seen after leaving the station. A hydraulic cement, equal to the famous Portland variety, is manufactured here. The stream is the Cimarron, which joins the Canadian and flows eastward across Texas, Oklahoma, and the Indian Territory to join the Arkansas.

The pueblo of Taos lies about fifty miles west. It is more conveniently reached from the farther side, and the visit to Taos is customarily made northward from Santa Fé, by way of the Santa Fé Southern Railway.

INTERMEDIATE STATIONS: Rayado, Colmor, Nolan, Levy.

Wagon Mound. — Altitude, 6,193 feet.

Formerly the seat of a Mexican frontier custom house, and its queer-shaped mountain, which may be seen from the train, was a landmark visible for many miles to travelers over the wearying and perilous old Santa Fé Trail. It is a small village of about 500 inhabitants.

INTERMEDIATE STATIONS: Tipton, Shoemaker.

Watrous. — Altitude, 6,413 feet.

Here begin the broad mountain-hemmed meadows to which the name Las Vegas is due. Fort Union, with a garrison, lies upon the right a short distance away.

INTERMEDIATE STATIONS: Kroenig's, Onava, Azul.

Las Vegas.— Chicago, 1,244 miles; St. Louis, 1,104 miles; Los Angeles, 1,021 miles; San Diego, 1,104 miles; San Francisco, 1,333 miles. Dining station. Junction with branch line to Las Vegas Hot Springs. Altitude, 6,399 feet. Population, 5,273.

This is the second city of New Mexico in population and commercial importance. It is one of the largest wool-shipping points in the United States, and in addition to this staple its mercantile houses handle a general business of large volume for an immense tributary and dependent country. It is a railroad division point, and a large number of men are employed in repair shops, freight yards, and tie-treating works. Wool-washing works, a brewery, and a steam flour-mill contribute to its industrial activity. Las Vegas contains the State asylum for the insane.

It is widely known as a health resort for consumptive patients, many of whom find here the precise conditions suitable to their needs. It stands on treeless meadows, underlaid by blue limestone and red and white sandstone. It is watered by the slender Rio Gallinas, which is Spanish for Turkey River. Las Vegas is exactly half way between St. Louis and San Diego.

INTERMEDIATE STATIONS: Romero, Sulzbacher, Bernal, Blanchard, San Miguel, Sands, Fulton.

STARVATION PEAK.

STARVATION PEAK.— There is a symmetrical, flat-topped mountain visible from numerous points along a distance of many miles, but most nearly to be seen from the neighborhood of Bernal, twenty miles below Las Vegas. This is Starvation Peak. Two or three gigantic crosses upon the summit give an air of solemnity to the bleak mass which is quite in keeping with the tale of dole which forms one of its traditions. Its early name was Bernal Peak, derived, like the name of the little village at its foot, from that of the first settler in the vicinity. It is said that about the end of the first quarter of our century the territory was generally involved in warfare with the Comanche and Navajo Indians, and the town of Bernal was attacked by the Navajoes. After a short siege the principal men of the town accepted an invitation to a council without arms, and were treacherously slain. The remainder of the settlers then fled toward the mountain, and about twenty of the number succeeded in reaching the summit. There they were secure from attack, but were besieged by the Indians below until they all died of starvation. Their bones were afterward collected by friendly hands and given burial, and the crosses were erected and maintained in their memory.

Thus runs one legend. The other maintains that the crosses were originally erected by the Brotherhood of Penitentes, and when their devotion flagged, some twenty-five years ago, a mysterious hermit appeared and made his home on the peak, engrossed in prayers and in exhortations to his numerous visitors to renew the former pious demonstrations. The crosses, which had fallen down, were replaced, and the penitential ceremonies received a new but short-lived impetus from the exhortations of the hermit.

The first version is the more romantic, but the second is perhaps the more plausible account, although it should be added that the Indians can not be persuaded to go upon the summit of Starvation Peak, presumably on account of a superstition grounded upon the tradition of some tragic occurrence. Still further confusion results from the existence of the ruins of stone fortifications on the summit, regarding which there is no discoverable definite legend. The oldest settlers do not pretend to know very much about the matter.

PENITENTES.— The Spanish name of this order, which seems to have originated in Europe several centuries ago, is *Los Hermanos Penitentes* (the Penitent Brotherhood), commonly abbreviated to Penitentes. It has many members among the Mexicans of New Mexico and southern Colorado.

Upon initiation of a member his back is cut deeply with a sharp piece of flint or obsidian. The incisions are given a symbolic meaning, and their number depends upon the enthusiasm of the novice. If he asks to be given "the five wounds of Christ," or "the ten commandments," or "the forty days in the wilderness," he is scoriated just so many times with the flint. The wounds are cut open afresh each year thereafter to increase the pain of the flagellations which are practiced. The scourging, or "discipline," consists of belaboring the bare back with a cruel whip, often made of cactus or soap-weed, and generally is performed by the penitent himself. It is no perfunctory ceremony, but a severe flogging, repeated for a self-imposed number of times, lacerating the flesh and drawing blood at every blow. One of the commoner demonstrations is a processional of such self-torturers. On other occasions the Penitentes stagger under the burden of heavy crosses, which they bear for long distances and to the point of exhaustion. The crosses are often twenty feet long and eight or ten inches square, weighing from 200 to 800 pounds. Sometimes only the upper part of the cross rests upon the shoulders, and the long upright is allowed to drag heavily on the ground. In other instances the entire weight bears on the shoulders and extended arms, each hand resting lightly upon the handle of a sword, the point pressing against the side of the poor zealot, whose arms can hardly support their load, yet can not relax without plunging one or both swords into his body.

These tortures, inflicted "for the love of God," are varied in many ways, all revolting; and the climax is reached in a veritable crucifixion, when men suffer themselves to be bound and, formerly, even nailed upon a cross and suspended for half an hour in an agony which not infrequently has proven fatal. Modern public sentiment has practically done away with the worst realism of this horrible rite, but not a few Penitentes are said to be still living in New Mexico who bear in their palms the marks of the crucifying spike.

The Catholic church, within whose pale they belong, has vainly tried to suppress the fanatic ceremonies of this extraordinary order, although they are slowly yielding to the sentiment of a more rational age. The Penitentes dislike publicity, and in their flagellations are accustomed to conceal their identity from any chance stranger by wearing hoods of black cloth. Their demonstrations begin with Lent and culminate on Good Friday; then they subside into unobtrusiveness as ordinary individuals for the remainder of the year.

Rowe.—Chicago, 1,290 miles; St. Louis, 1,150 miles; Los Angeles, 975 miles; San Diego, 1,058 miles; San Francisco, 1,287 miles. Altitude, 6,821 feet. Population, 315.

Attention is called to this station, half-way between Chicago and San Francisco, as being a convenient point of departure for the Pecos Ruin and the upper Pecos River, description of which follows.

THE PECOS RUIN.— Fifty miles below Las Vegas, on the rise to the pass of the Glorieta Mountain, there is visible upon the right, at a distance of several miles, an open valley in whose center stands a gaunt brown ruin. This ruin is plainly to be seen from the train at several points on either side of the station Pecos, although it too nearly resembles the earth in color to catch a careless eye. It is what is left of one of the first missions founded in New Mexico, approximately three and a half centuries old, and about it are strewn the ruins of an ancient Indian pueblo whose greater age may hardly be guessed. Not impossibly it was inhabited many centuries before the Spaniards came. The church ruin only is distinguishable from the train, and is not impressive in that view, but seen at close range it is augustly imposing. It is most conveniently reached by a drive of four miles from Rowe, a station five miles north of Pecos, and viewed nearly it possesses the valley — a lonely, slow-dying thing, weighted with tragic and mysterious memory. Upon a natural fortress-like elevation a few acres in extent, and rock-walled upon three sides, the razed pueblo lies scattered, an almost unintelligible heap of stones, with here and there a bit or an angle of wall standing. Upon the fourth side stand the dismantled adobe walls of the church. Every portable thing of particular value to the antiquarian or the merely curious has been carried away long ago, except scattered arrow-heads of flint and obsidian, a handful of which may still be picked up from the surface of the rock-strewn slopes in an hour's search.

The Pecos Church is supposed to have been built by the Friars about the year 1540, or simultaneously with Coronado's conquest, in accordance with their custom of locating their missions in the villages of the natives. In the Pueblo rebellion of 1680 it was partially burned and completely sacked, save for the oddly-carved beams and other crude architectural ornaments, which have since been stripped from the edifice. The number of arrow-heads still obtainable, after so many have been carried away, is sufficient evidence that this was often the scene of savage warfare. The course of old irrigating ditches is still discernible, and the plain which now supports only a few stray cattle and burros must once have maintained many hundreds of these agricultural people.

The Pecos tribe, reduced by some ill-starred fate to a mere handful, quitted this place half a century ago to dwell at Jemez, near the Rio Grande, west of Santa Fé.

Inquiry in this region easily elicits reputed traditions of the Pecos Pueblo, for there are aged Mexicans who apparently never in all their lives have been outside of this immediate locality; but it may be doubted if they are genuine derivations; they sound more like myths that have been falsely imputed. For example, such is the story that the Pecos Indians maintain that here Montezuma last reviewed his army before ascending into heaven, promising one day to return, and that so long as the tribe dwelt here a vestal flame was kept burning upon the altar in expectation of his coming. There is no good reason to believe that Montezuma is a god of the Pueblos. In any event the Montezuma myth is incoherent

A GREAT-GREAT-GRANDDAUGHTER OF CASTILE.

and elusive, if indeed it has anything of genuine Pueblo tradition about it, and it is cited here merely as an example of local legend relating to a people regarding whom about as much is actually known, concerning their past history and present inner life, as of the ancient Egyptians, or any other wholly problematical people that may be named.

THE PECOS RIVER AND NATIONAL PARK.—Far in the mountains upon the north the Pecos River rises, and flows southward through the reservation of the Pecos Pueblo, crossing the railroad just east of Rowe, and continuing southeastward to a junction with the Rio Grande in Texas. It becomes a large and important river during its course, but here is only a mountain stream, although much larger than any yet encountered in the Territory. Its uppermost portion is included in a large tract which has been set aside for a national park, whose lower bounds reach almost to the ruin. The park is a wildly beautiful country of forest, and meadow, and mountain, said to abound in game. The river swarms with trout. The word *pecos*, apparently corrupt Spanish for "freckles" (*pecas*), has been thought to be an allusion to the multitude of the speckled denizens of the stream, in the same manner that the word *blanquillos* (little white things) is used instead of *huevos* (eggs) in the Mexican vernacular. As far down as the vicinity of the pueblo, the fishing is of the very best. While the trout do not attain the large size boasted by eastern lakes and the more famous Colorado streams, they rarely weigh less than half a pound, and two-pounders are occasionally captured. They take the fly freely. The Pecos is shallow enough for continuous wading, except for occasional pools, and broad enough to give full play to the skill of the fly-fisherman. It is, moreover, a water-course of exceptional beauty, a succession of rapids, falls, and whirlpools through exquisite bits of woodland and meadow, and occasional gorges with perpendicular rock walls, whose splendors of form and color can hardly be exaggerated.

It is unfortunate that the average tourist is dependent upon what he can see from the car window for most of his impressions of New Mexico, as of Arizona. Let him, at least, remember that the conditions which commonly determine the precise route of railroad construction are cheapness and directness. Unavoidable obstacles do indeed arise, and then the railroad is forced through scenes of mountain beauty, such, for example, as this very ride over the Glorieta Range. But far grander scenes lie on every hand, avoided because their grandeur is made up of material that is decidedly adverse to railroad building.

INTERMEDIATE STATION: Pecos.

Glorieta Pass.—Altitude, 7,453 feet.

Glorieta means a summer-house, a bower; and its application here is probably no more than an allusion to the gentle verdured beauty of the scene. Here the forest is again encountered on the main line, for the first time since leaving the Raton Pass, 150 miles back. The whole length of the pass is nearly thirty miles, and is a natural park which art could hardly improve. Away to the north the mountains lie piled, the fragrant pines thickly set between. There are cuts through the rock, and deep water-hewn gorges. The air is cool, even in midsummer. Twenty feet below the summit, upon the eastern slope, is the little town of Glorieta. The western end of the pass is Apache Cañon, a savage notch where the mountain gives grudging passage. It must have been an admirable point for an ambuscade, from the Apache's point of view, and the name is unpleasantly suggestive of tragic doings, although trivial circumstances often determine the names of romantic spots. Distinct historical associations of a different kind, however, exist here. A battle took place on this ground in 1847, between Kearney's Army of the West and the Mexicans, and here in 1862 the Federal and Confederate forces met in conflict.

At the farther end of this cañon, near the track, a missionary priest named Lamy, afterward archbishop of Santa Fé, once taught the Indians in a little adobe school-house.

The Glorieta Mountain is the real water-shed of this region, and its western slope descends to the Rio Grande Valley. Thus it happens that the Pecos, taking rise very near the Rio Grande, wanders for hundreds of miles before finding a way to join that great stream.

INTERMEDIATE STATION: Cañoncito.

Lamy.—Chicago, 1,309 miles; St. Louis, 1,169 miles; Los Angeles, 956 miles; San Diego, 1,039 miles; San Francisco, 1,268 miles. Dining station. Junction with branch line to Santa Fé. Altitude, 6,475 feet.

The distance to Santa Fé is eighteen miles. The holder of a round-trip California ticket by the Santa Fé Route can obtain a side ride from Lamy to Santa Fé and return, without extra payment, upon application to the ticket agent at Lamy

Santa Fe.—Chicago, 1,327 miles; St. Louis, 1,187 miles; Los Angeles, 974 miles; San Diego, 1,057 miles; San Francisco, 1,286 miles. Junction with Santa Fé Southern Railway. Altitude, 7,019 feet. Railroad station, 6,954 feet. Population, 6,185.

The approach to the New Mexican capital is another ascent. It lies twenty miles from the Rio Grande, in the middle of a high plain rimmed by mountain peaks which, during many months of the year, are tipped with snow, although the climate of Santa Fé is characterized by extraordinary gentleness and equability. Its claim to being the oldest city in the United States (St. Augustine, its only contestant, dating from 1595) rests upon the discovery of a native village upon the same site by Coronado in 1540. This is perhaps not altogether an unreasonable claim, although it may be argued that in a world so old as ours, with the ashes of forgotten civilizations scattered everywhere beneath our feet, it will not do to rake over too much of antique dust in search of our beginnings. In any

STREET SCENE, SANTA FÉ.

event the Spanish city was actually founded in 1605, although some say 1598. Its population is about equally divided between Mexican and Saxon.

The older part of the town is typically Mexican, composed of little squat adobe houses irregularly strung along the sides of narrow streets. It is unwearyingly picturesque. Old men and old women sit placidly in the black shadows by the roadside, as if lounging were the only authentic business of life and they its hearty exemplars. Occasionally a woman issues from one of the houses to go a-visiting, her head and shoulders muffled in the black, fringed shawl which they call *tapelo;* or a dog barks; or a swarthy huckster appears aimlessly following the vagaries of a burro loaded to a small steeple-height with fire-wood or latticed boxes filled with garden-truck. Otherwise nothing appears to be doing. One suspects the problem of life is solved here on the old philosophic plan of requiring but little to subsist upon, and falls to wondering how the houses, primitive as they are, ever got themselves built. A seventh-day inactivity prevails. It is a city asleep, or mummified, rather, preserved almost unchanged for centuries by its gift of repose. It seems to be always drowsy noon, bathed in the brilliant sunlight which has no peer outside New Mexico. This sunlight is necessary to old Santa Fé. One can not conceive it in a land of fog and cloudy weather. The brown adobe walls gleam almost golden above their sharply-cut shadows. Here and there is a high-walled inclosure with ponderous gate of solid wood, through whose aperture may be had a glimpse of

SAN MIGUEL CHURCH, SANTA FÉ.

the brilliant green of dense foliage and the vivid variegated colors of flowers. These seem to declare the existence of a happy domestic life behind the adobe.

In the center of the cluster stands the Church of San Miguel, upon the street that bears its name. Built soon after the Spanish occupation, it was partly demolished by the natives in 1680, rehabilitated in 1710, and since further repaired into a resumption of its original appearance. It contains a very ancient copper bell, formerly in the turret, in which the date 1350 is cast.

Almost in the shadow of the church stands, among other houses, the one in which Coronado is believed to have lodged. This old house, until a year or two back, possessed the unusual distinction of a second story, now removed. It is inhabited by a Mexican family, and visitors are welcome to enter and leave what reckoning they deem proper after satisfying their curiosity.

Modern Santa Fé stands on the other side of the little dividing river, although much that is characteristically Mexican is mingled with it. The lower part of San Francisco Street is almost wholly lined by adobe structures, and its throng is a motley composition of Indians, Mexicans, and brisk business men of a different extraction. This was the scene of the transition period, of whose high romance chapters might be written if space permitted. The old Mexican town of prodigious mercantile importance as a receiving and distributing point was sapped by the diversion of traffic which naturally followed from railroad construction through the Territory. The exuberance of that era, when it was a central depot for overland caravans and stages, no longer pertains to Santa Fé, although it is an active and growing city.

At the side of the plaza stands the Palace, as old as Santa Fé itself, in which has been the home and office of every Governor of New Mexico since the first viceroy. Before the rebellion of 1680 the Holy Inquisition, *Santo Oficio*, held its functions there, and in the plaza in front of its placid walls many a Pueblo Indian has been executed. In the first decade of this century Lieut. Zebulon M. Pike, the explorer, was brought into its executive chamber to give an account of himself to Spanish authority, neither party dreaming that the United States would so soon preside there. At least, if Pike dreamed it he was very discreet, and after being detained for some months by a form of hospitality which was understood on both sides to be captivity courteously disguised, he was allowed to depart. A portion of the palace is now occupied by the collections of the historical society, which include innumerable archæological and historical treasures.

The Rosario Chapel, erected by Diego de Vargas, in pious gratitude for his victory over the Pueblos, is another antiquity. It stands upon an eminence nearly a mile from the heart of the city, where Vargas first looked down, with his little army, upon the town from which his countrymen had been repulsed for twelve years. By its side is the modern Ramona Indian school.

The Cathedral of San Francisco and the churches of Our Lady of Guadalupe and Our Lady of Light contain ancient paintings and wood-carvings, and the Territorial Library possesses the old Spanish records.

The penitentiary and Fort Marcy are other Government institutions located at Santa Fé.

Besides the Ramona school, the St. Catherine school and Dawes Institute are educational institutions for Indians.

Santa Fé Cañon, Monument Rock (on the border of the Pecos National Park), and the pueblos of Tesuque and Nambé are near objects of interest.

INTERMEDIATE STATIONS: Galisteo, Ortiz.

Los Cerrillos.— Eighteen miles beyond Lamy.

This is the location of large mines of both anthracite and bituminous coal. There are valuable gold mines in the vicinity, one of which, the Lincoln Lucky, shipped 200 car-loads of ore in 1892. There are also copper and turquoise mines.

INTERMEDIATE STATIONS: Waldo, Rosario.

Wallace.— Chicago, 1,340 miles; St. Louis, 1,200 miles; Los Angeles, 925 miles; San Diego, 1,008 miles; San Francisco, 1,237 miles. Altitude, 5,263 feet. Population, 124.

The pueblo of San Domingo lies at a distance of two or three miles on the other side of the Galisteo River, and can very conveniently be reached from this station, although it is usually included among the sights of the vicinity of Santa Fé.

San Domingo does not, however, rank high among the pueblos as an object of interest. The greater pueblos lie farther on along our route. The yearly feasts and rites of these strange people are, nevertheless, of great interest, regardless of the relative unimportance of the pueblo, and upon such occasions many New Mexicans flock together from immediately neighboring towns to witness the spectacle.

At Wallace the Galisteo joins the Rio Grande, and you fairly enter the great valley, whose course is followed as far as Albuquerque.

Mexican villages are plentifully strewn by the way. The life of the inhabitants of these villages is very simple and placidly happy. It goes on undisturbed by any of the changes that occur in what we call the world. There are births, and weddings, and deaths; that is the summary of exciting events. There are no lawyers or doctors, nor any politics. The only scholar is the priest. They have no theories; they try no experiments; and they often live to a very old age. But they are not barbarians. They possess an easy courtesy, a perfect understanding of even the statelier forms of politeness that is an inheritance with them, an integral part of the Spanish blood which, to a greater or less degree, flows in their veins.

INTERMEDIATE STATIONS: Elota, Algodones, Bernalillo, Alameda.

Albuquerque.—Chicago, 1,377 miles; St. Louis, 1,237 miles; Los Angeles, 888 miles; San Diego, 971 miles; San Francisco, 1,200 miles. Junction with Atlantic & Pacific Railroad. Altitude, 4,950 feet. Population, 5,518.

Metropolis of the upper Rio Grande Valley. Here, as at Sante Fé, there are two towns. In the old town, which lies a mile and a half from the new, there is a population of over 1,700. It contains an ancient cathedral and many interesting relics of old Spanish and Mexican days. The new town is only a dozen years old, having been founded in 1880.

Albuquerque lies in a lovely part of the valley, midway between the sightly Sandia Mountains on the east and a volcanic range on the west. Its neighboring attractions are the Coyote Mineral Springs, several small Mexican communities, and the pueblo of Isleta, besides numerous resorts in the mountains, all reached by enjoyable drives over excellent roads. There are many orchards and vineyards. It is an active business center, its immediate commercial sway extending over an area larger than New England. Besides the railroad machine-shops, there are two foundries, three flouring mills, a brewery, and an ice factory employing half a thousand men, and a score of smaller concerns engaged in manufacture.

Among its public institutions are included the University of New Mexico, a Government Indian school, a

Methodist college, the Southwestern Academy of the New West Education Commission, and St. Vincent's (Catholic) Academy. It has four large public school buildings, eleven churches, a free public library, and a commercial club.

Isleta.—Altitude 4,898 feet.

This pueblo lies a short distance north of A. & P. Junction, in plain view from the train. By necessity of train schedules, the through California passenger commonly passes it in the obscurity of the night. It is a fair sight, a huge rectangular terraced pile gleaming white in the sun, the peaks of numerous rough ladders showing in sharp relief. If the train were to pass in the day-time a few comely Indian maidens and a shriveled squaw or two would be on hand at the stopping-place to offer wares for sale, but otherwise the Pueblo Indian does not appear to pay much attention to the presence of the Caucasian. Doubtless he has his quiet joke, and a confident sense of superiority, but he is not curious. Of the outer world he knows little. He is mildly but exclusively engrossed in his own affairs. The daily presence of that disturbing factor, the railroad, does not affect the profound inertia of his type.

There are some twenty inhabited Pueblo villages in New Mexico, all in the northwestern division, with an aggregate population of about 8,000, comprising five tribal stocks, each of which possesses a distinct language: Quéres, Tiguas, Tehuas, Zuñis, and Jemez. The Moqui villages are in Arizona. Up to the time of the Spanish conquest the Pueblo Indians were in the habit of occasionally changing their abode, and there are in New Mexico the ruins of hundreds of stone pueblos so abandoned. The Spaniards allotted them reservations of land surrounding the sites upon which they were found, which were subsequently confirmed by the United States Government, and by that act they were permanently fixed in that place.

Isleta is Tigua. Its reservation contains a little more than 110,000 acres, and agriculture and fruit raising are very profitably followed by this community, which in a single year manufactures a thousand barrels of wine and sells thousands of dollars' worth of fruits. Pottery is purchased from the people of smaller pueblos, and blankets from the Navajoes, experience having taught these thrifty Tiguas that their own time can be more profitably employed in tilling the soil. The largest business controlled by any woman in New Mexico is here managed by an Indian woman of Isleta.

The Pueblo Indians are generally well-to-do, and many are possessed of considerable wealth. The costumes of the women are often quite costly.

Atlantic & Pacific Junction.—Chicago, 1,390 miles; St. Louis, 1,250 miles; Los Angeles, 875 miles; San Diego, 958 miles; San Francisco, 1,187 miles. Altitude, 4,891 feet.

Point of divergence via the Atlantic & Pacific Railroad, from the line which continues on down the Rio Grande Valley to El Paso, whence the Mexican Central proceeds to the City of Mexico. A few miles north of El Paso, at Rincon, the Santa Fé Route branches off again and continues through Deming, Benson, and Nogales to Guaymas, on the coast of the Gulf of California, in Sonora, Mexico.

Atlantic & Pacific Junction is the actual point of divergence, but Albuquerque is the nominal point, where connection of trains is made.

INTERMEDIATE STATIONS: Luna, Rio Puerco, San Jose, El Rito.

Laguna.— Chicago, 1,443 miles; St. Louis, 1,303 miles; Los Angeles, 822 miles; San Diego, 905 miles; San Francisco, 1,134 miles. Altitude, 5,786 feet. Population (Indian), 1,140.

The youngest of the pueblos, originally recruited from Acoma, Zuñi, Zia, and Cochití, in 1699. The train runs directly past it, affording a most excellent opportunity to the traveler of seeing one of these picturesque village habitations at close range.

It is perched upon a sterile hill, in a compact cluster. This form of habitation, it should be remembered, is not a freak of fancy, but the outcome of the needs of an harassed but far from timid people. It is a fortress, and the entrance by way of a ladder to the roof was a part of the defensive plan. From time immemorial the Pueblo Indians have been surrounded by enemies — Apaches, Navajoes, and the like — all nomads and robbers by nature. The Indians of the

SITTING IN THE SUN.

pueblos were very much unlike their foes; they were not predatory; they tilled the soil; they provided thriftily against future needs; and in consequence they always had something in their possession to tempt the cupidity of the Bedouin wanderers of mountain and plain. Such possessions they could not afford to abandon, and they were too brave to surrender them; hence the evolution of the terraced house.

These people work some arable watered land near by, and the children are usually out on the plain tending sheep. Little black-eyed, cotton-clad urchins may be seen among the rocks upon either side of the pueblo, and very modest comely maidens occasionally come down to the train to avail of an opportunity to make profitable disposition of pottery odds and ends. The traveler may thus procure a memento which, as such, is fairly worth its price; but as a specimen of the Indian's ornamental art in pottery it is usually quite inferior.

Cubero.— Six miles beyond Laguna. Altitude, 5,924 feet. Population, 418. Point of departure for Acoma pueblo.

Acoma.— Pueblos are much alike in structure and general appearance. Their individual interest is derived from natural environment and historical or legendary association. It is by virtue of both these distinctions that Acoma has become known to fame as the most poetic of all the pueblos, if not of all human habitations on this continent. The most practicable way of access is by wagon from Cubero, the distance being thirteen miles, although it is possible to go from Laguna or McCarty's. The first view of the valley of Acoma is from the summit of a divide which breaks suddenly down to its level. It is a scene of extraordinary, almost unearthly, beauty; a long, broad, steep-walled basin, carpeted with grass and green with growing crops, in autumn flaming with yellow blossoming thickets, and bordered by cliffs and quaintly eroded columns, buttes, and obelisks of red, yellow, green, and brown sandstone, the shadows of the towering peak of Los Pelones, above the horizon, marked in violet and amethystine hues.

In the midst stands the rock-flanked mesa which is surmounted by the pueblo of Acoma, a monolith that rises 350 feet above the floor of the valley, with a fairly level top at least a hundred acres in extent. The steep cliff sides of the mesa guard the pueblo more effectually than would cannon or an intrenched army. Numerous trails, feasible for a tribe of Indians that for unnumbered centuries has been bred to daily familiarity with such vertiginous passages, scale the rock, but only three may be safely attempted by a white man. One of these, constructed in recent years, is practicable for horses; that is to say Western horses. The other two are arduous enough to tax the address and endurance of the average mountaineer.

The inhabitants of Acoma are of the tribe of Quéres. The pueblo is not a single structure, but is built upon three parallel streets running north and south, the houses, except in one instance, fronting the east. They are connected, and present the appearance of long terraces of three gigantic stone steps, the second and third stories being commonly reached by way of a ladder and the intervening roofs, although there are now occasional doors in the lowermost story. Partition walls project at intervals of twelve or fifteen feet. Brightly decorated *tinajas*, or water-jars, are placed æsthetically here and there upon the roofs, and the chimneys are of pottery. Everybody is cleanly clad in white cotton and a blanket of gaudy hue, with leggings and moccasins, and a brilliant turban bound about the hair. All Indians are adepts in sign-language, and among the Quéres a conventional code of signs, conveyed by the peculiar disposition of the knot of the turban, is in vogue.

Three miles down the valley from Acoma stands a magnificent lone rock, nearly twice its height. This is the *Mesa Encantada*, or Haunted Mesa. Many centuries ago, according to the Quéres tradition, they dwelt upon that summit, to which a single trail of prodigious difficulty gave access. The entire face of the cliff which gave this solitary footing was undermined by an inundation, and fell upon the plain one day when every inhabitant except three old women was at work in the fields below. The mesa was rendered absolutely unscalable by the falling of the cliff, and those unfortunates perished of starvation within hearing of the lamentations of their kindred. After that catastrophe the present site was built upon, and in time the old table-rock came to be regarded as *encantada*, haunted by the spirits of the three ill-fated women.

It was the present pueblo that the Spaniards discovered in 1539, and even then the story of *Mesa Encantada* was a

AN UNPROGRESSIVE GRANGER.

very ancient legend. The Quéres did not get on well with their Castilian conquerors. They were at first disposed to treat them as belonging to a supernatural order of beings, but that illusion soon passed. A party of soldiers was decoyed upon the mesa and massacred, and Lieutenant de Zaldivar was sent by Oñate to administer punishment. In single file some fifty of those astonishing soldiers of Spain clambered upon the mesa and fought hand to hand for three days with the Quéres, and conquered them. That was in January, 1599. At the time of the memorable uprising, August, 1680, a Franciscan church had long been established at Acoma. The Pueblo tribes are by nature a religious people. Everything has to them some religious meaning or mystical association, even their gambling being preceded by an invocation. But the fact that missionaries were not spared in the general massacre of Spaniards indicates that their adoption of the Catholic faith was only superficial. The church was rebuilt nearly two hundred years ago, and is an immense structure, with walls 60 feet high and 7 feet thick. It has timbers 40 feet long and more than a foot square, which, together with everything else in Acoma, was brought on the backs of the Quéres up the trails from the plain below, at cost of incredible labor lasting through many years. The reservation contains nearly 96,000 acres.

Lava Beds.— For several miles in this region, lava beds lie on either hand, like the flow of a river. The craters are all extinct long since, although the eruptions frequently present the appearance of comparatively recent occurrence. The cinder cones near Flagstaff, in Arizona, wear a strikingly fresh look, some of those symmetrical black ash-heaps being almost bare of tree or twig, but it is in the very crater summits of such cones that the cave-dwellings are found, and they are admittedly prehistoric. Yet you will sink to your ankles in volcanic sand and gravel-cinder in climbing the slopes. Doubtless centuries have elapsed since this lava stream oozed from a fissure in the plain, and since the neighboring mountain-craters, which you may see from the car window, fired the sky with their glow.

San Mateo Mountains.— Northward from Grant's, a station thirty miles beyond Laguna.

Intermediate Stations: McCarty's, Grant's, Bluewater, Chaves, Mitchell, Summit.

Coolidge.— Chicago, 1,513 miles; St. Louis, 1,373 miles; Los Angeles, 752 miles; San Diego, 835 miles; San Francisco, 1,064 miles. Altitude, 6,996 feet. Dining station.

Continental Divide. Henceforward the rivers flow toward the west.

For several miles, on the north side of the track, is to be seen a line of red and gray palisades, the work of water. Here and there the face is marked by a long and narrow streak of white; sometimes there is a coping of green, and occasionally an isolated mass stands out in the plain.

Wingate.— Ten miles beyond Coolidge. Altitude, 6,736 feet. Point of departure for Zuñi pueblo.

Fort Wingate, with a garrison of soldiers, lies within sight, three miles distant upon the south. Close beside it stands the curious cathedral-shaped rock upon which the name "Navajo Church" has been bestowed, in recognition of its suggestive appearance.

The pueblo of Zuñi lies about forty miles south from Wingate. The reservation contains more than 215,000 acres. The pueblo is a five-story bee-hive, in pyramidal form, with clustering detached blocks.

The Zuñis number nearly 600. This is the tribe that was brought into especial prominence by Mr. Frank Cushing, who, as agent of the Smithsonian Institution, dwelt a long time among them, and upon one occasion conducted a number of their chief men on a tour of the Eastern cities, where they attracted no little attention, and doubtless since their return have been regarded as unconscionable liars, because of attempting to pass off stories of the white man's astonishing civilization as true.

Like all the Pueblo tribes, the Zuñis are industrious and courageous. They are rich in folk-lore and fanciful tradition. They sing, dance, and frolic in the intervals of labor. They are complex and ceremonious in religion, and are fond of secret societies. And the moral atmosphere of their community will bear favorable comparison with almost any community of the same size among the Caucasians. Other pueblos, however, are more cleanly than Zuñi.

Gallup.— Twenty-two miles beyond Coolidge. Altitude, 6,498 feet.

Location of the coal mines from which the Atlantic & Pacific Railroad draws its supply.

INTERMEDIATE STATION: Defiance.

Manuelito.— Thirty-eight miles beyond Coolidge. Altitude, 6,252 feet. Near the Arizona boundary.

A MEXICAN FIREPLACE.

One who desired to visit the cañons of the Rio de Chelly, with their remarkable cliff ruins, the exploration of which has been restricted to casual inspection by Government employes up to the present time, could make the journey from this point by way of Fort Defiance. It is to be hoped that special facilities will yet be provided to make this trip practicable for tourists. The celebrated portions of the Cañon de Chelly lie at a distance of upward of fifty miles north from Manuelito, and special arrangements would have to be made in advance by an intending visitor. It is mentioned here, in passing, merely as one of the marvels of this region, of whose existence, not to say whose features, comparatively few outside of scientific circles are aware.

ARIZONA.

HISTORICAL.— Here, as in New Mexico, are monuments of an ancient and mysterious people, but the pueblos, and possibly the cliff dwellings, are antedated by ruins of a semi-civilization which waxed and waned many centuries ago. That a multitude long vanished once dwelt in this titanic land is evidenced by the ruins of irrigating canals of enormous extent found in the southern part of the Territory. They were scientifically constructed by human hands, and utilized for the maintenance of hundreds of thousands of human beings. So much and no more is known. The throngs that populated the valleys have disappeared as mysteriously as have the Hittites, who are mentioned as a powerful nation in Holy Writ and in ancient hieroglyphs, but appear to have left no record beyond that casual contemporaneous reference. Casa Grande, also in the southern part, below Phœnix, which was an abandoned shell when the country was first invaded by the Spaniards, is regarded as a former habitation of the people of the Salt and Gila River valleys, and the excavations recently begun there are said to give promise of rich archæological treasure.

The antiquities of the northern portion are the cliff dwellings. Scores of these have been found, perched high on the steep walls of cañons and on the hill-tops that rise above the level of the broad arid plateaus. The builders of these, too, had vanished before the Spaniards came, only the Moquis, dwelling in their pueblos far to the north, and the wandering Apaches and Pimas, being left to represent mankind in all this wide land.

The world is a pretty ancient dust heap, wherever you may choose to stand, and written history is a serial story of which all save the last two or three chapters is missing; but a hiatus exists in Arizona that is not commonly brought so sharply to the sense. The impressive thing is not that it was anciently inhabited, for we have learned something from the mounds of Ohio and elsewhere about the antiquity of human life on our continent, but that oblivion should have covered these people like a wave, and for centuries these valleys, and plains, and cañons should have remained desolate, where once was an animated multitude — this gives the air of tragic romance.

The history of Arizona, like its topography, is convulsed, rent, gashed, whole volumes missing. It begins intelligibly with Marcos de Nizza, in 1539, for this was the route of the original northward exploration from Mexico. For more than two centuries after the Spanish discovery Arizona was a part of New Mexico, but the portion included in the present Territory was crossed and recrossed by those tireless world conquerors. The first settlement was made in 1685, in the neighborhood of Tucson. The missionaries then began their work of civilization, and mining and agriculture were undertaken in the face of Apache hostility. The suppression of the missions by Mexico early in our century practically surrendered the country to the Apaches, who promptly annihilated what remained of Spanish enterprise.

The acquisition of New Mexico by the United States, in 1848, included all of Arizona north of the Gila River; the remainder was purchased from Mexico, in 1853, for the sum of $10,000,000. The Territory of Arizona was created by Congress in 1863, and its first government was organized at Navajo Springs in December of that year. Shortly thereafter the capital was removed to Whipple Barracks, thence to Prescott, thence to Tucson, again to Prescott, and finally to Phœnix.

The bane of Arizona has been the Apache. He proved a well-nigh untamable wild man, as fierce and wary as the puma that still dwells in the mountains. He was destruction incarnate and a name of terror. He has at last been subdued and banished within a very few years, and, in consequence, upon this land the sunrise of prosperity is just breaking.

DESCRIPTIVE.— It is a land of high plains, rich valleys, pine parks, wide terraces, towering mountains, tremendous chasms, burnt-out volcanoes, lava-beds, deserts, painted rocks, mesas and buttes; aglow with color, overhung by an arch of deepest blue, enwrapped by a pure, cool, rarefied air, and encompassed by silence and a sense of immeasurable vastness. It is a marvel of geological revelation. The unparalleled gashes that rend the earth's crust perpendicularly more than a mile deep and many hundred miles long, as in the Grand Cañon of the Colorado, exhibit the rock series all the way down to the primitive formations. In ancient times that the geologist wots of, it was alternately the bed of salt and fresh water seas of vast extent, and although the sand-blast has carved curious shapes of stone, the mark of water is everywhere. Its erosion is traceable on the cliffs and in the cañons, which latter are largely due to its action. It has washed rock strata thousands of feet thick from the surface of thousands of square miles, and swept the detritus away to some distant ocean bourne. And as if by way of reprisal, water is now the scarcest commodity known in the greater part of Arizona. A living spring is a coveted treasure. A constant stream is better than a gold mine, if it can be availed of for irrigation.

In altitude it ranges from below sea level, on the south, to 13,000 feet above. Its actual dimensions are about 380 by 320 miles, embracing 113,020 square miles; the total population of a little more than 60,000 being restricted to small areas separated by wide untouched intervals. These intervals consist of mountain ranges, rich in mineral, of pine parks of magnificent timber, of rich valleys awaiting irrigation, of open tracts too arid for agriculture but valuable for grazing, and of genuine desert.

The deserts of Arizona, however, are neither monotonous nor lifeless. They are most emphatic in character in the southern portion of the Territory, yet even there picturesque and beautiful plant life is not wanting. The saguaro cactus (*Cereus giganteus*) is plentiful there, towering to a height of from thirty to sixty feet. Its diameter, whose maximum is about two feet, is nearly as great at the summit as at the base, and its fluted column, sometimes but not always branching, is of a deep green color, and is protected by innumerable stout spines. It is crowned by clusters of showy white flowers, and the fruit is red, containing saccharine and vinous qualities. This saguaro cactus grows, in proximity to water, at the rate of a foot per annum, but in the driest regions only a twelfth as fast. Yet even there it yields, on puncturing, a generous flow of water, somewhat unpalatable, but sufficient to quench the thirst of a needy traveler; and its pulpy part is edible. The echina cactus has a short, thick trunk, surmounted by yellow or crimson flowers. The cucumber cactus is fiercely thorny, with large crimson flowers and a fruit which contains an edible seedy pulp of pleasant flavor. The cholla is a variety of branching cactus, with loosely jointed limbs that easily part at the socket. Its thorns will pierce stout leather, and are scrupulously to be avoided. Another variety is the prickly pear, which is the most common cactus throughout the West. Its leaf-like segments grow without any apparent method, one out of another. There is also the fish-hook cactus, whose small spines are hook-shape. The agave, or century plant, and the yucca are exceedingly common, and their imposing spikes of large cream-colored flowers are very beautiful. The flower spike of the *yucca gloriosa* runs up to a height of ten or fifteen feet, and sometimes supports nearly a thousand blossoms. Among the more rare desert growths of Arizona is a lily that blooms about the time of Easter. The flower is white, streaked with pale green.

Of animals, the Gila Monster is peculiar to Arizona. This is a species of lizard which attains a length of nearly two feet, and presents a most repulsive appearance. It is found only in the south, in the heated valley of the Gila River, and is a subject of dispute in consequence of the alleged venom of its bite. It has been accused of emitting an acrid, poisonous breath when disturbed, and instances are offered which, if authentic, show that the bite of a Gila Monster is more to be feared than that of a rattlesnake. But it is not abundant, even in its habitat, and appears, in any event, to be entirely harm-

GIANT CACTUS.

less unless submitted to the indignity of handling, which its ferocious appearance does not encourage, whether it is venomous or no.

Our route traverses the upper portion of the Territory, at an elevation between 4,850 and 460 feet. It follows for some distance the Little Colorado River, and passes within easy access of the wonderful "jewel forest" of Chalcedony Park. It passes Winslow, where Moqui Indians often congregate, and crosses Cañon Diablo. It leads through Flagstaff, past the foot of San Francisco Mountain, in whose near vicinity are the cliff and cave dwellings, and north of which stretches the brilliant and terrible Grand Cañon, which ranks as the grandest spectacle known anywhere upon earth. It continues on past Bill Williams Mountain, threads the gentle beauties of Johnson's Cañon, and, after passing through a number of mining towns, comes to the Colorado River.

AN EARLY EXPLORER.

INDUSTRIAL. — The mining, smelting, and milling of ore constitute the chief industry, although agriculture and fruit raising are rapidly coming to the front. The silver mines have proven of enormous value, and the copper deposits are the richest in the world.

The lumber industry is active, and is based upon an incalculable supply of timber. The best quality of ornamental building-stone in the West is produced by the Peachblow sandstone quarries of Arizona.

There are upwards of 1,000,000 head of cattle in the

Territory, although the growth of that industry in the past few years has been checked by the cost of shipping to distant markets.

The greatest agricultural and horticultural development has been in the south, where undoubtedly the largest promise lies. The river valleys at low altitudes are almost tropical in character. For the past ten years nearly half a million dollars a year has been expended in constructing irrigating canals in Arizona.

INTERMEDIATE STATIONS: Allantown, Querino Cañon, Sanders.

Navajo Springs.— Chicago, 1,590 miles; St. Louis, 1,450 miles; Los Angeles, 675 miles; San Diego, 758 miles; San Francisco, 987 miles. Altitude, 5,626 feet.

A short distance from this station the government of the Territory was first organized, in 1863. No settlement was made, the first capital of Arizona consisting of a small tent encampment.

INTERMEDIATE STATIONS: Billings, Carrizo, Aztec.

Holbrook.— Chicago, 1,630 miles; St. Louis, 1,490 miles; Los Angeles, 635 miles; San Diego, 718 miles; San Francisco, 947 miles. Altitude, 5,072 feet. Population, 206. Point of departure for Chalcedony Park.

Situated at the junction of the Zuñi and Puerco rivers (not the Rio Puerco of New Mexico, which is on the Atlantic Slope). The confluence of these two streams forms the Little Colorado, which flows northwestward and empties into the Grand Cañon, its own channel at the point of junction possessing nearly the grandeur that characterizes that of the Colorado proper.

CHALCEDONY PARK.—About twenty miles southeast from Holbrook lies one of those marvels of which it is the characteristic of Arizona to be profuse. Chalcedony Park is a tract some 2,000 acres in extent, whose geological formation is sandstone resting on volcanic ash; and protruding from the sandstone, in water-worn basins and gulches, or entirely liberated and scattered over the surface, are innumerable petrified trunks of trees and their fragments, varying in size from mere chips and splinters to huge segments ten feet in diameter. It is believed that these trees, which appear to have been a species of pine or cedar, grew upon the shore of an inland sea, and after falling became water-logged, and the cell-structure was replaced by silica. Manganese and oxide of iron yielded a red, yellow, and black coloring matter, and thus the origin of this "jewel forest" is plausibly accounted for. These logs of stone have been curiously fractured, probably by the action of heat and cold, in a clean transverse cleavage, so that they appear exactly as if they had been neatly sawn apart into lengths which, in many instances, form discs only a few inches thick and many feet in diameter. All this vast heap of detritus, although the larger masses are not brilliant in the crude state, is most beautiful when polished, and the term "jewel forest" is hardly a misnomer, for every particle — and there are millions of tons — is chalcedony, cornelian, agate, chrysoprase, amethyst, topaz, and the like. In one instance one of these agatized trees, the trunk still intact, spans a cañon forty-five feet wide, fully fifty feet overlapping upon one side, and both ends imbedded in the sandstone.

Conveyance can be procured at Holbrook for the trip to this extraordinary spot.

INTERMEDIATE STATIONS: Putnam, St. Joseph, Hardy.

Winslow.— Chicago, 1,662 miles; St. Louis, 1,522 miles; Los Angeles, 603 miles; San Diego, 686 miles; San Francisco, 915 miles. Altitude, 4,848 feet. Population, 363. Dining station.

Just before reaching Winslow the course of the Little

Colorado is abandoned. Moqui Indians are frequently seen about the station. Their reservation and villages are some seventy miles to the north, and north and east of them lies the reservation of the Navajoes, which overlaps into New Mexico. Within the Navajo Reserve are the rivers San Juan and De Chelly, whose cañons and ruins of cliff dwellings are celebrated among scientists throughout the world.

SNAKE DANCE, MOQUI RESERVATION.

MOQUI SNAKE DANCE.—The serpent is singularly prominent in human history. Its trail stretches past innumerable milestones from our own original Eden to the desert villages of the aborigines of Western and Southern America. The Aztecs sculptured the snake upon their ornamental stones, and the Pueblo Indians indent their pottery with an imitation of its scales. But most singular among the tributes to the serpent is the snake dance, an astonishing annual rite formerly common to all the Pueblo tribes, but now practiced by the Moquis alone. For this ceremony, peculiarly abhorrent to any but Indian blood, hundreds of rattlesnakes are captured alive on the desert. This is accomplished in a singular manner by reducing them to a quiescent state by gentle strokes of a wisp, then dextrously depositing them in a leathern bag, where they are accumulated one by one. For three days preceding the snake dance the Indians who intend to participate abstain wholly from food, and partake only of a decoction whose secret is known to but three individuals in the tribe — the chief priest, the neophyte who is in training to succeed him, and the eldest woman. The revelation of the secret of this decoction, which appears to be a veritable neutralizer of the venom of a rattlesnake bite, is punishable by death. The snakes that have been collected are kept in a little corral until the hour of the dance, when the participants boldly enter, and seizing a snake recklessly in each hand, and sometimes taking one in their mouths, leap into the ring and begin the barbaric performance of weird chant and uncouth contortion. The snakes swing to and fro, twisting their fat sinister bodies about the arms of their captors, and striking out angrily with their wicked fangs. The dancers are repeatedly bitten, but except that the priest administers another dose of the antidote, no attention is paid to the occurrence. A small local inflammation, and possibly a temporary indisposition after the excitement of the dance is ended, are the only ill effects that result.

The rattlesnake is one of the animal gods of the Indians, and in their quaint folk-lore occupies a relation to the other animals that suggests Brer Rabbit of Uncle Remus, although mystic magical powers are ascribed to it. The dance is a ceremony to propitiate the snake-god, who is believed to be influential in directing earthly events, and upon the conclusion of the rite all the reptiles are reverently restored to liberty.

Mr. Keam, the Government agent for the Moquis, states positively that the snakes are neither unfanged nor drugged, nor in any manner deprived of the natural exercise of their venomous function.

INTERMEDIATE STATION: Dennison.

CAÑON DIABLO.

Cañon Diablo.—Chicago, 1,688 miles; St. Louis, 1,548 miles; Los Angeles, 577 miles; San Diego, 660 miles; San Francisco, 889 miles. Altitude, 5,421 feet.

The name is Spanish for Devil Cañon. It is simply a hideous gash in the level plain, 540 feet wide and 222 feet deep, extending for many miles. At a little distance it can not be seen at all. If it were closed up the projections on one edge would fit with tolerable accuracy the notches on the other, and it has the appearance of having been caused by a rending of the crust of the earth in cooling. It is crossed over an ingeniously constructed bridge.

In the Harvard Mineralogical Museum is a meteorite of 150 pounds weight, studded with minute white diamonds, which was flung by one of Hendrick Hudson's crew somewhere aloft in the Arizona sky and picked up in the bottom of this cañon.

INTERMEDIATE STATIONS: Angell, Walnut, Cosnino.

MISTLETOE.—Nearing Flagstaff, some distance beyond the crossing of Cañon Diablo, the road runs through a park of small cedars and piñons, where on every hand thick bunches of this pretty parasitic plant cling to the boughs in great profusion.

Flagstaff.—Chicago, 1,721 miles; St. Louis, 1,581 miles; Los Angeles, 544 miles; San Diego, 627 miles; San Francisco, 856 miles. Altitude, 6,886 feet. Population, 963. Point of departure for Grand Cañon of the Colorado, San Francisco Peaks, cliff and cave dwellings, and Oak Creek Cañon.

A United States cavalry corps was encamped on this spot one 4th of July, and in honor of the day the national colors were hoisted to the top of a tall pine tree, which was stripped of its branches and made to serve as a gigantic flagstaff. The old pine, thus amputated, has disappeared, but the vigorous little town that has sprung up on its site has succeeded to the name. A large aggregate capital is vested in different enterprises here. It is the distributing point for a broad country through which stockmen and miners are scattered. One store alone carries a stock of general merchandise that is valued at over $150,000. It lies in the midst of a beautiful pine park, on whose wide intervals large numbers of sheep and cattle graze. The great saw-mills of the Arizona Lumber & Timber Company are located a mile south of the center of the town. This concern employs about 500 men. The red sandstone of the Flagstaff quarries is classed among the handsomest and most valuable of building-stones. In the quarry it is soft and easily worked, but on exposure to the air it quickly hardens. Portland, Los Angeles, and Denver have each imported from these quarries stone for the construction of costly public buildings.

The noble four-peaked mountain behind the town,

SAN FRANCISCO MOUNTAIN, ARIZONA.

upon the north, which has been conspicuously in sight for the past hundred miles, is the San Francisco Mountain.

Flagstaff is the gateway to scenes whose grandeur is impossible of adequate description, and to more sights of novelty and unaccustomed interest than any other town in the world. All these, fragmentarily described in the following pages, are easily accessible and should on no account be omitted by the traveler who can spare the time requisite for their examination.

GRAND CAÑON OF THE COLORADO.—The Colorado River,

sweeping down through southern Utah and across northern Arizona, has carved a series of unprecedented channels some four hundred miles long. Midway, in Arizona, occurs a climax 217 miles in length, to which, by way of crowning distinction, the name Grand Cañon was given. Its brink is closely neighbored by a growth of pines such as are seen around Flagstaff, and it is as sudden and inconsequent a chasm as Cañon Diablo. But, taking the Diablo Cañon as a unit, the Grand Cañon is thirty times as deep and one hundred and twenty-five times as wide. It is not, however, a mere notch. It is thronged with hundreds upon hundreds of brilliantly colored mountainous bulks, as tall as yonder San Francisco Mountain, whose peaks rise only to the level of your feet as you stand upon the rim.

To convey some slight notion of the scene thus outstretched before the observer, the present writer can do no better than to quote from an attempted description written and published by him after the partial familiarity gained by a week's stay in and around the Grand Cañon had made such an undertaking appear possible in part:

The beholder is at first unimpressed by any detail; he is overwhelmed by the *ensemble* of a stupendous panorama, a thousand square miles in extent, that lies wholly beneath the eye, as if he stood upon a mountain peak instead of the level brink of a fearful chasm in the plateau whose opposite shore is thirteen miles away. A labyrinth of huge architectural forms, endlessly varied in design, fretted with ornamental devices, festooned with lace-like webs formed of talus from the upper cliffs and painted with every color known to the palette in pure transparent tones of marvelous delicacy. Never was picture more harmonious, never flower more exquisitely beautiful. It flashes instant communication of all that architecture and painting and music for a thousand years have gropingly striven to express. It is the soul of Michael Angelo and of Beethoven.

A cañon, truly, but not after the accepted type. An intricate system of cañons, rather, all subordinate to the river channel in the midst, which in its turn is subordinate to the total effect. That river channel, the profoundest depth, and actually more than six thousand feet below the point of view, is in seeming a rather insignificant trench, attracting the eye more by reason of its somber tone and mysterious suggestion than by any appreciable characteristic of a chasm. It is nearly five miles distant in a straight line, and its uppermost rims are 3,000 feet beneath the observer, whose measuring capacity is entirely inadequate to the demand made by such magnitudes. One can not believe the distance to be more than a mile as the crow flies, before descending the wall or attempting some other form of inch-worm measurement. Mere brain knowledge counts for little against the illusion under which the organ of vision is doomed here to labor. That red cliff upon your right, fading through brown, yellow, and gray, to white at the top, is taller than the Washington Monument. The Auditorium in Chicago would not cover one-half its perpendicular span. Yet it does not greatly impress you. You idly toss a pebble toward it, and are surprised that your aim fell short. Subsequently you learn that the cliff is a good half-mile distant. If you care for an abiding sense of its true proportions, go over to the trail that begins beside its summit and clamber down to its base and back. You will return some hours later, and with a decided respect for a small Grand Cañon cliff. Relatively it is insignificant; in that sense your first estimate was correct. Were Vulcan to cast it bodily into the chasm directly beneath your feet, it would pass for a bowlder, if indeed it were discoverable to the unaided eye. Yet the immediate chasm itself is only the first step of a long terrace that leads down to the innermost gorge and the river. Roll a heavy stone to the rim and let it go. It falls sheer the height of a church or an Eiffel Tower, according to your position, and explodes like a bomb on a projecting ledge. If, happily, any considerable fragments remain, they bound onward like elastic balls, leaping in wild parabola from point to point, snapping trees like straws, bursting, crashing, thundering down until they make a last plunge over the brink of a void, and then there comes languidly up the cliff-sides a faint, distant roar, and your bowlder that had withstood the buffets of centuries lies scattered as wide as Wycliffe's ashes, although the final fragment has lodged only a little way, so to speak, below the rim. Such performances are frequently given in these amphitheaters without human aid, by the mere undermining of the rain, or perhaps it is here that Sisyphus rehearses his unending task. Often in the silence of night a tremendous fragment may be heard crashing from terrace to terrace like shocks of thunder-peal.

The spectacle is so symmetrical, and so completely excludes the outside world and its accustomed standards, it is with difficulty one can acquire any notion of its immensity. Were it half as deep, half as broad, it would be no less bewildering, so utterly does it baffle human grasp. Something may be gleaned from the account given by geologists. What is known to them as the Grand Cañon District lies

A COWBOY.

principally in northwestern Arizona, its length from northwest to southeast, in a straight line, being about 180 miles, its width 125 miles, and its total area some 15,000 square miles. Its northerly beginning, at the high plateaus in Southern Utah, is a series of ter-races, many miles broad, dropping like a stairway step by step to successively lower geological formations, until in Arizona the plat-form is reached which borders the real chasm and extends southerly beyond far into the central part of that Territory. It is the theory of geologists that 10,000 feet of strata have been swept by erosion from the surface of this entire platform, whose present uppermost formation is the carboniferous; the deduction being based upon the fact that the missing permian, mesozoic, and tertiary formations, which belong above this carboniferous in the series, are found in their place at the beginning of the northern terraces referred to. The theory is fortified by many evidences supplied by examination of the district, where, more than anywhere else, mother earth has laid bare the secrets of her girlhood. The climax in this extraordinary example of erosion is, of course, the chasm of the Grand Cañon proper, which, were the missing strata restored to the adjacent plateau, would be 16,000 feet deep. The layman is apt to stigmatize such an assertion as a vagary of theorists, and until the argument has been heard it does seem incredible that water should have carved such a trough in solid rock. Briefly, the whole region appears to have been repeatedly lifted and submerged, both under the ocean and under a fresh-water sea, and during the period of the last upheaval the river cut its gorge. Existing as the drainage system of a vast territory, it had the right of way, and as the plateau deliberately rose before the pressure of the internal forces, slowly, as grind the mills of the gods, through a period not to be measured by years, the river kept its bed worn down to the level of erosion; sawed its channel free, as the saw cuts the log that is thrust against it. Tributaries, traceable now only by dry lateral gorges, and the gradual but no less effective process of weathering did the rest.

Beginning on the plateau level on the cañon's brink, the order of the rock formations above the river, according to Captain Dutton, is as follows :

1. Cherty limestone, 240 feet.
2. Upper Aubrey limestone, 320 feet.
3. Cross-bedded sandstone, 380 feet.
4. Lower Aubrey sandstone, 950 feet.
5. Upper red wall sandstone, 400 feet.
6. Red wall limestone, 1,500 feet.
7. Lower carboniferous sandstone, 550 feet.
8. Quartzite base of carboniferous, 180 feet.
9. Archæan.

The total vertical depth is more than a mile.

Of the descent to the river, down the cañon wall:

For the first two miles the trail is a sort of Jacob's ladder, zigzagging at an unrelenting pitch down a steep and nearly uniform decline caused by a sliding geological fault and centuries of frost and rain. It is safe and practicable for pack animals and for sound pedestrians, ladies having occasionally made the descent; but at present it necessitates too hurried a scramble in places to attempt it confidently on muleback. At the end of two miles a comparatively gentle slope is reached, known as the First Level, some 2,500 feet below the rim; that is to say — for such figures have to be impressed objectively upon the mind — five times the height of St. Peter's, the Pyramid of Cheops, or the Strasburg Cathedral; eight times the height of the Bartholdi Statue of Liberty; eleven times the height of Bunker Hill Monument. Looking back from this level the huge picturesque towers that border the rim shrink to pigmies and seem to crown a perpendicular wall, unattainably far in the sky. Yet only one-half the perpendicular descent, and less than one-third the entire distance of the trail to the river, have been accomplished. For more than three miles now riding on horse or muleback is entirely practicable. Hance's Rock Cabin lies only a short distance ahead, where dinner and rest are to be had under the shade of cottonwoods by the side of a living spring. Farther on, the trail continues down a widening gorge plentifully set with shrubs and spangled, in season, with the bloom of the yucca, prickly pear, primrose, marigold, and a score of unfamiliar showy flowers, white, blue, red, and yellow, surprisingly fresh and vigorous, above a dry, red, stony soil. Soon the course of a clear rivulet is reached, whose windings are followed to the end. The red wall limestone gives place to dark brown sandstone, whose perfectly horizontal strata rapidly rise above the head to prove the rate of descent along the apparently gentle decline. Overshadowed by this sandstone of chocolate hue the way grows gloomy and foreboding, and the gorge narrows greatly. The traveler stops a moment beneath a slanting cliff 500 feet high, where there is an Indian grave and pottery scattered about. A gigantic niche has been worn in the face of this cavernous cliff, which, in recognition of its fancied Egyptian character, was named the Temple of Sett by the celebrated painter, Thomas Moran. A little beyond this temple it becomes necessary to abandon the animals. The river is still a mile and a half distant. The way now narrows to a mere notch, where two wagons could barely pass, and the granite begins to tower gloomily overhead, for we have dropped below the sandstone and have entered the archæan — a frowning black rock, streaked, veined, and swirled with vivid red and white, smoothed and polished by the rivulet and beautiful as a mosaic. Obstacles are encountered in the form of steep interposing crags, past which the brook has found a way, but over which the pedestrian must clamber. After these lesser difficulties come sheer descents, which at present must be passed by the aid of ropes. The last considerable drop is a forty-foot bit by the side of a pretty cascade, where there are just enough irregularities in the wall to give toe-hold. The narrow cleft becomes exceedingly wayward in its course, turning abruptly to right and left and working down into twilight depths. It is very still. At every turn one looks to see the *embouchure* upon the river, anticipating the sudden shock of the unintercepted roar of waters. When at last this is reached, over a final downward clamber, the traveler stands upon a sandy rift confronted by nearly vertical walls many hundred feet high, at whose base a black torrent pitches in a giddying onward slide that gives him momentarily the sensation of slipping into an abyss.

Dwarfed by such prodigious mountain shores, that rise immediately from the water at an angle that would deny footing to a mountain sheep, it is not easy to estimate confidently the width and volume of the river. Choked by the stubborn granite at this point, its width is probably between two hundred and fifty and three hundred feet, its velocity fifteen miles an hour, and its volume and turmoil equal to the Whirlpool Rapids of Niagara. Its rise in time of heavy rain is rapid and appalling, for the walls shed almost instantly all the water that falls upon them. Drift is lodged in the crevices thirty feet overhead. For only a few hundred yards is the tortuous stream visible, but its effect upon the senses is perhaps the greater for that reason. Issuing as from a mountain-side, it slides with oily smoothness for a space and suddenly breaks into violent waves that comb back against the current and shoot unexpectedly here and there, while the volume sways tide-like from side to side and long curling breakers form and hold their outline lengthwise of the shore, despite the seemingly irresistible velocity of the water. The river is laden with drift, huge tree-trunks, which it tosses like chips in its terrible play. * * *

Returning to the spot where the animals were abandoned, camp is made for the night. Next morning the way is retraced. Not the most fervid pictures of a poet's fancy could transcend the glories then revealed in the depths of the cañon: inky shadows, pale gildings of lofty spires, golden splendors of sun beating full on façades of red and yellow, obscurations of distant peaks by veils of transient shower, glimpses of white towers half-drowned in purple haze, suffusions of rosy light blended in reflection from a hundred tinted walls. Caught up to exalted emotional heights the beholder becomes unmindful of fatigue. He mounts on wings. He drives the chariot of the sun.

Since the foregoing was written the Hance Trail has been greatly improved, and a new trail constructed a little farther west, and it is now practicable to cover most of the trip to the river and return on horseback.

The distance from Flagstaff to the Grand Cañon is sixty-five miles. Except in winter a stage runs three times a week, namely, on Monday, Wednesday, and Friday, to the grandest accessible point on the cañon rim, which is the point of view in the foregoing description. The entire distance is covered in twelve hours, over an excellent and romantic road, and the stage returns to Flagstaff the following morning. There is a dinner camp midway, at Cedar Ranch, and ample accommodations for food and comfortable lodging at the stage terminus on the rim of the cañon, where visitors may remain as long as they desire.

The office of the Grand Cañon Stage Company is a little building next the railroad depot, by the side of the station platform.

SAN FRANCISCO PEAKS.—Agassiz, 12,794 feet above the sea, is the highest of the four peaks of San Francisco Mountain, but the only practicable trail for the tourist is the one recently constructed by Mr. A. Doyle of Flagstaff to the pinnacle of Humphrey's Peak, 12,750 feet above sea level. The distance from Flagstaff is about eleven miles, and there is a good carriage-road for seven miles. The remaining distance, to within a few yards of the topmost crag, is accomplished on horseback over a safe trail.

The carriage-road leads smoothly through pines and exquisite groves of aspen, and gives place to a bridle-path at the foot of a steep grass-grown slope. From every successive angle of the trail that climbs this slope a wider panorama is unfolded, and objects far out on the plain seem to creep nearer to the mountain's foot. Above the terrace, pines and firs shade the way, and the trail winds along the rim of a gorge where the avalanches of winter have torn tree and root and earth away down to the floor of rock. The timber line is very high, and for only a few hundred feet do the peaks stand bare of vegetation, although the last mile of the trail is taken up in solving the difficulties of this portion of the ascent. There are long doublings to ameliorate the pitch of the slope that sweeps far downward at a very acute angle with the perpendicular. A short final clamber on foot over crags brings one to the top, a real apex, on which only a small party can find simultaneous footing.

From this point the entire circle of the horizon can be surveyed for a distance of from eighty to upwards of two hundred miles in every direction.

To the north, past the edge of Agassiz Peak, lies the Coconino Forest and Basin, and beyond them, fifty miles away, may be seen the farther wall of the Bright Angel Amphitheater, in the Grand Cañon, a dimly glowing splendor of colors; and thirty miles beyond that the Buckskin Mountains rise above the level of the Kanab Plateau.

Swinging toward the right, the Navajo Mountains are next seen, 200 miles away, and to the northeast the Navajo Reservation is visible, and the Painted Desert gleams faintly, like a faded rainbow. Next, the Moqui villages, and to the east, past Fremont Peak, lava beds, O'Leary's Peak (10,000 feet), Sunset Crater, the Little Colorado River, and the plateau and desert for 130 miles.

To the southeast the White Mountains are seen, 200 miles distant. To the south, past Mount Elden, and beyond Flagstaff, Apache Maid Mountain, forty miles; Mormon Mountain and Lake, and a group of nearly a dozen other lakes: Hay, Vail's, Big and Little Horse, Cow, Deep, Long, Dry, Rogue, Ducksnest, etc.; the Mogollon Plateau, Baker's Butte, eighty miles; The Four Peaks, 160 miles, and the Superstition Mountains near Phœnix.

To the southwest, the Verde Valley, the Jerome Smelters, Oak Creek Cañon, Squaw Peak, Granite Mountains, near Prescott, 100 miles; Bradshaw Mountains, 140 miles, and Juniper Mountains, 150 miles.

To the west, Mounts Kendrick (10,250 feet), Sitgreaves (9,500 feet), and Bill Williams (9,264 feet), and, beyond, a vast country wanting in determinable landmarks. Turning from this magnificent survey to a study of the mountain itself, a half-mile ride along a lower ridge with smooth slopes brings you to the edge of the crater, a deep cavity with rugged, blistered rims, looking much like the photographs of the large craters on the moon. The descent into the crater is arduous, but entirely feasible for both horse and man, the sides being buried deep in volcanic gravel and dust. In the bottom is a small living spring. There is no wall to the crater upon the northern side. There it breaks down into a beautiful cañon, thickly grown with evergreen trees and flowering plants, overhung by towering side-cliffs of ruddy color, for this mountain is not, as was long believed, composed entirely of volcanic rock. Looking upward toward the distant rims, they lift uncouth shapes against the sky — bent and twisted forms, with huge orifices, like rude doors and windows, as if they might be the tottering walls of some ancient castle. It is as if you stood in some forgotten corner of a dead world, until again your glance falls to the refreshing green of tree and fern, and the bright hue of flowers, and you hear the murmur of the tiny rivulet that cheers them here in the midst of desolation.

The trip to Humphrey's Peak can easily be made in a day, and is well worth the making. Mr. Doyle furnishes conveyance and horses, and acts as guide, for a reasonable consideration.

CLIFF AND CAVE DWELLINGS.—Eight miles southeast

CLIFF DWELLINGS, ARIZONA.

from Flagstaff, in the same park of yellow pines, are the most numerous cliff dwellings in the rugged, beautiful Walnut Cañon. They occupy a level on both sides of the narrow gorge where the harder strata had resisted the erosion of water and the weathering of time, and had formed projecting shelves with recesses between. A rough wall of rock fragments laid in mortar, and extending from the edge of the lower to the upper ledge, formed the front of the dwellings, which were subdivided into from three to five compartments. These dwellings, while the rooms are usually small, are numerous enough to have sheltered a population of several hundred, and being situated nearly half-way down the wall were, while not inaccessible, easily defended. Such articles as are now in use among the Pueblo Indians have been found in these long-abandoned habitations, and it is not improbable that their ancient inhabitants were the parent stock of the Pueblo tribes; but that is not positively known. Whoever he was, that ancient man, he is an interesting and sorrowful figure, for there is something very pathetic about these deserted cliff dwellings, perched between earth and sky in a lonely cañon, old refuges against rapine in the days when the hand of the stronger was ever raised against the weaker. They were certainly hiding-places, either for a timid or a much harassed handful of people, or for the wives and children of warriors in time of battle. The dense tragic veil of obscurity that hides the history of the earliest occupants of our country can never be lifted. They, like ourselves, were birds of passage, flown from the common nest of humanity in Asiatic wilds, impelled by unrest, or driven by relentless foes, and perhaps in the end exterminated, leaving a few crude trinkets to survive all memory of the hands that fashioned them.

The cave dwellings are north of Flagstaff about nine miles, by the side of the stage-road leading to the Grand Cañon. They are the simplest conceivable human habitations, consisting only of natural caverns formed by the spout-holes of a crater, on the summit of a small volcano. In some instances these black holes, which vary from the size of a mere closet to that of a commodious room, are roughly walled about with loose rock for defense. Fragments of pottery are abundant, and appear to be identical with that found in the cliff dwellings; but whether the last named were contemporaneous, or a subsequent evolution, has not been determined. There is abundant local evidence that the cave dwellings were long inhabited, and apparently by a considerable population. Scientists have never estimated the age of either at less than five or six centuries, and back of that the gulf of uncertainty widely yawns.

BOTTOMLESS PITS.—A disturbing event occurred in 1891 out on the plain by the side of the road to the cliff dwellings. One morning three yawning pits were discovered where, the day before, solid earth had been. Such examination as could be made with the aid of available lengths of rope revealed no bottom, and the pits were named accordingly. In the lapse of time the caving of the earth has partially filled them, or perhaps has only superficially bridged or choked the ugly narrow chasms, except in one instance, where an adventurous cowboy has recently penetrated 150 feet obliquely downward, first securely anchoring himself by a rope from above. Though not worth going far to see, they possess a local interest. Their cause is conjectural.

OAK CREEK CAÑON.—Fifteen miles south from Flagstaff the channel of Oak Creek reaches its climax of impressiveness and beauty. It is a narrow, or "box," cañon with walls perhaps a thousand feet in height. The clear deep pools and foaming rapids of the "creek" contain myriads of trout, which are not commonly found in this region, where the streams are usually of a turbid character distasteful to this king of small game fish. The trout-fishing of Oak Creek is really excellent, and the cañon itself is impressive, in spite of the fact that the chaotic giant upon the north makes all others seem puerile by comparison.

VOLCANIC CONES AND LAVA BEDS.— It is claimed that

from the first thousand-feet elevation on San Francisco Mountain 300 extinct volcanoes can be seen. In any event, upon the north they are very plentifully scattered, and the road to the Grand Cañon leads past a great number. Many are perfectly formed cones, deeply covered with black and red cinder. Some of them are prettily set with shrubby cedar trees at regular intervals to their summits, appearing like the intelligent work of a landscape gardener. Others are almost entirely bare of vegetation, and the lusterless black cones tipped and streaked with red seem to be touched by a perpetual ruddy ray of sunset light. Sunset Crater and Peachblow Mountain are names that were applied in recognition of this remarkable aspect. These two volcanoes are singularly beautiful in the landscape, although they are nearly as barren as a heap of dry coal-dust.

Large patches of lava also cover the plain, upon the north, looking at a distance like the dense shadow of a cloud, or the desolate charred path of a widespread conflagration.

It must have been a grand, though terrible sight, when the plutonic forces of this vast region were in active operation.

PAINTED DESERT.— This is a weird, desolate plateau far distant upon the northeast. It is destitute of water or vegetation, and its surface is covered with isolated peaks, buttes, and columns of sandstone worn into fantastic shapes by the sand-blast. It is a region of wonderful mirages, in which are said to be depicted palaces, gardens, colonnades, temples, fountains, lakes, islands, fortifications, groves, orchards, cattle-herds, and human beings. It is supernatural ground to the Indians, who have always carefully avoided it.

The Painted Desert is visible from the San Francisco

peaks, and the view has an uncanny and shadowy beauty. It is delicately colored with blue, red, yellow, and green, softened and harmonized by distance.

INTERMEDIATE STATIONS: Riordan, Bellemont, Cinder Pit, Rhodes, Challender, Davenport.

Williams.—Chicago, 1,755 miles; St. Louis, 1,615 miles; Los Angeles, 510 miles; San Diego, 593 miles; San Francisco, 822 miles. Altitude, 6,750 feet. Population, 199. Dining station.

The name of this station was derived from Bill Williams Peak, which is distinguishable upon the south, and the peak in its turn is indebted to some early pioneer whose personality and deeds appear to have otherwise faded from memory.

It is practicable to visit the Grand Cañon from this point, where conveyance can be found, but the stage-line from Flagstaff is the only one indorsed by the Santa Fé Route, as it reaches the point of grandest outlook yet made accessible, and the best facilities and accommodations for the tourist have in consequence been provided on the Flagstaff route.

Three miles beyond Williams is the station Supai, and beyond that for a number of miles, extends a very pretty and varied gorge known as Johnson's Cañon.

INTERMEDIATE STATIONS: Supai, McLellan, Fairview.

Ash Fork.—Chicago, 1,778 miles; St. Louis, 1,638 miles; Los Angeles, 487 miles; San Diego, 570 miles; San Francisco, 799 miles. Altitude, 5,129 feet. Junction with Santa Fé, Prescott & Phœnix Railway to Prescott and Phœnix.

PRESCOTT, PHŒNIX, AND THE SALT RIVER VALLEY REGION.—Southward from Ash Fork stretches the Santa Fé, Prescott & Phœnix Railway, at the time of writing newly constructed and in operation to the city of Prescott, a distance of sixty miles, and in course of construction onward to Phœnix, a further distance of 137 miles, to which latter city it is expected to be in operation before the winter of 1894. The completion of this railroad through the rich mining regions surrounding Prescott, and through the smaller alluvial valleys to the immensely productive lands along the Salt River at and near Phœnix, is a matter of great import to the development of Arizona and to a large number of home-seekers in other parts of the country, whose attention is turned inquiringly toward the new Southwest. The region thus opened on the north to quick rail communication with the outside world offers much, therefore, of interest to the settler and the investor, and is worthy of some comment for the benefit of the mere traveler. But inasmuch as the railroad is not yet completed between Prescott and Phœnix, this somewhat wide gap being at present crossed by stage, the topic will here be treated less methodically than are the subjects relating to the direct trip to California.

Immediately below Ash Fork for a distance of twenty-five miles the Santa Fé, Prescott & Phœnix Railway leads through mountain scenery, and then descends to Chino Valley, a grazing region, where alfalfa and small fruits are cultivated on the irrigated portions. At a distance of twenty-five miles farther on the road passes out of Chino Valley at Granite Station, from which point large quantities of copper matte (impure metal smelted from the ore but not refined) are shipped to Chicago and New York from the United, Verde, Boggs, and other copper mines which lie from twenty to twenty-five miles distant. A little beyond this station the road threads an extraordinary upheaval of granite forms, covering an area nearly two miles square, which much resembles in freakish character the Garden of the Gods in Colorado. This locality, known as Point of Rocks, was an almost impregnable lurking-place of Apaches in earlier troublous times in the history of the Territory. Whipple Barracks, a military post, lies a short distance beyond. This post was established some forty years ago, and contains a garrison of four companies. It is regarded as one of the most healthful locations among Government posts.

Prescott.—Distance from Ash Fork sixty miles. Altitude, 5,350 feet. Population (city), 1,759.

This prosperous city is the center of a vast mining country, in which gold predominates over other metals. Large herds of cattle find ample grazing in the adjacent valleys, and there, also, are many small segregated farms within a radius of from ten to twenty miles. In nearly all the draws of the mountains are streams, such as the Lynx, Granite, Weaver, Hassayampa, etc., in the sand-bars of all which placer gold is found in paying quantity. It has been claimed that many thousand men could find profitable employment in this industry of gold-washing in Yavapai County alone.

The summer climate of Prescott is delightful. Unlike the summer months in California, July, August, and September here are visited by frequent rains. There are no troublesome insects. The winter is temperate. Light snow occasionally falls, but seldom remains on the ground for a sufficient period to afford sleighing. To this locality come, in the summer, the pleasure-seeking residents of the more southerly and less elevated regions, to dwell in tents and cottages.

Prescott is situated in the north central portion of Yavapai County, of which it is the seat. It is attractively placed upon a moderate hillside that dips to Granite Creek, and is girt with pines and cedars. Founded early in the '60s it is one of the oldest of the towns of modern Arizona. It possesses two public schools, a Catholic school, a hospital under charge of the Sisters of Mercy, half a dozen churches, and two banks. There are several saw-mills, a planing-mill, stone-cutting and ore-sampling works, and an electric-light plant.

Southward from Prescott the Sierra Prieta Range is crossed at an altitude of 6,600 feet to Skull Valley, whose grim name is due to the large number of Indian skulls that long marked here the scene of a considerable conflict between the aborigines and the early Caucasian settlers, in which the latter were victorious. The valley is a dozen miles long, and affords grazing for many cattle. Placer gold was found in the high bars on the east side of this valley in 1885, the pay dirt being on the surface; but there being no water within a distance of two miles, and there in practicable quantity only in the winter months, work has never been extensively prosecuted, although the gravel is said to yield $2 per cubic yard in flat leaf gold. A few miles to the south is a larger deposit of better grade, where workmen make good wages in winter, although handicapped by the necessity of hauling the gravel three miles to be sluiced. And it will suffice to say that over a large area in this part of Arizona placer gold is not uncommon, but is only fitfully worked by reason of the scant water supply. From Skull Valley the west slope of the Bradshaw Mountains and the Walnut Grove mining regions are easily accessible. At Walnut Grove, on the Hassayampa River, are the remains of a great storage dam, which burst a few years ago, nearly two-score persons losing their lives in consequence. This dam will shortly be rebuilt, preparations being already under way. The area of the original reservoir was more than a square mile, and the water in some portions was 100 feet deep. It was utilized for both mining and irrigating.

From Skull Valley, at an approximate altitude of 4,600 feet, the railway route passes into Kirkland Valley, a basin of equal size. Here also hay and grain are raised in quantity, and large herds of cattle are concentrated from outlying ranges for shipment.

APACHE INDIANS.

Bell's Cañon is the point of interest next following. Here, more than a quarter century back, a Government paymaster was waylaid and slain by Apaches, thus bequeathing his name to the spot. Old Camp Date Creek an abandoned military post, follows. Just as Skull and

Kirkland valleys are the determined distributing points of supplies for the adjacent mining localities, so Old Camp Date Creek will serve the Santa Maria region, the scene of rich and extensive gold discoveries in recent times; likewise the Hillside mine properties.

Ten miles beyond Date Creek the supply point for the Congress Mine and the Weaver and lower Hassayampa districts is reached. In the Weaver district is the far-famed Rich Hill, where a Mexican, searching for lost horses belonging to his employer, found a nugget of such size and value that legend has long since claimed it for its own, and sets its worth at a fabulous amount. Rich Hill became famous for its placer gold, yielding larger nuggets than any other camp in Arizona, but quartz ledges also exist in the vicinity. There was a considerable rush from California to this locality early in the '50s.

Twenty miles farther on is Wickenburg, supply point for the Vulture Mine and the Harquahala and Castle Creek districts. It is stated that the Vulture yielded over $9,000,000 in gold in former days, but is now nearly inoperative for want of timber, which the railway will soon bring to this as to other properties which await the assistance of cheap transportation facilities. The difficulties attending the development of these mines will be better apprehended when it is stated that the lumber necessary for timbering the shafts has hitherto been brought from Puget Sound by vessel to the Southern California coast, thence by the Southern Pacific Railroad to a point in Southern Arizona on the banks of the Gila River, and then freighted by wagon from sixty to seventy-five miles across a waterless desert.

From Wickenburg the projected railway follows the course of the Hassayampa through Box Cañon, where the river is crossed, and a few miles farther on the Agua

Fria Valley is entered. This promising valley is some ten miles wide from north to south, and thirty miles long, and is almost wholly capable of irrigation. In Agua Fria Valley, twenty miles beyond the crossing of the Hassayampa, is Hot Springs Junction, 106 miles from Prescott. This is the point of divergence to Castle Creek Hot Springs, twenty miles away. These springs are unimproved, and the surroundings are crude, but the residents of the region have unbounded faith in the future of the locality as a resort for invalids and pleasure-seekers. Many hundreds of people annually find their way to these springs, despite their comparatively difficult accessibility. There is a small hotel, but visitors commonly camp in the neighborhood. The bathing is performed in a large rock-walled basin, which has been created by long erosion of the flowing water. The temperature of the springs is from 100° to 110°. The waters are claimed to possess a distinct medicinal virtue, and are resorted to for the healing of rheumatism and blood diseases, and for recuperation from mining casualties. No analysis is at hand.

The Agua Fria, like all western rivers, is a capricious stream, sinking from sight in many places during the dry season, and at other times swelling to a deep turbulent current, which can not be safely forded. It divides the valley which bears its name from that of the Salt River, the crossing being only twenty-four miles distant from Phœnix.

There is no more wonderful garden spot in America, perhaps in the whole world, than the Salt River Valley. It contains many hundred thousand acres of irrigable land, more than 200,000 acres of which have already been brought into the highest state of cultivation. It is settling up rapidly, and will sustain a large population. It may be said to extend to Yuma, on the California boundary.

Maricopa County, of which Phœnix is the seat, contains about 250 miles of modern canals, exclusive of lateral ditches; 600,000 acres of land are capable of reclamation under the present water development, and 240,000 acres have actually been reclaimed. The largest artificial waterway in the Territory is the Arizona Canal, which is forty-one miles in length and thirty-six feet in width at the bottom, with a carrying capacity of 1,000 cubic feet per second. This is situated in the northern part of the valley, where also are the Grand Canal, twenty-seven miles; Maricopa Canal, twenty-six miles; and Salt River Valley Canal, nineteen miles, besides Farmers' Canal and St. John's Canal, of a smaller dimension. On the south side are the Mesa Consolidated, forty miles; Highland, twenty-two miles; Tempe, twenty miles; Utah and Eureka, sixteen miles, and San Francisco. The Arizona Canal taps the Salt River a short distance below the confluence of the Verde, at a point where a crib dam 1,000 feet in length raises the water of the river about ten feet. Twenty-two miles from its head the water of the canal falls perpendicularly sixteen feet over a ledge of solid rock, furnishing power estimated at more than 2,000 horse-power. A mile below this fall a cross-cut canal connects the Arizona with the Grand, Maricopa, and Salt River Valley canals. In a course of 4½ miles this cross-cut canal makes twenty-four falls of from four to six feet each, thus furnishing an additional amount of water power. The commercial value of these falls is, however, as yet prospective.

Concerning hay, grain, stock and fruit farming, etc., in the Salt River Valley, the following brief observations, condensed from reliable sources, will be of interest to the inquirer:

Not less than 50,000 acres of alfalfa are now planted,

capable of producing 250,000 tons of hay per annum, but only a small portion of this immense possible crop ever reaches the baler, as thousands of range steers are brought in from the mountains every year to be fattened on alfalfa pasturage. Alfalfa is a profitable crop, reliable and easy to raise. Every acre commonly produces five or six tons annually. It is mown from three to five times, dried on the ground, and by means of hay-carriers and derricks hoisted into great ricks. The price for such hay in the stack varies from $4 to $7 per ton.

Barley leads the grain crops, taking the place of corn, which is little grown, and used almost wholly for fattening swine. In 1893 the area devoted to barley in this valley was 30,000 acres. This grain is a favorite with farmers on account of its freedom from rust and smut, and its unfailing productiveness. Barley land is usually irrigated during October or November, and planted about the beginning of cold weather. A yield of forty bushels to the acre may be looked for, and the price ranges from 75 cents to $1.50 per 100 pounds.

About 8,000 acres of wheat are planted annually, the local flour mills absorbing the product. Oats are planted to a limited extent for hay, and the wild variety overruns all neglected grain fields. Beets, carrots, turnips, pumpkins, squashes, watermelons, and cantaloupes grow to a very great size, and yield heavily. Gardening, however, is principally in the hands of the Chinese, who supply the town residents.

The valley is exceedingly well adapted to breeding and training race-horses, no winter housing being necessary, and this industry is profitably followed. The cattle business is of considerable importance, many farmers finding their profit in buying the lean cattle of the back ranges and fattening them upon green or stacked alfalfa at a cost of $5 per head. Cattlemen, in their turn, rent such pasturage at $1 a month per head. Dairying is remunerative, by reason of the rich nutriment of alfalfa feed; and there are not less than 3,000 stands of bees in the county, the fragrant blossoms of the mesquit, alfalfa bloom, and a multitude of flowering shrubs yielding a rich booty to those proverbial improvers of shining hours.

But the Salt River Valley will find its greatest wealth, as it has already found its widest fame, in its semi-tropical fruits. The orange, lemon, fig, date, apricot, peach, nectarine, plum, pomegranate, grape, and a host of smaller fruits and berries grow here in perfection, and some of them, notably the orange, mature several weeks in advance of the California product, which fact should give the Arizona fruit a distinct advantage in eastern markets.

The area at present planted to orchards and vineyards is about 20,000 acres. There are orange trees in the valley that have been in bearing for ten years, but the first orange orchard of any importance was planted under the Arizona Canal, nine miles from Phœnix, in 1889. It covered sixteen acres. There are now about 600 acres of orange orchards, some 200 acres having begun to bear, and the acreage planted is yearly increasing. The fig orchards in the neighborhood of Phœnix are very extensive. The favorite variety is the White Adriatic. A large packing-house in the vicinity is entirely devoted to fig drying. Of raisin grapes there are thousands of acres in bearing, of which the Muscat of Alexandria, Muscatel, Gordo Blanco, Malaga, and Sultana are the chief varieties. The conditions of soil and climate are understood to be congenial to the olive, but the trees that have been planted have not yet reached the age of bearing.

Phœnix.—Distance from Ash Fork, 197 miles. Altitude, 1,100 feet. Population (city), 3,152. Junction with Maricopa & Phœnix Railroad.

This, the capital of Arizona, is situated in the center of the southern half of the Territory. It stands upon a gently sloping plain some two miles distant from the Salt River. On either hand, to the north and south, lie the mountains, at a distance of about ten miles. It was laid out in 1872. Immigration came slowly until the town was connected with the Southern Pacific Railroad upon the south by the Maricopa & Phœnix Railroad in 1888. Since that date the rate of increase in population has been rapid, until, in 1893, the number of inhabitants is estimated at 10,000. The streets are regularly laid out from north to south and from east to west, the latter being named for the Presidents of the United States and the former being numbered; those upon the east of Center Street being known as streets, and those upon the west as avenues. The main streets are 80 to 100 feet in width, and many are pleasantly shaded by large trees. Water flows at the side of every street, and a good waterworks system supplies domestic needs. Illumination is supplied by gas and by electric lights, which latter are used not only in the principal stores but in many private residences as well. There is a complete telephone system. Street-car lines traverse the most important parts of the city. Among the business blocks the newest are pretentious in proportions and attractive in design. There are three public schools, seven or eight churches, and numerous sectarian, charitable, and secret organizations, among which are Masons, Odd Fellows, Workmen, Knights of Pythias, Select Knights, Chosen Friends, Good Templars, and the Grand Army of the Republic. Also three daily and weekly newspapers, three public halls, four hotels, two ice factories, three planing-mills, three lumber-yards, an iron foundry, a flour-mill, and four banks. The Territorial Insane Asylum is three miles distant.

The thriving town of Tempe is a near neighbor of Phœnix, only nine miles distant. This is the site of several manufactories and a normal school.

Mesa City, a town of Mormon settlement, lies eighteen miles distant from Phœnix. It is actively engaged in the manufacture of cheese, wine, and brandy, and in fruit raising, drying, and canning. In 1892 Mesa City produced 30,000 gallons of wine and 4,000 gallons of brandy.

The climate of the Salt River Valley marks a high temperature in summer, the mercury sometimes rising to 110°. It will be well, however, to bear in mind a fact emphasized elsewhere in this book in treating of the climate of the arid regions of the West, namely, that the degree of heat shown by the thermometer does not necessarily indicate one's personal comfort or discomfort. To say that the agriculture of a given locality is dependent upon irrigation is only another way of stating that the air is dry and the precipitation of moisture slight. This means absence of humidity, which, quite as much as a high temperature, constitutes the unpleasantness of hot weather in localities where the rainfall is abundant and the air surcharged with moisture. The inhabitants of humid regions, in consequence, are accustomed to mount to physical discomfort in exact proportion as the mercury climbs its tube, and experience has taught them to associate misery with a high temperature. Such teaching is true only in the locality where it is taught. It becomes false under different conditions, such as are presented by a dry, pure, elevated air. Except in certain sunken basins, at or below sea level, it would be difficult to find in the whole arid West a locality which in hottest midsummer could afford the terrors which are well-known to the cities of New York and New England. A land of almost perpetual sun, dog-days and sunstrokes are strangers here. Midsummer is unquestionably a hot season in the Salt River Valley, but there are few days when the workman can not labor with comfort in the fields. It is distinctly a healthful region, the death-rate being very low in spite of the fact that a yearly increasing number of invalids resort to Phœnix and vicinity. An almost total immunity from the diseases elsewhere common to children is reported. The county is free from malaria, and a record of two years shows only half a dozen cases of typhoid fever. Rheumatic, consumptive, and asthmatic patients are particularly benefited by residence here. When the weather grows uncomfortably warm the mountains are near at hand and afford prompt relief to such as are free to avail themselves of the respite.

The following is the meteorological summary of Arizona for the year 1892–3, based on reports from about forty stations in various sections of the Territory. It represents the average meteorological conditions for the several months.

MONTHS.	Mean temperature for the Territory.	Average precipitation for the Territory (inches and hundredths).	WEATHER CHARACTER OF DAYS.			
			Clear.	Partly cloudy	Cloudy	Rainy.*
1892.						
July	83.7	1.29	11	10	9	5
August	83.0	1.15	16	9	6	4
September	77.7	0.17	20	6	3	1
October	63.4	0.81				
November	54.4	0.15	23	4	4	1
December	43.6	0.54	21	4	5	3
1893.						
January	47.7	0.36	22	5	4	1
February	50.3	0.85	15	7	6	2
March	52.8	2.24	16	8	7	6
April	61.6		22	6	2	
May	69.9	0.85	24	4	3	2
June	82.0	0.01	23	5	2	

* Days with 0.01 inch or more.

PREHISTORIC RUINS.— When the soldiers of Cortez were subduing and plundering the Aztecs in Mexico the valleys of the Salt and Gila rivers were barren, the rust of antiquity already lying upon half-buried canals stretching mile after mile across the plain, where once artificial streams had watered productive acres for a numerous people, long since disappeared. Ruins of their "cities" are abundant, no less than twenty-six having been discovered, nearly buried with earth and debris, in the immediate neighborhood of Casa Grande, Pinal County, which is the most celebrated of all. In these ruins has been found a large quantity of pottery, domestic implements, weapons, stone mills and axes, bracelets, and other trinkets of shell and onyx, etc., and the neighboring cliffs are covered with chiseled and painted hieroglyphs. Stone fortresses and caves have also been discovered in the mountains, which were doubtless inhabited by the same or a similar people. The skill exercised in the construction of the ancient canals of Arizona, of which numerous examples are found in the Salt River Valley, is evidenced by the fact that the modern engineer has not disdained to make use of considerable portions of them. In truth, the new canals, in some instances, are nothing more than the old ones re-excavated.

The traveler who is curious in such matters will find abundant material to gratify his curiosity in this neighborhood. In this instance the present writer is unable to contribute anything derived from his personal observation, and is indebted to a recently published article written by Mr. J. H. McClintock of Phœnix for particulars of these ancient relics:

> In the Salt River Valley was, without doubt, the seat of the highest development of Arizona's prehistoric tribes. Scattered over the valley are thousands of mounds that mark where the ancients' castles

and houses of cement and adobe once stood. Long lines of irrigating canals led from the river to the broad plains that stretch away for a score of miles on either side. Occasionally there are seen the ruins of what were plainly great citadels, their walls, for a dozen feet or more, still standing, though covered with the debris of the upper stories.

The only systematic and satisfying exploration of these mines was in 1887, by Frank Hamilton Cushing, in charge of the Hemingway Archæological Expedition. This skilled ethnologist, for his field of operations, fixed upon a buried city about seven miles south of Tempe. This Western Pompeii he termed "Los Muertos," in English, "The City of the Dead." The writer was at the time a near resident, and watched the progress of the work with the utmost interest.

The field chosen for investigation turned out all the most sanguine could have hoped for. Within its limits many long, low, gravelly knolls and other elevations, covered with a rank growth of mesquit and sage-brush, proved, under the searching spades of Mr. Cushing's workmen, the debris of hundreds of houses, one and two, possibly three, stories in height, while the apparently natural arroyos that crossed the lines of these foundations were demonstrated irrigating canals of no small capacity. In fact, a large city, of which, on the arrival of Mr. Cushing's party, not one corner-stone or trace of a wall could be found, was partially exhumed from the earthy debris of its own decay, and from amidst its now low foundations were gathered almost numberless implements and remains of art, from a study of which almost whole chapters have been deduced relative to the domestic, civil, and religious life of the community that once inhabited it.

The number of inhabitants is beyond even approximate conjecture, but the era of their residence seems in all probability to have antedated, or to have been contemporaneous with, the Norman conquest of England. It seems strange, and conveys the idea of great age, to see the roots of the largest and oldest mesquits where they had penetrated the chambers of these long-deserted houses now laid bare, but though a dozen such trees may have grown to maturity and fallen to dust on these same spots, the sum of their ages would be naught compared with the time that has been required to level these high buildings almost to their very foundations, and to rot away every trace of the woodwork which once abundantly entered into their structures, save such as is left on fallen or deeply buried fragments of mud and plaster. Indeed, whole vessels of hard-burned earthenware, found by Mr. Cushing, which as bread and meat receptacles were evidently set in close, well-plastered cysts or cells of adobe, have, nevertheless, so far crumbled away as to be beyond restoration save by the artist's methods.

The city seems to gradually thin out to the suburbs and towards the small farm-houses, the burned floors of which have been found scattered about more than two miles northeast, east and southeast of the citadel or temple-mound. Within the intervening two miles in those directions diggings were made at various intervals, and in every place designated by Mr. Cushing or excavated under his personal directions, not only walls and foundations were found, but also valuable antiquities, by the clearing away of the debris of centuries.

The investigations led to the conclusion that the race who inhabited these now leveled buildings were of a superior cast, were a people in whom industry and the instincts of government were inherent and highly developed. Both skill and enterprise are shown by the numerous great irrigating canals and ditches that lie spread out, like true arteries, which once carried fertility and life not only to these but to all parts of the valley; indeed, beyond points as yet untilled by our people. Their canals, one or two of which certainly exceed in length, if not in size, the Arizona (the largest canal of this day), indicate vast communities of people working under an organized corporative rather than a despotic system, since they were all dug by the aid of no other hard implements than hoes, mattocks, and axes of chipped or ground stone, and since the sole method of conveying earth to the banks seems to have been by means of wicker barrows, conical burden-baskets thrown over the shoulders, and roughly-woven fiber mats, impressions of the borders of nearly all of which were detected in the mud along these banks wherever, being near houses, it happens to have been hardened by fire or otherwise.

Those who have ever traced the course of any of the old main acequias have noticed, scattered on the banks, the immense number of partially rounded black basalt, or diorite bowlders, or stones. It will be found that this kind of rock is not in any native deposit of the lower valleys. It has been imported from the distant mountains or from the river bed, whose cobbles nearly always were broken in half or otherwise shaped by the ancients and used as the chipping-stones wherewith the implements above referred to were sharpened, until, their more angular edges being worn away, they were cast aside upon the banks of the canal useless, save as the testimonials to later generations of the prodigious labors they helped to perform.

Returning, to speak of the city, the houses were irregularly placed, rather according to the suitability of the topography than according to the regularity of the thoroughfares, though considerable attention has been given to the latter, since in some instances they passed directly through, or even sometimes, evidently like tunnels, under the blocks of buildings. The dwellings were scattered rather promiscuously, but, singularly enough, they all face very nearly to the cardinal points or the compass, or, in exceptional cases, were laid out with reference to the central ruin or great temple mound.

The material of the houses was always adobe, usually formed by hand, like large and small stones. The floors were of mud mixed with ashes, beaten down and sometimes burned, and the roofs were of the same material, supported, as is shown by many indentations and impressions and occasional charred remains, by rafters of mesquit and cross-mattings of cane, cornstalks, or small, neatly-trimmed osiers, or sometimes, as in the case of the outer dwellings, near the farms, by simple brush, making practically the same sort of roof as is extensively used in the valley at present. Even, too, in the latter kind of buildings, thatching was in vogue, of which was seen the remains in one small building, consisting of quite a deposit of straw, twigs, and corn leaves, or stalks, preserved to the sight, though not to the touch, from the destructive tooth of time by carbonization.

Water was supplied to the town continually by four, possibly more, good-sized ditches, crossing it at almost regular intervals, and connected by several smaller ones, some of which passed before the very doorways of the very largest group of houses.

The active shovels of Mr. Cushing's men scooped the earth from a number of public ovens. They were great pits dug into the earth and lined with a thick, carefully-formed plastering of mud and natural cement, which, in some instances, having been melted down by excessive heat, shows slag, inclosing fragments of rock, thrown in to master the fire, and which exhibit a decided copper stain. The pits are in shape similar to an inverted cone or a great hopper, and are of varying sizes; one which was particularly noted was about fifteen feet in diameter and seven feet deep.

The Zuñis have cooking pits somewhat like these, which in their language are named " Mi-ak-thli-na-a-k'o-we," literally, " green ripening oven caves." They are used after the following fashion: After heating to a high degree the walls, by filling them with fuel both dry and green, to the very brink, and burning, usually for a day or two, many of the brands and embers are hauled out by means of long poles, and such of the embers as remain, which are very considerable, are either closed in by large flat stones or covered over by smaller ones. Green cornstalks and leaves, or certain branches, amongst which those of the cedar or juniper may be mentioned as favorites, are thrown in upon these stones and piled up along the hissing walls, which are frequently sprinkled with water; then corn or the other food which, usually green, is to be ripened or cooked, is heaped in, also being frequently sprinkled, and a covering similar to the lining is made. Over this stones and earth are thrown and the whole is sealed, as it were, with mud plastering. Then more fire is kindled on the surface and the cooking or steam-baking is continued from one to three or four days, according to the quantity of food contained.

The ovens of these ancients were always more extensive than those their modern representatives have used — evidently in an identical manner. By their means almost any green vegetable matter was rendered sweet and delicious, and by drying could be preserved in palatable form for any length of time. If proof other than this general similarity were needed relative to the use of these ancient fire-pits it might be found in the fact that in them were found charred remains of corn, mescal, and other green foods.

The main walls constituted a temple as well as a citadel, the residence of the superior priesthood. It was surrounded at a distance of sixty feet, more or less, by a sun-dried mud wall, which was high and straight, originally, on the foundations, and which, though pushed out of shape by the growth of mesquits and the weight of fallen buildings, are still tolerably straight, and so thick that a team and wagon might be driven along the greater part of their extent. The space inclosed by this wall is partially covered by rooms of varying sizes, and there seem to have been two or three open courts, notably one at the southeastern angle, which were presumably used for the sacred dances and dramas and other public religious ceremonials of the priests.

The central structure covered a large extent of ground and was certainly four, perhaps more, stories in height. The ground floor was reached in the excavation.

The walls were thick and of carefully-formed adobes, as were also the two medium walls and the double walls at either end, all extending to and adjoining the great wall surrounding the whole. The interior walls were, many of them, comparatively thin, being built up of little hand-made adobes, placed while still soft between upright, nearly equidistant poles or posts of mesquit. Some of the partitions were formed of coarse cane matting, secured to the upright posts and plastered on either side with thick coats of mud, a prehistoric and most ingenious instance of "lathing and plastering." The wood and the matting are to-day disintegrated, dust or powdered charcoal alone remaining of them, but on the hardened clay may be seen the impress of the woven and matted work and in the walls the deep holes where the wooden pillars once stood.

Though windows and port-holes have been found far up in the external walls, no doors penetrated them, and thus we may infer that the houses were reached by ladders as in Zuñi to-day. Within, however, in addition to the same openings, doorways are not infrequently encountered. These doorways were closed in a number of ways, most usually by means of heavy portieres of matting or fiber, or by means of doors hung from spindles turning at top and bottom in wooden or stone sockets, and sometimes by means of flat stones opening and closing vertically, and fastened with heavy braces of wood.

Among the many proofs found confirming the archaic relation between these ancient people and the ancestry of the Zuñis of northwestern New Mexico, is the circumstance that the thick earthen lids of the burial urns and other vessels when found show on their lower surfaces the impression of a coarse, flat, cane matting identically such as is used to-day by the Zuñis for the reception of their sheets of wafer or paper bread, which mats are to-day, as they were in forgotten times, used also in the fashioning of flat masses of clay or other plastic material.

The same implements, too, and especially the same paraphernalia, were in vogue amongst these same ancient people that may be seen in use in Zuñi at the present time. Portions of the fire-hardened, wooden belt looms and woof-sticks, as well as one or two quaint bobbins, were found. Portions of scoop-shaped spatulæ and polishing stones, the regular possessions of Zuñi matrons (the potters of to-day), have also been found. It might be inferred that, like their modern representatives, the women of this ancient city were expert in all the household arts of the Zuñis, in the making of the fine paper bread, in the molding of vessels of clay, and in the weaving of belts and blankets and other garments, for amongst the other articles of daily use thus far gathered are hundreds of whorls of fine stone or ground earthenware, which served to twirl the tall spiked spindles on the winter evenings of long ago.

Shells are abundant, more than twenty marine species having been found, indicating frequent communications with the seacoast. The small oliva (of special significance) and other snail-like shells are particularly common. Many fragments and complete fetiches of green, blue, red, and other finely colored stones, often of spirited execution, and many finely carved ornaments of suggestive shapes in shell were also found.

Death and the dead seem to have had few terrors for these people, for mixed in their daily associations were the urn-graves of their friends and relatives and the adobe sarcophagi of their priests. Their worship, as shown by the sacred implements and by numerous mystic symbols, was practically the same as that of the Zuñis, and may be explained as a reverence of all natural forces personified or deified. Each individual of the sacred priestly or esoteric societies which Mr. Cushing has found existed among them, was attached to some particular patron or deity whose protection was sought by the wearing of carvings representing or symbolizing him or her.

The priests, from fasting and from continued researches into occult science, as well as from inherited spiritual rank, were thought to have the power of communication with the invisible world, to be able at any time to disengage their souls from fetters of clay, and, having this power, it was deemed unnecessary to aid the flight or disembodiment of their spirits at death. On the other hand, the commoner people, having no such power, must needs be cremated, that the entire soul might be liberated without delay or even partial detention from its earthly tenement. This will explain why so comparatively few skeletons were found. Thirty-two skeletons, three or four of which are those of children, and two or three only those of women — none the less of sacred rank — were found, each usually having at its head a pitcher, a drinking-bowl, and a trencher, in which were placed the food and drink to serve for the brief journey to the earliest home or council of the dead.

Sometimes it was deemed necessary to provide vessels for use in the other world; in such a case the jars or cups whose spirits were to accompany the dead were "killed" by boring through their bottoms a good-sized hole, or by more violent means.

Five skeletons were found, in an excellent state of preservation, within the great temple mound. One of them is of a man whose mental powers must have been of the first order, certainly of his day, the skull of a man who might have been in times of war a Napoleon, in times of peace a Gladstone among them. With jutting forehead, strong jaws, and perfect, large teeth, the skull is one over which Professor Fowler would have grown ecstatic. Another was of a man who died at an age of quite, if not over, 100 years. The sutures of the skull were, in places, consolidated and the entire dental and alveolar formations had disappeared. Both were about six feet in height.

Then, a remarkable treasure, by the side of a little priest child, in addition to finer pottery than usual, was found, carven in earthen, a small rude image of a dog. This was one of Mr. Cushing's choicest treasures, as it alone seemed to show connection — possibly ancestral — of these ancients with the Toltecs and their successors the Aztecs; since, in the tombs of the so-called "nobles" or warrior-priests among the latter famed nation, it was customary to place a Mexican dog. Amongst the Zuñis no less than with the Aztecs the dog was held (as is the horse now) as the type of geographic knowledge, it being able to return through any country and from any distance to the place of its nativity. Mr. Cushing attributed the historic custom of the Aztecs of slaughtering a dog and placing it in the grave of a person of consequence — "as a guide to the soul"—to this conception. Here, whither the custom seems to have been brought, or whence, as he thinks, it was more likely taken, the dogs were either rare or their lives held in high esteem, since the figure of one was made to serve instead of the actual animal.

The bones of the skeletons lay in vaults just large enough to contain the bodies. The receptacles were of clay, cemented from without. They were, in nearly all instances, placed in a corner of a room supposed to have been occupied by their tenants in life, and the floors show evidence of having been either filled in until level with the top of the tomb or else the tomb was built up until the ceiling was reached. Owing to this peculiar custom the level of the rooms of each story was not uniform, some of the chambers being filled to the depth of several feet, nor do the walls seem built with any other than accidental reference to the original plan of the main structure, at least in the upper stories.

The burial of the commoner people was materially different. In the first place, as above stated, the remains were incinerated; they were then placed in the burial urns, covered with saucer-like lids, miniature earthen vessels placed beside, and the whole covered with earth to the depth of from one to several feet. Several cemeteries have been laid bare, each having dozens of these funeral caskets of all the various shapes in actual use in their day buried in them. The burial plats are scattered all over the pueblo, and seem to show that every family or small clan had a separate and convenient place to deposit their dead near the walls of their block or blocks of dwellings. The level of the country has, in Mr. Cushing's opinion, not risen during the intervening centuries; it has, on the contrary, been, in some places, lowered through the action of the wind and rain, and many of these ancient burying places have thus been opened to the elements and the vessels destroyed, scattering much of the pottery so common to the valley.

In none of the interments, either of the common people or of the priests themselves, not excepting those of war, are actual weapons found, merely ceremonial representatives of them, which, while indicating an elaborate martial organization and a thorough understanding of the art of war, show that the latter was always defensive or at most retaliative. Strictly in keeping with this are the huge pierced stones found near the exterior walls, which were suspended over portals and other passages as means of defense, while in the far northern towns and cities of this same people, along the valley and tributaries of the Colorado Chiquito, huge machine missiles take the place of these stones of defense, and the dead warrior-priest, in addition to his supplies of food, water, and other appurtenances, was furnished not infrequently with actual weapons, and his shrine received symbols of the same as its most fitting offerings.

Much the same character of "desert" ruins are to be found all over southern Arizona, where there existed a chance to divert the waters of even distant streams.

INTERMEDIATE STATIONS: Pineveta, Crookton.

Seligman. — Chicago, 1,805 miles; St. Louis, 1,665 miles; Los Angeles, 460 miles; San Diego, 543 miles; San Francisco, 772 miles. Altitude, 5,247 feet.

Junction with Prescott & Arizona Central Railway

INTERMEDIATE STATIONS: Chino, Red Mesa, Aubrey, Yampai, Nelson.

Peach Springs. — Chicago, 1,842 miles; St. Louis, 1,702 miles; Los Angeles, 423 miles; San Diego, 506 miles; San Francisco, 735 miles. Altitude, 4,780 feet. Dining station.

In the vicinity of the station dwells a tribe of Indians whose hillside "wickiups" are visible from the train. The squaws are unconscionable beggars, and will spurn any offering smaller than a nickel, which, by the way, is the lowest denomination of money freely current in the extreme West.

The Grand Cañon is accessible from this point, too, at a distance of only twenty-three miles, but the trip is hardly worth the making, in view of the better facilities and the infinitely grander view afforded by the Flagstaff route, except in winter, if the Flagstaff route should be closed. The road from Peach Springs leads over a rough way to the bottom of the side cañon of Diamond Creek, through which it is necessary to proceed about four miles to reach the main cañon, and then the panoramic view is not obtainable.

INTERMEDIATE STATIONS: Truxton, Crozier, Hackberry, Hualapai, Berry.

Kingman. — Chicago, 1,893 miles; St. Louis, 1,753 miles; Los Angeles, 372 miles; San Diego, 455 miles; San Francisco, 684 miles. Altitude, 3,326 feet. Population, 322.

A mining town. Rich mines lie behind the village, several miles distant among the hills. The broad simple landscape exerts a charm no less than fascination upon those who reside in this region. The miners love it with a hearty affection, and are homesick for it when away. If you chance to see it in the hour of twilight, when the horizon seems to shed a soft aurora above the dusky quiet land, and the outline of the hills is sharply marked against the sky, you will feel something of its subtle, masterful quality. It shuts out all the feverish, hurrying world, without requiring any surrender of manly energy.

INTERMEDIATE STATIONS: Hancock, Drake, Kaster, Yucca, Franconia, Powell.

THE COLORADO RIVER. — Next to the Columbia this is the principal American tributary to the Pacific. The Spaniard Alarçon discovered it in 1540, and ascended a considerable distance from the Gulf of California by boat; and in the same year one of Coronado's lieutenants reached it overland from New Mexico. As a curious sidelight upon the sublime guess-work that guided the discoverers of that period, it may be mentioned that Cabrillo, the discoverer of the California coast, in 1542, heard of this river, and sailed north as far as Cape Mendocino in search of it. In 1857 Lieutenant Ives made a lengthy exploration of it for our Government, and near this point, about 450 miles from the mouth, encountered a populous and warlike tribe of Indians, the Mojaves, who tilled these meadows and made their home in this locality. They were intelligent, almost gigantic in stature, and feared by other tribes. They are now reduced to a pitiful and disgusting handful, of which enough will be seen at Needles Station, nine miles beyond the river crossing. The cantilever bridge at this point, altitude 560 feet, is the second largest in America. Its clear span is 660 feet. Formerly the crossing was several miles above, over a pile bridge, but the treacherous, shifting nature of the stream compelled the railroad to build down here among the obelisks, where permanence is assured.

The rock spires upon the left are known as The Needles. The largest are taller and farther away than they look. They form the head of the beautiful Mojave Cañon, into which the river at once plunges. Lieutenant Ives' description of this cañon, upon the occasion when he forced the sturdy little "Explorer" through its rapids, is worth reading, although no convenient means has yet been afforded the tourist to look upon its splendors:

A low purple gateway and a splendid corridor, with massive red walls, formed the entrance to the cañon. At the head of this avenue frowning mountains, piled one above the other, seemed to block the way. An abrupt turn at the base of the apparent barrier revealed a cavern-like approach to the profound chasm beyond. A scene of such imposing grandeur as that which now presented itself I have never before witnessed. On either side majestic cliffs, hundreds of feet in height, rose perpendicularly from the water. As the river wound through the narrow inclosure every turn developed some sublime effect or startling novelty in the view. Brilliant tints of purple, green, brown, red, and white, illumined the stupendous surfaces and relieved their somber monotony. Far above, clear and distinct upon the narrow strip of sky, turrets, spires, jagged statue-like peaks and grotesque pinnacles overlooked the deep abyss.

CALIFORNIA.

HISTORICAL.— On the 27th day of June, 1542, Juan Rodriguez Cabrillo, with two vessels, set out from Navidad, a Pacific Coast port of New Spain about 300 miles north of Acapulco, Mexico, to explore the upper coast and take possession of the country. On the 17th day of September in that year he sailed into a bay to which he gave the name of San Mateo. This was the bay of San Diego. The pilot, Ferrel, kept a diary of the expedition, and relates that here they saw cabins and flocks of goats; so it is clear that there was then an Indian village at the point where the city of San Diego now stands. Thence they proceeded northward, occasionally observing a few Indians in canoes, and great signal smokes on the mainland. On the shores of what is now called San Pedro Bay they had their first interview with the California

Indians, who manifested no little fear of the Spaniards. Some of the crew went ashore to catch fish in a net, and the Indians let fly at them with arrows, wounding three men. This was the only Indian hostility that occurred throughout Cabrillo's expedition, and next day it was explained by the statement that another Spanish exploring party was penetrating the interior of Upper California at the same time, and had killed many of the natives. Ferrel describes these Indians as "well-disposed and advanced," and covered with the skins of animals, although these serious-minded mariners did capture two naked youngsters and clap shirts on them. From this point Cabrillo proceeded to explore a number of the northernmost Channel Islands, where many Indians were found, who treated the Spaniards kindly. These islands have long since been abandoned by the natives, who were described by Ferrel as inferior to the tribes on the mainland, subsisting wholly on fish and living swinishly.

Cabrillo's course was irregular and uncertain. He was a pioneer, and in such work as the discoverers cut out for themselves in that audacious era, the most skillful navigator was little more than a professional guesser. Moreover the two vessels were without decks, and were driven hither and yon at the pleasure of the storm, often separated, and both occasionally forced to take a southward tack to the Channel Islands for rendezvous and repairs. When the winds again were favorable they took up the task once more. The expedition wintered on the Isla de Posesion (afterward Juan Rodriguez, and now San Miguel Island), where on the 3d day of January, 1543, Cabrillo died and was buried. Ferrel succeeded him in command, and by the 1st day of March following had pushed as far north as the present southern boundary of Oregon. There tempestuous weather separated the vessels and drove them southward, not to meet again until twenty-five days after. The expedition then returned to Navidad.

Ferrel's narrative is difficult to follow, and for the

CALIFORNIA LIVE OAK.

most part monotonous; but it has occasional passages that are full-flavored, like the following:

Toward night the wind freshened and shifted to the south-southwest. They ran this night to the west-northwest with much difficulty, and Thursday at daybreak the wind shifted to the southwest with great fury, and the seas came from many parts, which harassed them much, and broke over the ships, which not having decks, if God should not succor them, they could not escape; and not being able to lay by, of necessity they ran aft northeast toward the land; and now holding themselves for lost they commended themselves to Our Lady of Guadalupe, and made their wills, and ran thus until 3 o'clock in the forenoon with much fear and labor, for they saw that they were going to be lost, and already saw many signs of the land which was near, as small birds, and logs very fresh, which floated from some rivers, although from the dark and cloudy weather the land did not appear. At this hour the mother of God succored them with the grace of her son, and there came a violent rainstorm from the north, which made them run all that night and the following day until sunset to the south with the foresails lowered; and because there was a high sea from the south it broke over them each time by the prow, and passed over them as if over a rock, and the wind shifted to the northwest and the north-northwest with great fury, so that it made them run until Saturday, the 3d of March, to the southeast and to the east-southeast, with such a high sea that it made them cry out without reserve that if God and his blessed mother did not miraculously save them they could not escape. Saturday afternoon the wind moderated and remained at the northwest, for which they gave many thanks to our Lord.

This exploration had no immediate results. For sixty years thereafter California lay fallow. During that interval, namely, in 1579, Sir Francis Drake, cruising in the Golden Hind, stumbled upon this coast and named it New Albion. Philip III. heard of Drake's exploit, and fearing that the country would be lost to Spain ordered it fortified. Sebastian Vizcaino, therefore, in 1602, discovered the bay of Monterey and rediscovered and surveyed the harbor of San Mateo, which, as the survey was made on the 12th day of November — St. James' "day" in the church calendar — was thereupon named San Diego, which is Spanish for the name of that saint. Nevertheless, the actual occupation of California did not begin until 1769, when Fra Serra and his companions came to San Diego to found missions.

The early history of California is therefore a history of the missions. The region was known as Alta (Upper) and Baja (Lower) California, the latter division corresponding generally to the peninsula in Mexican territory which still bears that name. The mission work of the Spaniards was begun upon the peninsula by the Jesuits, in 1697. In 1748, or thereabouts, a priest of the Franciscan order, named Junipero Serra, came to Mexico with two or three companions of his sect and devoted himself to general missionary labors. In 1797 the Jesuits were expelled from the California peninsula and their privileges given to the Franciscans. Serra was a man of profound piety, and although fifty-six years old, and lame, possessed indefatigable energy. The opportunity thus offered was one he had long dreamed of, and he promptly proceeded to take advantage of it. After a short stay on the peninsula, Serra and his companions withdrew to Alta California, in 1769, and made that the scene of the vast missionary work that was projected.

James W. Steele gives the following sketch of the beginning and end of the Franciscan missions in his delightful "Old Californian Days":

There were sixteen persons in the land party with which Serra was. There was still another land party, and two more were to go by sea in two ships. None of the four parties knew anything about it. They were taking the chances that a part of some one of them would get there. A man of those times named Galvez had charge of the outfitting and practical part. It was to him that California is to this day indebted for a considerable addition to the resources found when, after seventy-nine years, an eminently enterprising people became interested. He ordered the carrying of the seeds of everything that would grow in Spain, together with 200 head of cattle. Of these came the herds that were afterward so much at home, and of the seeds and cuttings came much that is most profitable and beautiful in California now. There was, besides, a very complete assortment of holy vessels, crosses, banners, and things necessary to the uses and services of the church. There are even strong evidences that so heavy and inconvenient a thing as a church bell, several of them, was thought of and included.

If the reader has any idea whatever of the country near the coast in South California, and of the southern part of it where it joins the peninsula of Lower California, and then can imagine it in a state of nature, covered with cactus and sage, crossed by a jumble of mountain ridges, waterless save in hidden places, and absolutely pathless, he can have some conception of the rigors of this tramp from Villacata to San Diego. We may remember that there was a double pur-

OLD CALIFORNIA HACIENDA.

pose in it, the first of which was the colonization of California, and secondly, the conversion of those who, in the cant of that day, both Puritan and Catholic, were known, as by the Mormons now, as "Gentiles."

At the end of the written instructions of Galvez, which were intended to govern the expedition, he stated, among other things, that one of the objects of the enterprise was to protect the country from the ambitious views of foreign nations. This is very Spanish, for the beautiful wilderness of California was then more utterly unknown than are now the scenes of Stanley's explorations in the heart of Africa, and probably its latest foreign visit had been that of Drake, one hundred and eighty-nine years before.

Indeed, the only knowledge of where they were going was obtained from such record as had been made of the survey of Admiral Vizcaino, in 1602, a hundred and sixty-five years before. The two points that attracted especial attention were San Diego and Monterey, both named and described by him for the first time. Yet so closely was this first definite scheme of colonization and conversion planned, that there were orders to plant a mission and garrison first at San Diego, then at Monterey, and then one half-way between to be called Buena Ventura, a favorite Spanish name meaning " good luck."

The expedition having been divided into four bodies in all, Serra insisted upon accompanying one of the land parties, and this, seemingly, for the reason that he had a lame leg, acquired in walking from Vera Cruz to the City of Mexico twenty years before. All the degrees of martyrdom seem to have been fully appreciated in those times. One of the ideas of the age may be partially illustrated by the fact that Serra never did anything for this difficulty in all the years after, but either aggravated it or was indifferent to it. . . .

The present writer must, in all sincerity, state his entire ignorance as to precisely where in the upper part of the peninsula of Lower California Villacata was situated, but the missionaries left there on March 24th and arrived at San Diego on May 13th. The party with which Serra was, however, did not reach there until six weeks later, and when they came they found everybody sick with scurvy, and many dead. The ships were there. One of them, the San Carlos, which arrived last, lost all her sailors but two. The San Antonio, the other, which sailed a month and a half later than the San Carlos, reached San Diego twenty days the soonest. There was some difficulty in finding the place. An age of discovery and maritime adventure could not furnish any better sailors than that. She also lost half her crew by that fatal malady, now almost unknown. . . . .

Padre Serra was an enthusiast. He beat his bare breast with a stone, and burned it with a lighted torch, to illustrate to the Indians the pains and penalties of hell. But neither he nor any of his brethren ever made a mistake in the location of a mission, and they are invariably the best locations in the California of to-day. Walking barefoot over those thorny miles, possessed with a burning desire to baptize, longing only to preach the everlasting gospel, one of the most devoted men who has ever followed in the footsteps of the founder of the Christian faith, he yet knew where the land was good, where the wild grapes grew, where there were roses which reminded him of those that in his youth he had seen in the braids of the maids of old Castile. . . . . Serra was a man who believed. He believed it all. He had the original theological ideas, and all of them, which now seem so incongruous in a practical and doubting world. He knew. In all his days he never wavered in the idea that he should convert the heathen of California, and yet he knew nothing of the task before him. He was an enthusiast who remained so regardless of difficulty, or fact, or report, or actual demonstration. And there was, therefore, never a missionary enterprise before or since so successful as this. Here are some data, not given from the religio-spiritual view point, which was Serra's, but from the temporal one of his brethren and successors:

During sixty-five years only thirty thousand Indians are actually known to have been in the church at one time, and these were engaged in the mission establishments, kept and lodged there, and occupied in profitable industries. Yet the early beginnings grew into establishments at that time unequaled elsewhere, and since impossible anywhere. There are no reliable facts showing how many heathens were all the time outside and unconverted. Some have said there were 120,000. In fact their number has never been precisely known. . . . .

In 1834 the line of missions was about 700 miles long, from San Diego northward to the latitude of Sonoma. They lay contiguous and adjoining. Their sites were the most eligible spots of the sunniest land the world knows.

Seven hundred thousand cattle grazed on the mission pastures, with 60,000 horses and an immense number of other domestic animals.

A hundred and twenty thousand bushels of wheat were raised annually, besides all other crops.

The usual products came under the following heads: wheat, wine, brandy, soap, leather, hides, wool, oil, cotton, hemp, linen, tobacco, salt, soda.

Two hundred thousand head of cattle were slaughtered annually at a net profit of $10 each.

Gardens, vineyards, and orchards surrounded or were contiguous to all the missions except the two most northern ones.

The total average annual gains of the missions from sales and trade generally was more than $2,000,000. This on an uninhabited and distant coast where commerce in our sense was unknown. The value of live-stock alone was, in 1834, $2,000,000.

There was, besides all these resources, a "pious fund" in Mexico, constantly accumulating, which had belonged to the Jesuits and was now the property of these missions. It amounted to $2,000,000. Towards the end the Mexican government could not resist the temptation of borrowing from this, and finally General Santa Ana confiscated it bodily.

It now appears that the Spanish government had a theory upon which these missions were established. It was, that after ten years the Indians would become citizens, living in agricultural communities on lands secured to them, and self-supporting and perhaps prosperous. They intended to use the missions to this end. The final acts and decrees which secularized them seem to hint at this original intention, and to consider the time ripe for its fulfillment. The present conclusion is that this theory of the capacity of the American Indian for citizenship was a false one, to which there is only one exception in all the annals of our history. To him nothing now remains of all the fathers taught him. He does not remain himself. Through what means the remnant of him became what it is, may be found by reading a glowing chapter in Mrs. H. H. Jackson's volume, "Glimpses of Three Coasts." . . . Contemporary testimony is to the effect that he knew about as little as any being that ever bore the human form, and that the padres made the most of him, spiritually and temporally. . . . . Most commentators upon those times allege that the Indians were in reality slaves; that they were flogged and forced in the name of religion; that those outside would not come into the fold, and those inside could not get out. It seems certain that when the heroic soul of Junipero Serra departed at Monterey, in 1784, the end for which he had endured and prayed was lost sight of, and the human love of ease and gain arose uppermost in all minds. Thus the briefest history of South California develops one of the saddest stories to be found in the annals of Christian endeavor. It was a work wrought almost in vain. There are no results. There is just a splendid story spoiled, a lofty and pious life wasted, and the doom of a race sealed by the mere effort to civilize and save them. For hardly more than one hundred years have passed, and the few wretches one encounters, living in huts and wandering through the country at sheep-shearing time, are almost the entire visible remnants of the thousands that blackened the hills to watch the entrance of the San Carlos or the San Antonio, under Point Loma, or who ran, scared away, when the soldiers fired their pieces as an accompaniment of that first mass at a spot facing the port where the corner-stone of a fatal civilization was laid on the western coast, on July 16, 1769. . . .

More than a score of missions were established by the Franciscans in California, in the following order:

San Diego, July 16, 1769.
San Carlos de Monterey, June 3, 1770.

A RUINED MISSION.

San Antonio de Padua, July 14, 1771.
San Gabriel Archangel, September 8, 1771.
San Luis Obispo de Tolosa, September 1, 1772.
Dolores de Nuestro Padre San Francisco de Assis, October 9, 1776.
San Juan Capistrano, November 1, 1776.
Santa Clara de Assis, January 18, 1777.
San Buenaventura, March 21, 1782.
Santa Barbara, December 4, 1786.
La Purisima, December 8, 1787.
Santa Cruz, August 28, 1791.
Nuestra Señora de la Soledad, October 9, 1791.

San Jose, June 11, 1797.
San Juan Bautista, June 24, 1797.
San Miguel, July 25, 1797.
San Fernando Rey, September 8, 1797.
San Luis Rey de Francia, June 13, 1798.
Santa Inez Virgen y Martyr, September 17, 1804.
San Rafael, December 14, 1817.
San Francisco de Solano, April 25, 1820.

In 1834 the Mexican government secularized the mission properties, reserving lands to the Indians in indefinite terms. After the departure of the padres, incoming settlers deprived the Indians of their lands, and their condition became such that the attention of philanthropic minds was directed to them. Before the novel "Ramona" had been conceived, Mrs. Helen Hunt Jackson had studied the condition of the California Indians, as special agent of the United States Government, and it was largely due to her untiring efforts that a law was passed providing for a division of reservation lands among them.

Early in the second decade of the present century California threw off the Spanish yoke and became a territory of the new Mexican republic. By 1846 many Americans had crossed the plains into California, and in that year they rebelled against Mexican rule. Fremont, accompanied by Kit Carson and a handful of men who composed his exploring party, came into conflict with the Mexicans about the same time, and open warfare began.

United States war vessels which were upon the coast captured Monterey, Santa Barbara, and San Diego. On the 6th of December of that year (1846) the little Army of the West, having marched from the Missouri River to San Pascual Valley, which lies thirty miles distant from San Diego, was met by a Mexican force, and the bloody little battle of San Pascual was fought, in which nineteen officers and men were lost by the Americans, who, nevertheless, succeeded in effecting a junction with Commodore Stockton at San Diego. Shortly after, the Saxon conquest of California was complete, and in 1848 it was formally ceded by Mexico to the United States. It was admitted as a State in 1850.

In 1848 gold was discovered by James W. Marshall at Sutter's Mill (Coloma), about forty miles north of Sacramento, and within two years thereafter the fame of the discovery had attracted a vast multitude of fortune-seekers. When, out of the chaos of the few years immediately following, order was brought, the modern California became possible. Its development since that time has been no less than phenomenal, and the enormous value of precious metal which in the past it has yielded, and in the future will continue to yield, has become a minor consideration; for the agricultural and horticultural possibilities of the State are beyond all calculation.

DESCRIPTIVE.— The length of California, from north to south, is 770 miles, and its breadth is from 150 to 330 miles. Its area is 156,592 square miles, and next to Texas it is the largest State in the Union. It has more than a thousand miles of seacoast. In altitude it ranges over 15,000 feet; that is to say, from below sea-level to 15,046 feet, which is the height of the pinnacle of Mount Whitney. This is the highest mountain-peak in the United States, excepting Alaska, and overlooks the sunken region of Death Valley, which lies directly east and not far away.

The entire shore-line of the Atlantic coast from Boston to Charleston and all the area included in ten of the original States are required to measure the extent of California, many of whose counties are large enough for kingdoms in the Old World. It is mainly composed of mountains and valleys, and has two great ranges, the Sierra Nevada and the Coast Range. The first named fences the eastern border, and has an altitude of from 8,000 to 15,000 feet; the second is from 2,500 to 4,000 feet in height.

The extreme north is marked by a densely wooded mountainous country. In the middle lies the Great Valley, renowned for fertility. And in the extreme south there is much of desert and bleak mountain alternated with lovely fruitful valleys and timbered ranges.

Here are many of the world's marvels. The Yosemite Valley, with its magnificent scenery of forest, cliffs, rock-sculptures, and extraordinary waterfalls, nestles in the Sierra Nevada at an altitude of over 4,000 feet. Farther north in the same range lies Lake Tahoe, a beautiful and much-visited sheet of water, divided by the Nevada boundary. And there are innumerable passes, and gorges, and small valleys, between towering individual peaks and volcanic plains, and cones, redwood forests and giant *sequoias*. The Coast Range offers bare or tree-dotted slopes, dense forests and valleys of well-watered agricultural lands.

A rough topographical sketch of California would conspicuously show an elongated narrow basin, lying nearly north and south between the two ranges, and pointed at each end. The northern point is approximately marked by Mount Shasta, a bald volcanic peak 14,440 feet high, and near the southern point stands Mount San Bernardino. The valley thus roughly inclosed is actually about 450 miles long, and, including the foot-hills, from 75 to 100 miles broad. Northward through the southern half flows the San Joaquin River, and southward through the northern half flows the Sacramento. These two meet opposite San Francisco and flow into the bay as one. This vast interior basin is, by common usage, referred to as if it were really composed of two separate valleys, which are named after their respective rivers. Here the fame of California as an agricultural and fruit-raising State took rise, and for a good many years was monopolized. Until about twenty years ago Southern California (by which is understood the region comprised in the six southern counties of San Bernardino, Los Angeles, Ventura, Santa Barbara, Orange, and San Diego) was, except in the immediate neighborhood of the missions, little better than a desert. In that short space the southern part of the State has become even more famous than the northern, by reason of the superior equability of its climate and its better adaptability to the culture of the citrus fruits (orange, lemon, citron, etc.). The word desert, as applied to any portion of our West, must be understood to refer to the absence or scantiness of vegetation in consequence of the lack of water. There is no richer soil to be found anywhere than that which composes the Great American Desert. But the amount of rainfall is in many parts insufficient to support vegetation, and for the same reason the streams are few and generally small; and in consequence artificial watering, as practiced in irrigation, is generally necessary, although there are many large and profitable fruit-growing and general farming ranches in California in localities where irrigation is not required. The commercial value of a large and permanent water supply here, therefore, is very great. It is the only desirable thing with which nature has not been lavish.

CLIMATE.—Within the ten degrees of latitude comprised in the boundaries of California are included enormous areas of seacoast and interior desert, between which lie long, sinuous mountain ranges, here and there rising to lofty, frigid peaks, or broken by gaps, with numerous interlying sheltered valleys. Latitude, altitude, mountain barriers, the proximity of the sea, and the effect of the Japanese ocean current, flowing southward from the Alaskan coast, all enter into the question of climate. The State has two general climatic divisions, the line of separation being practically the same as for the geographical division, extending from Point Conception, a high promontory of the Coast Range west of Santa Barbara, eastward along the Sierra Madre arm of that range. North of that promontory the general direction of the shore line is east of south, and it is closely followed by the Japanese current already mentioned. South from Point Conception the coast turns rather abruptly toward the east, and then bends southeastward in a long arc. Here begins the Santa Barbara Channel, running between the mainland and the neighboring chain of islands. Point Conception and these islands ward off the cool Japanese current from the retreating coast, and within the channel the water is perceptibly warmer. The heated air of the interior valleys rises during the day, and induces an inward draft of air from the sea, which, by reason of the deflection of the Japanese current as above described, is warmer along the coast south of Point Conception than it is north of that point. And every night, continuing through the early morning, this air-current returns seaward, having been cooled and stripped of moisture upon the interior desert levels after nightfall. This pendulum-swing of the wind, blowing inland laden with inspiriting qualities derived from the sea, and returning heavily charged with ozone and the balsamic odor of pines, considered in connection with the configuration of mountains, valleys, and mesas, is the key to innumerable differentiations of climate within the two broad divisions above mentioned. The vast interior plain of the San Joaquin and Sacramento valleys is entirely walled in between the Sierra Nevada and Coast ranges, except for one outlet opposite San Francisco Bay. This basin, thus largely cut off from the ameliorating effect of the ocean breeze upon the one hand and the breeze from the high desert regions upon the other, experiences greater extremes of heat and cold than any other portion of the State west of the Sierra. It has also less rainfall, for the reason that the intervening ranges rob the rain-clouds of much of their moisture in their progress toward this region. The coast has a more equable temperature, but is subject to evening fogs from the sea.

It follows that the nearest approach to perfection of climate in California is generally to be looked for in the southern part of the State, that is to say, in the region outside of the great walled valley of the interior south of the deflection of the Japanese current; and if one is sensitive to an occasionally fog-laden air, a short distance back from the sea. It is, however, true that the topography of a number of localities in Northern California presents conditions which in effect are practically the same.

The tourist will find this a land of delightfully temperate weather in the main, sunny, stimulating, and healthful at all times; a land where he can escape the inclemencies of the northern winter, and in summer abide in comfort. It has become famous as a winter resort simply because of its greater natural beauty and attractiveness, and its contrast with harsh regions of the north temperate zone in that season; but the California summer is only less agreeable. There are two seasons, the rainy and the dry. The rains are usually restricted to the period between the latter part of October, or early part of November, and the end of April. The rainy season is the most delightful time of the year, the precipitations being commonly separated by periods of perfect weather. At San Diego the average rainfall for a period of sixteen years was only 10.95 inches per annum; at Point Conception, for eight years, it was 12.21 inches; at Santa Barbara, for nineteen years, 17.83 inches; at Santa Monica, for three years, 16.13 inches. Inland points make showing as follows: Los Angeles, nine years, 17.64 inches; Colton, ten years, 9.84 inches; Riverside, five years, 9.37 inches; San Bernardino, sixteen years, 16.17 inches. It can not rain very industriously where so little water falls. But the records also show the average number of clear, fair, and cloudy days in each year, and the average number of days on which rain fell at San Diego through a period of fifteen years was only thirty-four yearly. In the long dry interval of summer, vegetation, except where artificially supplied with water, languishes, the hillsides turn brown and the roads become very dusty; but when the first rains come the grass shoots anew, herbage springs up freshly, and shortly the hills are buried in a tangle of odorous bloom well-nigh incredible to one who had looked upon them a few short weeks before. Whole fields are ablaze with the orange flame of the poppy, which is the floral emblem of California; violets and a score of familiar blossoms carpet the ground thickly, and there is a profuse blooming of myriad plants peculiar to California, or at least unfamiliar to the newcomer, and not easy of identification by means of the standard books on botany to which he is accustomed.

The nights, even in midsummer, are chill, and in midwinter the days are spring-like and friendly. In the coldest weather heavy flannels or heavy outer wraps are not worn, but light flannels and woolens are worn throughout the year. The northern visitor unaccustomed to California will do well to wear in winter the same clothing that he would wear at home, substituting a light overcoat or wrap for a heavy one; and in summer avoid the mistake of being insufficiently clad. There are no sudden changes of temperature, but it is always a little cooler than it seems to be, and the winter tourist is only too often accustomed to overheated apartments and finds the interior of hotels, houses, shops, and theaters in California incomprehensibly chilly during the first few days of his stay. The trouble is merely that he has been habituated to an unnecessarily high temperature within doors. Let him keep warm, and in a short time he will become accustomed to a normal and healthy temperature and be the better for it.

The ocean air is humid, but not heavily laden with moisture, as is evidenced by the fact that it abstracts moisture from instead of lending it to other objects. Meats and fish are dried for export in the open air on the seashore, grasses cure upon the root, perspiration is insensible, and water is cooled by hanging in an earthen vessel exposed to the air. It is a not uncommon belief among invalids that humidity is hostile in its effect upon certain diseases, among which phthisis is included, but it is only proper to state that eminent California practitioners, at least, make an emphatic distinction between such humidity as the moisture of pure sea air and that which exudes from the soil. It is certain that not a few cases of advanced consumption have found the most favorable conditions for permanent arrest of the disease upon the very shore of the sea, as at San Diego. Others appear to derive greater benefit from a greater altitude and a drier air. And it would seem that all the favorable conditions that climate can afford are to be found at one or another locality in Southern California, on either island, peninsula, valley, foot-hill, mountain or desert. The invalid is advised to abandon at once any notion that because he does not experience the sensation of tropical warmth the conditions may not be suitable. It is not the least of the merits of this climate that it is opposed to languor and stirs to out-of-door activities. In this particular the very sensitive need only be cautioned to wear sufficient clothing and to confine out-of-door exercise to the warmer hours of the day.

The healthfulness of California is strikingly evidenced in the longevity of the native Indians, many individuals being still alive at ages ranging from one hundred to one hundred and forty years.

The following tables, selected from the latest published reports of the California State Agricultural Society, will give the reader a fair general idea of the kind of weather that prevails here, so far as brief meteorological statistics will serve:

SAN DIEGO.

SUMMARY OF WEATHER FOR 1890.

Months	Mean Temperature.	Mean Maximum Temperature.	Mean Minimum Temperature.	Days Tempt. above 90°.	Days Tempt. below 32°.	Total Rainfall.	Greatest Rainfall in any 24 hours.	Maximum wind Velocity.	Clear Days.	Fair Days.	Cloudy Days.	Rainy Days.
January	51°	58°	41°	0	0	2.99	1.32	28m	1	11	5	9
February	54	62	46	0	0	1.70	1.04	30	13	3	12	9
March	56	65	48	0	0	.41	.38	24	11	9	11	4
April	59	65	52	0	0	.05	.03	20	9	8	13	2
May	60	66	55	0	0	.08	.04	21	12	7	12	3
June	64	71	57	2	0	None.	None.	21	15	15	0	0
July	68	74	63	0	0	None.	None.	20	18	9	4	0
August	70	75	64	0	0	Trace.	Trace.	23	14	7	10	0
September	69	75	63	0	0	.65	.37	24	18	1	11	5
October	65	71	55	1	0	.01	.01	21	23	3	5	1
November	64	76	52	1	0	.72	.72	21	23	5	2	2
December	61	69	52	0	0	1.61	1.23	26	14	5	12	6

NEW GUIDE TO THE PACIFIC COAST.   177

LOS ANGELES.
SUMMARY OF WEATHER FOR 1891.

MONTHS.	Mean Temperature.	Highest Temperature.	Lowest Temperature.	Rainfall.	Mean Humidity.	Maximum Velocity of Wind.	Cloudless Days.	Partly Cloudy Days.	Cloudy Days.	Rainy Days.	Light Frosts.
January	56°	80°	34°	.25	48	19m	18	11	2	1	10
February	53	71	33	8.56	70	24	10	7	11	12	2
March	58	82	40	.41	70	24	14	10	7	4	0
April	59	86	42	1.26	72	16	10	13	7	3	0
May	62	74	47	.31	78	18	4	20	7	2	0
June	66	89	49	None	73	16	15	14	1	0	0
July	74	*109	54	Trace	73	15	8	23	0	0	0
August	75	96	54	None	75	13	9	22	0	0	0
September	73	100	52	.06	69	20	17	13	0	1	0
October	66	89	46	None	75	16	10	20	1	0	0
November	61	85	40	None	73	12	20	10	0	0	0
December	53	75	33	1.99	58	28	19	9	3	4	8

*Highest recorded. The normal maximum is 94°.

RIVERSIDE.
SUMMARY OF WEATHER FOR 1890.

MONTHS.	Mean Temperature.	Highest Temperature.	Lowest Temperature.	Total Precipitation.	Clear Days.	Fair Days.	Cloudy Days.	Rainy Days.	Light Frosts.
January	43.1°	66.5°	26.5°	4.28	16	8	7	10	16
February	50.2	82.0	28.0	1.76	17	6	5	9	7
March	53.3	83.0	32.0	.55	11	14	6	4	2
April	58.0	93.0	35.5	.06	9	16	5	1	none.
May	62.6	96.5	38.5	.17	9	15	7	2	none.
June	67.1	108.0	43.5	none.	14	16	none.	none.	none.
July	76.1	109.0	50.5	none.	27	3	1	none.	none.
August	74.1	105.0	52.5	.55	20	8	3	2	none.
September	69.1	104.0	49.0	.71	20	4	6	5	none.
October	63.1	97.0	38.0	.07	25	3	3	1	none.
November	57.8	95.0	35.5	.33	26	3	1	1	none.
December	54.0	78.0	33.5	3.07	14	9	8	5	1

SANTA BARBARA.
SUMMARY OF WEATHER FOR 1891.

MONTHS.	Mean Monthly Temperature.	Mean Maximum Temperature.	Mean Minimum Temperature.	Rainfall, Inches.	Hourly Movement of Wind, Miles.	Relative Humidity.	Clear Days.	Fair Days.	Cloudy Days.
January	54.4	61.5	47.5	0.45	3.4	59	28	3	0
February	52.6	59.2	47.5	7.92	4.5	74	15	5	8
March	56.6	64.5	50.0	1.56	4.6	71	22	4	5
April	56.3	62.8	51.2	1.57	4.1	75	22	3	5
May	59.0	64.0	55.7	0.30	3.8	76	10	4	17
June	62.5	70.5	56.2	0.00	4.3	72	24	5	1
July	67.0	78.2	61.5	0.00	3.8	78	21	6	4
August	69.1	76.5	63.0	0.00	3.5	75	26	3	2
September	69.3	77.5	73.0	0.15	3.5	69	23	4	3
October	63.0	72.5	58.2	0.00	3.0	75	17	8	6
November	58.8	65.5	53.0	0.00	2.6	70	22	5	3
December	51.9	61.5	43.5	2.43	4.7	61	24	4	3

The mean temperature of the year was 60°, differing by less than one-tenth of a degree from the normal.

The highest temperature during the year was 96°, and lowest 33°. There were thirty-six days when the temperature rose above 80°, and thirty-five nights when it did not fall below 60°.

Of the 365 days in the year, 254 were clear, 54 fair, and 57 cloudy.

Rain fell on twenty days, with a rainfall of 14.38 inches, being 2.7 inches below the average. Between the 18th of April and the 4th of December, a period of 230 days, the entire rainfall was less than half an inch.

The average rainfall for twenty-four years was, in inches: January, 3.76; February, 3.80; March, 2.16; April, 1.45; May, 0.33; June, 0.11; July, none; August, trace; September, 0.10; October, 0.77; November, 1.69; December, 3.97.

FRESNO.
SUMMARY OF WEATHER FOR 1891.

Average temperature .... 63°
Highest temperature .... 114°, in July.
Lowest temperature .... 26°, in January.
Days temperature above 90° 87
Days temperature below 32° 20

Mean humidity .... 55 per cent.
Total precipitation .... 8.94 inches.
Clear days 235
Fair days 98
Cloudy days 32
Days .01 inches of rainfall 41
Thunder-storm 1

SAN FRANCISCO.
Summary of Weather for 1891.

Average temperature .... 56.6°
Highest temperature .... 100°, June 29th.
Lowest temperature .... 37°, December 25th.
Average humidity .... 80 per cent.
Total precipitation .... 21.11 inches.
Maximum velocity of wind .... 48 miles, Feb. 22d.
Clear days 185
Fair days 100
Cloudy days 80
Rainy days 81
Snow-storms 0
Thunder and lightning 0
Days temperature above 90° 3
Days temperature below 32° 0

SACRAMENTO.

Weather Review for:	1882.	1883.	1884.	1885.	1886.	1887.	1888.	1889.	1890.	1891.
Average temper'ture	58.5	58.8	58.8	61.2	58.8	59.9	60.6	60.9	59.4	59.5
Highest temperature	99.8	103.5	100.0	105.5	105.0	100.0	107.5	104.0	102.0	106.0
Lowest temperature	27.0	22.0	21.0	34.2	27.5	28.0	19.0	31.0	29.0	26.0
Average humidity	66.0	69.0	70.7	67.8	70.1	63.7	67.1	69.8	68.0	66.0
Total precipitation	18.04	13.48	34.92	20.72	18.17	13.43	18.46	27.48	20.95	15.63
Maximum velocity of wind	36	36	36	36	44	40	48	42	42	39
Clear days	249	263	239	227	262	267	238	218	237	230
Fair days	76	76	68	88	76	74	75	91	59	90
Cloudy days	40	26	59	50	27	24	52	57	69	45
Days of precipitation	70	54	76	62	57	56	63	77	55	61
Snow-storms	3	2	0	0	0	0	3	0	0	0
Electric storms	4	2	2	6	3	2	3	7	2	2
Light frosts	69	33	31	24	30	18	6	18	19	17
Killing frosts	12	40	22	0	10	26	14	14	10	23
Days temp. above 90°	43	45	22	49	45	48	58	51	28	57
Days temp. below 32°	5	27	13	0	4	9	12	7	5	11

INDUSTRIAL.— California produces more gold, more wool, and more fruit than any other State in the Union. Gold to the value of a few millions has been taken from Southern California, but the great placer fields lie along the foot-hills of the Sierra Nevada in the northern part of the State. A total of about $1,275,000,000 in gold has been taken from California and about $40,000,000 of silver. From 1850 to 1855 the annual output of gold averaged $55,000,000, but it has greatly decreased in recent years. The yearly product is lessened about $10,000,000 in consequence of the law forbidding hydraulic mining in the greater part of the State, because the voluminous washing away of large bodies of earth by that process injured the agricultural lands and the navigable rivers which received the enormous floods of detritus. Efforts are periodically made to have this prohibition rescinded, but thus far without success.

In other minerals the State has proven exceedingly rich, copper, lead, iron, graphite, coal, petroleum, asphaltum, gypsum, borax, salt, sulphur, asbestos, soda, nitre, etc., being largely produced. The commoner building-stones are also plentifully quarried. Some 30,000 men are engaged in the different branches of mining.

The annual wheat yield is about 35,000,000 bushels. Dairies produce 15,000,000 pounds of cheese and butter. The conversion of cattle into beef reaches the value of $30,000,000. The wool industry yields over 30,000,000 pounds; 15,000,000 gallons of wine are manufactured, of which 3,000,000 gallons are converted into sweet wine and brandy.

Hay and root crops are very valuable, and sugar is a large commercial item, many thousand acres being devoted to the sugar-beet. Hops and tobacco are raised in considerable quantity, although the rank growth of tobacco in California is not favorable to the best quality.

There are millions upon millions of fruit trees in bearing, and an enormous number of new orchards are planted every year. The fruits, berries, and nuts of the upper north temperate zone grow side by side with the orange, lemon, lime, pomegranate, prune, olive, fig, almond, peach, apricot, persimmon, and guava. The English walnut and the palm thrive in the same garden, and the strawberry and the banana are neighbors.

The time of the year at which the principal fruits of California are ripe is noted below:

Oranges	Christmas to July.
Lemons	All the year.
Limes	All the year.
Figs	July to Christmas.
Almonds	October.
Apples	July to November.
Pears	July to November.
Grapes	July 15th to December.
Peaches	June 15th to Christmas.
Apricots	June 15th to September.
Plums and prunes	June 1st to November.
Cherries	June.
Japanese persimmons	November.
Guavas	Nearly all the year.
Loquats	May 15th to June 15th.
Strawberries	Nearly all the year round.
Raspberries	June 15th to January.
Blackberries	June 15th to September.
Currants	May 15th to June 15th.
Watermelons	July to October.
Muskmelons	July to October.
Mulberries	July to December.
Nectarines	August.
Olives	December to January.
Pomegranates	September to December.
Quinces	October to December.

For the general information of the inquiring reader some account of the methods and profits of a few of the most important fruit, berry, and nut-growing industries of the State is appended. The figures given have been collated from sources which are believed to be reliable, but are not furnished with any intent of persuading the reader that his fortune surely lies in an orchard or vineyard in California or elsewhere. The fruit business is by no means all poetry, and not every investment is rewarded by success. Intelligence and eternal vigilance are essential in this as in other enterprises for the making of money. An orchard is generally prompt to resent neglect or wrong treatment, and it is all-important to secure a proper location in the beginning, where soil and local climate are suitable. And it is well to remember that the greatest successes in fruit raising are naturally accomplished by the expert growers, and that assumed success is the basis of the figures quoted.

The Orange.—The orange trees now growing in California number nearly 4,000,000, of which 94 per cent (3,720,257 trees) are in the six southern counties, as follows:

San Bernardino County	2,287,200
San Diego County	204,026
Ventura County	63,700
Los Angeles County	987,102
Orange County	134,029
Santa Barbara County	44,200

These counties, comprising the region known as the Citrus Belt, now export approximately 4,000 car-loads of oranges, and for every tree in bearing there are three not yet productive. The Washington Navel, brought from Brazil and first domesticated at Riverside, is the favorite. The Seedling is also very popular at Riverside. This tree is slower in maturing, and bears smaller fruit, but larger crops, and it is very long-lived. The Mediterranean Sweet, Valencia, Malta Blood, and Tangerine complete the list of principal varieties grown.

The length of time required for an orange orchard to come into full bearing, and the cost of bringing it to that point, is considerable. The land, in the first place,

ORANGE GROVE, CALIFORNIA.

costs more than farm land in the Eastern States, but it gives very much greater returns for well-directed effort. Two hundred and fifty dollars an acre is regarded as a fair average price for orange land in Southern California, with ample irrigation facilities attached, in a district where the cultivation of the citrus fruits has proven a success. In many places of long-established reputation the prices range from $450 to $750 per acre. The expenditure involved in rearing an orange orchard to the end of the third year, when it should pay interest upon the investment at the rate of 10 per cent, is approximately as follows :

Ten acres of land	$2,500
Preparing the ground	50
One thousand trees	1,000
Planting complete	50
Water first year	30
Care of orchard first year	200
Incidentals	70
	$3,900
The two following years, counting interest at 8 per cent, will cost	1,320
Total cost after three years	$5,220

It is assumed in the above computation that the trees planted are two-year-old buds on three-year-old roots. Five years thereafter each tree should bear from one to one and a half boxes, and the total crop of the ten acres should be worth from $2,000 to $3,000. Six hundred dollars an acre net profit, however, has been realized from full-bearing orchards.

The Lemon.—The culture of the lemon is much the same as that of the orange, and the profits do not greatly differ. Lemon culture in California was long retarded by the difficulty of curing the fruit, as, although it has a seemingly tough rind, it is very sensitive to rough handling, and can spoil quickly. It is now successfully cured, all its quality being retained for many months after picking, and in consequence the producer is not compelled to sacrifice his crop at unprofitable prices, but can wait for a good market.

Southern California has 397,792 lemon trees, 96 per cent of all that the State contains. Less than one-fourth of these are in bearing, yet the product is already 800 carloads a year. The Lisbon and the Eureka are the leading varieties.

The Grape.—Enormous quantities of choice grapes are grown for table use, and for raisins, wine, and brandy. The mission lands gave to the successors of the Spaniard a palatable grape, but this has been supplanted by many improved varieties, of which there are the Flame Tokay, Champagne, and Black Hamburg for the table, the Muscat and Seedless Sultana for raisins, and the French and Spanish varieties for wine and brandy.

To plant, irrigate, and care for a raisin vineyard to the end of the second year costs about $85 per acre. The yield in the third year is 50 boxes; fourth year, 100 boxes; fifth year, 200 boxes; and after that there is a small increase. Raisins are worth from $1 to $1.50 a box. The

A CALIFORNIA GRAPEVINE.

cost of cultivating is $15 per acre, and of curing and packing 40 cents per box. In many localities the raisin grape is raised without irrigation. The fogless interior valleys are best adapted to this industry. Two and a half million boxes was the raisin product of California in 1891.

The Prune.— Prunes are grafted on plum stock, and are planted about twenty-five feet apart, at the rate of 100 trees to the acre. The fourth year after planting the yield is about 10 pounds per tree, the fifth year 60 pounds, and the sixth year 120 pounds. Thereafter the yield ranges from 150 pounds to 300 pounds. They are not picked, but shaken from the tree, at intervals covering most of the month of August, the ripest hanging most loosely to the stem. Prunes are dried before shipment. The ripe fruit — called " green " to distinguish it from the dried article — is dipped in a wire basket into boiling water to which concentrated lye has been added, and then laid upon trays and dried in the sun. A finishing gloss for market may then be added by dipping in pure boiling water. This process is for those that are dried whole. They are also split and stoned before drying. The French and the Silver prune are favorites.

The California product of prunes is 20,000,000 pounds. The cost of rearing a ten-acre prune orchard to the end of the fourth year, the land costing $150 per acre, has been figured at $2,750. From the fifth year onward a net profit of from $150 to $300 per acre may be expected.

The Olive.— The olive tree reaches a maximum height of twenty feet. It has evergreen leaves and minute white blossoms in small clusters. The fruit is of a black-red color when ripe, and very bitter. Over twenty varieties are enumerated by the French. It is propagated very easily, by grafting upon seedlings, or from truncheons, from cuttings of stems and roots, and from suckers, layers and protuberances, planted in the ground. It begins to bear in from three to five years from planting of one-year-old rooted cuttings. In seven years the yield should be a gallon of olives to a tree, and increases steadily for many years. Olive trees live and are fruitful for centuries. There are some now in existence in the Old World which are believed to antedate the Christian era.

The primitive man who first tasted an olive, and in the bitterness of that experience had faith to persist in discovering a use for it, is worthy of as great an admiration as he who first ate an oyster. Fair as a plum in its appearance, the essence of gall is not more execrable than its taste.

In most American homes, in regions where the olive does not grow, it is commonly used as a relish, and the taste is acquired rather than natural; and the liberal use of its oil is not common there. This is accounted for by two reasons. First, the common pickled olive of commerce is not the oil berry, and is consequently deficient in flavor and nutriment. Secondly, what is termed olive oil in the Eastern States is, many chances to one, largely composed of the oil of cotton seed, mustard seed, and the peanut, or other adulterants. It is, therefore, not to be wondered at that the articles which go by the name of olive oil have not recommended themselves more favorably to the average American palate.

The Franciscan friars brought with them cuttings from the choicest olive trees in Spain, and the Mission olive contains five times as much oil as the Queen olive. It is a soft-fleshed, oleaginous berry, grateful to the palate when properly pickled, and may be freely eaten without satiety or injury. It is a food claimed to be as nutritious as the best beef, pound for pound, and day laborers can work indefinitely on no other diet than this bitter berry, soaked in lye, washed in water, and plunged into brine.

The manufacture of olive oil is a nice process, requiring the absolute exclusion of deleterious odors, which it is quick to absorb. The ripe berries, having first been partially dried, are ground to a pumice and repeatedly placed under heavy pressure. The oil thus expressed falls into tanks of pure water, from whose surface it is collected. The further process of ripening and filtering requires skill and a rigid observance of proper conditions.

These products in California are greatly superior to the imported articles. Up to the present time they have been almost wholly consumed within the State, but it seems probable that the greater output of the thousands of young orchards now growing will find a ready market in other States by reason of superior merit alone. Pickled olives here are worth about 75 cents per gallon, and the oil about $5. The berry yields from 10 to 20 per cent of its weight in oil. A fully developed tree has been known to yield sixteen gallons of oil. Its longevity gave rise to the old Italian proverb that "He who plants an olive orchard leaves an inheritance for future generations." It may be counted upon for 300 years of productiveness. It thrives on hillside soil without irrigation, but while it is in many respects hardy and free from parasitic pests, it is easily injured by rough handling. At seven years from planting the gross return per acre has been figured at $500.

The literature of the olive contains much that is of interest. It begins, of course, at the point when Noah's dove went back to the ark with an olive branch, for such a beginning has so manifest an advantage in establishing at once a respectable antiquity for the subject, no writer seems willing to forego it. The olive must have been treasured high in the hearts of mankind, even at that remote epoch, to be identified with so momentous an occasion, and ever since the flood it has stood for an overture of peace and good will among men. Its leaves were the laurel wreath of the Greeks, typical of vitality and longevity, and were mingled in the triumphal crowns of Roman heroes. It also possesses the dignity of intimate association with Christian story, as Gethsemane means an oil-press, and stood upon the Mount of Olives. For thousands of years the olive has yielded food, light, and medicine for innumerable generations, a staple luxury to the rich and a cheap and sufficient nutriment to multitudes of the poor who have scarce known the use of meat except by hearsay. It was native to Palestine and Asia Minor, from which countries it was early carried to Northern Europe, Western Asia, and Northern Africa.

TWENTY MINUTES FROM AN ORANGE GROVE.

It was brought to South America and Mexico two centuries ago, and introduced into our South Atlantic States not long before the Revolution. The Mission fathers brought it to California. Ancient history, both sacred and profane, abounds in allusions to it. The oil mentioned in Holy Writ was that of the olive. The Good Samaritan poured it into the wounds of the poor wayfarer, and the Wise Virgins filled their lamps with it. The Greeks used it for outward application in their gymnasiums, for Athens was a center of olive culture, and the Romans imitated them in its use; and not a few prominent physicians in California regard anointing with olive oil as a valuable adjunct in the art of healing.

The Walnut.— The valleys of Southern California are particularly favorable to the culture of the walnut, of which there are many varieties, differing in hardness of shell, of which the "improved soft-shell" is regarded as most profitable. A deep alluvial soil, with good drainage, is best adapted to this nut. The trees grow to a large size, and should be set at least fifty feet apart to insure separation when the full growth has been attained. The soft-shell walnut tree begins to bear when five years old, and at ten years is in full bearing, in proportion to its capacity, although it continues to increase in size for many years thereafter. At sixteen years of age a walnut tree should have produced a total of 1,000 pounds of nuts, which are worth from 7½ to 8½ cents per pound. The nuts are dried in trays and assorted by running through a grader. The largest bearing walnut orchard in the world is one of 200 acres at Carpinteria, in Santa Barbara County. From Rivera, near Los Angeles, forty-seven car-loads of walnuts are shipped annually.

The Almond.— The almond tree differs from the apple, peach, cherry, and plum in the particular that it is always grafted or budded. The other trees named usually produce more and better fruit when similarly treated than if allowed to mature from the seed, but the fruit of their seedlings is sure to be marketable at some price, and often turns out to be a superior variety. The seedling almond, however, while subject to the same possibility, usually proves worthless, and its fruit is often deadly poisonous. There is a tendency to frequent reversion to antecedent types throughout the animal and vegetable kingdoms, technically known as atavism, and this tendency is particularly strong in the almond, as if its evolution had been too recent for the approved type to have become firmly set. And even among carefully budded or grafted trees there will occasionally be some that never bear at all, or bear nuts that are worthless.

The almond blooms early in spring and matures late in the fall. It belongs to the same family as the peach, but its quality goes to the pit, or nut, instead of to the flesh of the envelope, or drupe. It has no parasite enemies, and is easily cultivated. The varieties are differentiated, like those of the walnut, by the thickness or fragility of the shell, the paper-shell variety being most highly esteemed. After husking, the nuts are sun-dried and bleached with the fumes of sulphur before they are ready for market. The almond is the most precious of orchard products, pound for pound, and American consumers yearly spend more money for this than for all other nuts together. The tree is said to be somewhat capricious as to locality, although it will thrive on land that is too poor for peaches or apricots. It bears in four years from planting, and yields a net profit of $100 per acre. The almond does not yet count among the important products of California, but has begun to receive more general attention than was formerly accorded to it.

The Fig. — Although the fig tree thrives generally in Southern California, most of the orchards are still young, having been planted within the last half-dozen years. It fruits young, cuttings generally bearing a few figs the next year after planting. Ten tons have been gathered from an acre of sixteen-year-old trees, worth $50 a ton delivered at the local curing establishment.

The Apricot.—The apricot is a fruit that does well near the coast. It follows the strawberry and cherry in order of ripening. From $75 to $150 an acre net profit from an orchard five years old is considered a fair average. The apricot is largely canned and dried.

Peaches, nectarines, apples, pears, cherries, guavas, persimmons (Japanese), loquats (Japanese plums), pomegranates, and enormous quantities of strawberries, blackberries, raspberries, gooseberries, etc., are commonly raised, and pineapples, dates, and bananas are grown on a small scale in favorable localities.

Ostrich Farming.—There are perhaps half a dozen ostrich farms in Southern California. The enterprise is by no means a purely fanciful one. These birds thrive and multiply and yield valuable plumes as well among the California hills as in their native Africa, and the pioneers of the experiment maintain that in time the industry will prove profitable and comparatively general, not only in this State but in parts of Arizona and New Mexico as well. The largest farm is between Oceanside and Fall Brook, about twelve miles from the former.

The ostrich is a mere other-hemisphere curiosity when viewed in a menagerie. Here, where he roams with scores of his fellows over 160 acres of grass-grown hills, he is at home, and his habits and personality become an easy and entertaining study. A three-months'-old "chick" is no chicken in appearance, for it stands fully four feet high and looks as if it might have had at least two birthdays. Nevertheless, the female does not mature until four years old, nor does the male until five.

The color of the young birds is brown in general effect, and the hen remains of that hue. The cock, as he nears maturity, turns a deep, glossy black, with a row of pure white plumes among those of jet; down the front of each leg is a stripe of brilliant red, and a ring of the same

OSTRICHES, CALIFORNIA.

color surrounds his big, savage eyes, for the cock ostrich is a ferocious creature at times, and even the hens must be handled with skill. As fast as the birds pair, the couple are confined in a paddock about an acre in extent. The hen begins to lay soon after the rains come, one egg every other day until the nest — a careless excavation three feet across, scratched in the sand — contains anywhere from eight to fifteen eggs, according to her humor, or her ability to count.

The cock does the principal part of the labor of setting. Every afternoon exactly at 4 o'clock he relieves his mate, and never quits the nest until 8 o'clock next morning, thus giving the female a short watch of only eight hours out of the twenty-four, and all daylight at that. The practice, however, is to remove the eggs to an incubator as fast as laid, and in that case the hen will lay as many as twenty-five or thirty before taking a rest.

An interval of five or six weeks ensues, and then she resumes laying. Thus the ostrich farmer counts upon three periods of productiveness from his breeders in a year, aggregating from seventy-five to ninety eggs from each laying hen, although, as in the case of fowls, not all the eggs are fertile. The eggs hatch in forty days here — two days sooner than in Africa. The unmated birds are allowed to herd, and are called the "feather troop."

The plumes are plucked once in eight months. The first plucking takes place when the chick is six months old. The feathers then are small and of an inferior quality, and are used in the manufacture of feather dusters. In the vernacular of the African Boers, these first feathers are "spadones." At one year old the chick yields feathers fit for use in trimmings. At two years a respectable plume is obtained, and thereafter the ostrich is a ripe and regular plume-producer. Of plumes there are four rows on each wing, and in each row twenty-six plumes, every one after its own kind, both in color and size, in any given row. The tail plumes are termed "boos."

An ostrich-plucking is an interesting operation. The regular "feather troop" are rather docile if unmolested, but highly excitable, and are dangerous kickers on small provocation unless they are first blindfolded. Consequently they are called into a paddock and fed, and while they are busily engaged in picking up the corn or chopped beets that have been thrown them, two trained men quietly approach and dexterously seize a bird by the neck and at the same instant thrust a long hood, not unlike a huge stocking, over its head.

It is then forced into a railed inclosure about three feet square and a gate is shut behind it. Thus hooded, the ostrich requires muscular men to hold it, but it rarely shows fight. The plumes are then carefully snipped off one by one, and the stub of the quill allowed to remain until its juices have been diverted into other growing feathers and it has become transparent to the eye. This requires but a few days, and then the stub is pulled out. After plucking, the bird's thigh is daubed with red paint before it is turned loose, and when the quill stubs have been extracted a second marking is made, so that a glance will discover the condition of any bird in the troop.

When, however, a breeding cock is to be shorn of his plumes, the operation requires more nerve, address, and strength. He is as dangerous as a vicious bull at almost any hour of the day. If you but approach his paddock closely he will generally trot up to the fence and peer over and down upon you, opening his short, stout beak with a hiss, and looking bullets and bludgeons at you out of his wicked eyes. He fights with his queer, two-toed, hoof-like feet, and kicks forward, something as a pugilist delivers his blow, sometimes from a standstill and sometimes while running upon his adversary.

Owing to the pugnacious temper of the breeding cock, therefore, the ordinary stratagem of throwing it food is of no avail. When the hour for his plucking arrives, he is taunted and challenged to come to the fence and fight, if by any chance he does not propose it himself, and in the melee he is caught around the neck by strong arms and hooded. He is then harmless, although the combined strength of two men is exhausted by the time his plucking is finished.

The average weight of a full-grown cock is 175 pounds. Each bird yields at a plucking, on an average, one and one-fourth pounds of plumes. Some of these are the "prime white," and sell for $75 a pound at wholesale, although as much as $7.50 is sometimes received for a single plume of super excellence.

Others are the "long black," next in value, the "long drab" (from the female), "medium," and "short." The average value of a plucking from a single bird is $35, and as it is plucked three times in two years the value of the annual product in plumes is about $50 for each bird.

The life of an ostrich is commonly thirty years. They are sold at from $30, the price of a chick, to $300 for a three-year-old bird. A breeding pair is valued at $1,000.

PRINCIPAL POINTS OF INTEREST.

INTERMEDIATE STATIONS: Mellen, Beal.

Needles.—Chicago, 1,955 miles; St. Louis, 1,815 miles; Los Angeles, 310 miles; San Diego, 393 miles; San Francisco, 622 miles. Altitude, 476 feet. Dining station.

Approaching this desert station the hovels of the Mojave and Chimehuevi Indians are seen on the flats by the wayside. There are about 800 of the Mojaves remaining. The men are well built and are not bad looking for Indians. They are fleet runners and capable of covering an extraordinary distance in a short time. The women are unprepossessing. A number of Mojave squaws are always seen at the station on arrival of trains, eager to sell pottery, toys, and bows and arrows to tourists. This tribe lost its formidable character thirty years ago, when Colonel Hoffman of the regular service gave it a crushing defeat. Lieutenant Ives found stanch and manly characters among them, but they are now a disreputable, beggarly lot, offering another example of the singular demoralization of the Red Man that has resulted from contact with a superior race.

THE MOJAVE DESERT.— Westward from Needles the Atlantic & Pacific Railroad runs for 240 miles over the Mojave Desert, to the station Mojave. This is merely a section of the Great Desert belt which in this longitude extends across the whole of the United States from north to south, and intercepts every transcontinental railroad. Except in the extreme north this desert belt is very warm in midsummer, through the day. The greater part of the Mojave Desert is, however, commonly crossed in the night by the trains of the Santa Fé Route, the schedule being purposely arranged to escape the discomforts of a transit by day. But even by day there is enough of interest in the scene to reward one for its heat and fatigue. Rock, alkali, scoriæ, cactus, yucca, and sage-brush are invested with a certain charm by reason of the absence of animation from all the landscape, and the eye ranges far to huge mountain masses upon the horizon, blue with distance. It is not a desert in the sense of being an unbroken waste of sand, but a vast barren, extremely arid and apparently hopeless. Only at long intervals is there a cluster of human habitations. The desert lies like a grim barrier against approach to the garden of California, a thing stripped of its terrors only by the locomotive. This route by the way of The Needles was never a thoroughfare until the railroad was built. The Forty-niners went to California overland, by routes far to the north and to the south; across the desert, indeed, but by no short cut. If the old-time caravans could have arrived thus far without molestation by Indians, it is doubtful if they could have found water with sufficient frequency to support life in traversing this desolate tract. But the age of steam has subdued it. It has no longer power to disturb the traveler's sleep for a single night.

INTERMEDIATE STATIONS: Java, Klinefelter, Ibex, Homer, Blake, Fenner, Edson, Danby, Cadiz, Bristol, Amboy.

Blake is a junction point with the Nevada Southern Railway, recently constructed and now in operation to Manvel, a distance of thirty miles.

Bagdad. — Chicago, 2,046 miles; St. Louis, 1,906 miles; Los Angeles, 219 miles; San Diego, 302 miles; San Francisco, 531 miles. Altitude, 782 feet. Dining station.

INTERMEDIATE STATIONS: Siberia, Ash Hill, Ludlow, Lavic, Haslett, Newberry.

Daggett. —Chicago, 2,114 miles; St. Louis, 1,974 miles; Los Angeles, 151 miles; San Diego, 234 miles; San Francisco, 463 miles. Altitude, 2,000 feet.

North of Daggett lies Death Valley, often erroneously spoken and written of as located in the vicinity of Salton, on the Southern Pacific Railroad, in the extreme southern part of California. It is a sunken basin 285 feet below sea-level, surrounded by mountains. Its lugubrious name was derived from the experience of a company of Argonauts, and Amargosa (Bitter) River, Furnace Creek, Funeral Mountains, and the like are also descriptive of the locality. In the early days of the excitement following the discovery of gold in California, thousands of gold-seekers made their way overland by every available route. One of these routes led through Salt Lake City, and across nearly a thousand miles of alkali plain and desert that intervened between the Mormon settlements and the Sierra Nevada Range. One party, numbering about seventy, including women and children, was induced to deflect southward from the regular wagon trail across

Nevada, in the belief that more abundant water would thus be found, and the hardships and perils of the journey much abated. It was a march to death. One after another the oxen died of thirst and starvation, and one after another of the party succumbed and was buried in the sands of the relentless desert. On arriving at the summit of the Funeral Range it became necessary to cross a deep valley which stretched between that range and the Para-

CAJON PASS.

mint Mountains, and they descended hopefully in the delusion that the white reflection from the bottom indicated the presence of a body of water. They found only alkali marshes, salt hillocks, and sand-dunes. There the destruction of the party was completed, save only two men, Bennett and Stockton, who succeeded in reaching the California settlements. The rest perished, either within the valley or in the wilderness, over which they scattered panic-stricken in a mad individual search for water. That episode gave the valley its name, and the story is rendered more pathetic by the subsequent discovery by prospectors of fresh-water springs not far from the spot where the tragedy culminated. Similar instances of death from thirst within reach of unsuspected means of salvation have occurred elsewhere on the desert. In some arid localities water lies very near the surface of barren sands, and has been known to form a pool by "seeping" into the slight depression made by the tread of a gathered bunch of buffalo or cattle. In Texas a party of emigrants once perished of thirst upon a spot where those who discovered their bodies struck water in digging their graves.

Twenty years ago silver and gold were discovered in Death Valley, on the slopes of the Paramint Range, and the evil reputation of the place was enhanced by the dismal fate of not a few prospectors who wandered too far from the infrequent water-holes. Large deposits of borax were also discovered there, and a line of freight wagons was established between the valley and Daggett for the transportation of this commodity, afterward abandoned because of the great cost of teaming across a mountainous desert where for seventy-five miles at one stretch from Daggett there is no sign of water, and because the fearful heat of summer in the furnace-like basin permitted the work to be carried on only through a portion of the year.

In 1891 the region was scientifically explored by naturalists employed by the United States Department of Agriculture. The mountains are described by one of the party as brilliantly colored masses of black, yellow, blood-red, gray, and brown. Yuccas, cacti, and in the upper cañons many varieties of wild-flowers, in season, abound. The waters of the Amargosa, after flowing for eighty miles, are completely absorbed by Death Valley. They are strongly impregnated with soda and borax, and are exceedingly poisonous to drink. Some of the noblest mountain-peaks in the world are there visible, but the tourist might almost as reasonably leap into the crater of Vesuvius as to commit himself to the perils of a visit to the spot. The world probably does not contain a more terrible region.

Barstow.—Chicago, 2,124 miles; St. Louis, 1,984 miles; Los Angeles, 141 miles; San Diego, 224 miles; San Francisco, 453 miles. Altitude, 2,105 feet. Dining station. Junction with Southern California Railway.

Trains for Southern California here turn south, and for those trains the time here changes one hour.

Barstow is an unimportant distributing point for scattered mining properties.

INTERMEDIATE STATIONS: Waterman, Hinckley, Harper, Kramer, Rogers, Bissell.

Mojave.— Chicago, 2,195 miles; St. Louis, 2,055 miles; San Francisco, 382 miles. Altitude, 2,737 feet. Dining station.

This is merely a junction point with the Southern Pacific Railroad, and the end of the Atlantic & Pacific Railroad. Trains from Los Angeles to San Francisco pass through Mojave, and the through cars destined to San Francisco over the Santa Fé Route are attached to those trains at this point.

Here the time changes one hour, as it changed at Barstow for trains turning south from that point, Barstow being a southern boundary, and Mojave a southwestern boundary, of the mountain division of standard time.

The plan of this guide-book now reverts to Barstow and accompanies the traveler destined to Southern California. On page 238 the journey to San Francisco is resumed.

BARSTOW TO SAN BERNARDINO.—Northwest of Los Angeles an arm of the Coast Range, known as the Sierra Madre, and also as the San Bernardino Range, stretches eastward for 100 miles to Mount San Bernardino, beyond which it turns taperingly to the southeast. Leaving Barstow the northern slope of this range is climbed, crossing the Mojave River, and the passage made through Cajon Pass at an altitude of less than 4,000 feet, although San Bernardino Peak itself rises to a height of more than 11,000. The approach to the pass is not particularly impressive, except by reason of the sterility of the adjacent country and the extraordinary rockiness of certain localities. There are points where it would seem impossible to have brought horses or mules in making the original railroad survey, in consequence of the dense litter of sharp rock fragments. A few small stations are scattered along the ascent of this slope, which are tributary to mining properties a dozen miles distant from the railroad. There are deposits of gold, silver, tin, and iron, and valuable quarries of Verde Antique marble. Oro Grande and Victor are examples of such stations, thirty-one and thirty-seven miles, respectively, from Barstow. Hesperia, forty-five miles from Barstow, is the seat of a small colony devoted to raisin growing. In the vicinity of Hesperia the *Yucca brevifolia* is particularly abundant. This æsthetic tree is often erroneously called a palm.

INTERMEDIATE STATIONS: Cottonwood, Point of Rocks, Oro Grande, Victor, Hesperia.

Summit.—Chicago, 2,180 miles; St. Louis, 2,040 miles; Los Angeles, 85 miles; San Diego, 168 miles. Altitude, 3,819 feet.

This is the summit of Cajon Pass, whose descent, immediately following, affords through many miles a series of mountain views of great beauty. Between Summit and Cajon, the station six miles beyond, are roofed terraces on both sides of the track, an engineering device to prevent the softening of the earth in times of heavy rain and the consequent landslides that formerly filled up these deep cuts and completely blocked the railroad.

INTERMEDIATE STATIONS: Cajon, Keenbrook, Irvington.

Highland Junction.—Two miles north of San Bernardino. Altitude, 1,138 feet. Junction with the Belt Line, known as the Kite-shaped Track, of which further mention will be made in its place.

San Bernardino.—Chicago, 2,205 miles; St. Louis, 2,065 miles; Los Angeles, 60 miles; San Diego, 143 miles. Dining station. Altitude, 1,075 feet. Population, 4,012. Diverging point of short line to San Diego from main line to Los Angeles.

San Bernardino was settled by Mormons more than forty years ago, but its greatest growth has been attained in the last half-dozen years. It is environed by many orange orchards and vineyards. Fruit-canning and the manufacture of flour, lumber, bricks, and carriages are among its industries, and it contains the customary shops and engine-houses of a railroad division point. It possesses handsome residences and business blocks, and excellent hotels.

The peaks of Mounts San Bernardino (11,800 feet) and San Antonio (10,894 feet) are visible from the station, and a third conspicuous object is a gigantic bare spot, 1,300 feet long and 450 feet wide, on the mountain slopes six miles away, presenting a striking likeness to a stone arrow-head. It marks the location of Arrowhead Springs, an attractive and popular resort.

Stages regularly run to Arrowhead Springs and also to Bear Valley, a mountain resort thirty miles from San Bernardino, where trout-fishing is reported to be had in Bear Valley Lake, and good shooting in the forest. Here is the reservoir of the Bear Valley Irrigation Company.

From San Bernardino the railroad line runs due west to Los Angeles, and thence southeast to San Diego. The short line cuts off a portion of this corner, saving a distance of forty-four miles, and through cars to San Diego are commonly run over this intercepting line, which meets the other at Orange, thirty-one miles below Los Angeles.

The traveler journeying direct to San Diego by way of the short line is referred to page 224.

SAN BERNARDINO TO LOS ANGELES.—Against the foot of the Sierra Madre or San Bernardino Range is nestled a chain of towns, most of which are small, and do not greatly differ in character. Some are the centers of colonies, simultaneous settlements of irrigable tracts, where by virtue of combined effort a greater development and one more profitable to the individual has resulted than would have been possible to unaided individual enterprise. All the California fruits in varying quantity are cultivated, and fruit-drying and packing, and winemaking, are common industries.

Rialto.—Four miles from San Bernardino. Altitude, 1,201 feet. Population (precinct), 329.

Etiwanda.—Eleven miles. Altitude, 1,143 feet. Population (precinct), 231.

Rochester.—Fourteen miles. Altitude, 1,120 feet.

North Cucamonga.—Sixteen miles. Altitude, 1,115 feet. Population (Cucamonga Precinct), 416.

The village of Cucamonga is two miles distant upon the south.

North Ontario.—Twenty miles. Altitude, 1,212 feet. Population (Ontario Precinct), 1,229.

The street-car line through Euclid Avenue, connecting this station with the city of Ontario, seven miles distant, is a gravity line. The mules employed to haul the cars up grade to the station coast back with the passengers on a truck that trails behind. Euclid Avenue extends for fifteen miles from Ontario toward Mount San Antonio, to the foot of the range. San Antonio Cañon, in the foot-hills, is a much frequented spot for trout fishermen and for summer campers, who are attracted by the wild beauty of the place, to which a lofty waterfall, a sycamore-shaded stream, and an abundance of flowers contribute.

Claremont.— Twenty-four miles. Altitude, 1,143 feet.

Seat of Pomona College.

North Pomona.— Twenty-five miles. Altitude, 1,074 feet. Population (township), 5,010.

Connected with the city of Pomona by a steam motor road and an electric railway. The different varieties of berries here receive special attention and are exported in large quantity. Pomona is also an active manufacturing city.

Lordsburg.— Twenty-seven miles. Altitude, 1,041 feet.

A Dunkard (German Baptist) colony.

San Dimas.— Twenty-nine miles. Altitude, 941 feet.
Glendora.— Thirty-three miles. Altitude, 747 feet.
Azusa.— Thirty-six miles. Altitude, 616 feet. Population (township), 1,851.
Duarte.— Thirty-nine miles. Altitude, 497 feet.

San Gabriel Cañon, three miles distant, is a favorite mountain resort.

Monrovia.— Forty-one miles. Altitude, 434 feet. Population (township), 2,557.
Arcadia.— Forty-three miles. Altitude, 492 feet.

Located on the Lucky Baldwin ranch.

Santa Anita.— Forty-five miles. Altitude, 604 feet.

Also on the Baldwin ranch, which, by reason of its large orchards, vineyards, wineries, and race-horse stables, is visited by many tourists. It is only five miles distant from Pasadena, and is included among the features com-

SIERRA MADRE VILLA, SAN BERNARDINO VALLEY.

prised in the many pleasant carriage-drives from that city.

Chapman.— Forty-six miles.
Lamanda Park.— Forty-seven miles. Altitude, 735 feet.

The location of wineries whose aggregate annual product is nearly half a million gallons. Carriages from the

Sierra Madre Villa Hotel meet trains at this station. San Gabriel Mission is three and a half miles away.

Fair Oaks.— Forty-eight miles.
Olivewood.— Forty-nine miles.
Pasadena.— Chicago, 2,255 miles; St. Louis, 2,115 miles; Los Angeles, 10 miles. Altitude, 829 feet. Population, 4,882, township, 7,222.

Connected with Los Angeles by two steam railroads, over which frequent trains are run through the day.

Pasadena is a city of residences, and the established winter home of many eastern people of wealth and culture. It is one of the most attractive towns in California, a perpetually blooming garden.

This is the point of departure for the most popular mountain trip in the State.

PASADENA MOUNTAIN RAILWAY.— More than five thousand tourists are said to have visited the summits of the Sierra Madre every year prior to the initiation of the mountain railway, while still the ascent was wholly made with burros. Mount Wilson, the site of the new Harvard Observatory, and Mount Lowe, each more than 6,000 feet above sea-level, lie just north of Pasadena.

The Pasadena Mountain Railway, part of which is already completed and in operation, is projected to the pinnacle of Mount Lowe. The first section of this railway, from a connection with the Los Angeles Terminal Railroad at Mountain Junction to Rubio Cañon, is operated by electricity. At the foot of Echo Mountain, in Rubio Cañon, begins the second section, a stout cable road, which climbs the steep incline to the Echo Mountain House, rising 1,400 feet vertically in 3,000 feet of progress.

The Echo Mountain House is 3,500 feet above sea-level, upon the crest of the semi-detached mountain from which its name was derived. The slopes at the foot of this mountain, for hundreds of acres, are covered in season with the flaming blossoms of the poppy — a mass of solid color so vivid that it has for centuries served as a beacon by day for mariners fifty miles out at sea. The point was named Las Flores (The Flowers) by the sailors, and the name has become permanent. Flowers, vines, ferns and mosses, rugged rocks, innumerable woodland nooks, and cascades diversify the mountain slopes and levels within a few minutes' walk of the hotel, on every hand, and there

ALTADENA.

is more than enough to reward a trip to the summit of Echo Mountain, even if one should not care to make the entire journey to the upper peaks of the Sierra Madre. Beyond that point, numerous bridle paths diverge and good trails lead to the summit. The enterprise includes the erection and maintenance of another hotel on the pinnacle of Mount Lowe.

In Rubio Cañon is a pavilion, where vocal and instrumental concerts are given, and where moonlight parties from Pasadena, Los Angeles, and other neighboring cities and towns frequently resort. There is also a waterfall and a fountain illuminated at night by electric lights.

Raymond.— Two miles west of Pasadena station. Altitude, 748 feet.

Named for the imposing Raymond Hotel, which stands upon an eminence near at hand, commanding a full circular sweep of the valley. The hotel is visible from the train upon the left.

INTERMEDIATE STATIONS: South Pasadena, Lincoln Park, Garvanza, Highland Park, Morgan, Water Street, Downey Avenue.

Los Angeles.—Chicago, 2,265 miles; St. Louis, 2,125 miles; San Diego, 127 miles. Altitude, 270 feet. Population, 50,395. Junction with Southern Pacific Railroad and Los Angeles Terminal Railway.

This is the principal city of Southern California, its assessed wealth being $46,000,000. It has 90 miles of graded and graveled streets, 10 miles of paved streets, 80 miles of cement sidewalks, and 90 miles of street railroads. The city is lighted entirely by electricity. The residences are of the cottage style, and are commonly surrounded by lawns and gardens, in which the orange, magnolia, date palm, cypress, pepper, and eucalyptus contrast their different shades of green with the brilliant hues of geraniums, roses, and innumerable other cultivated flowers of choice variety. The hot-house blossoms of the East here overrun hedges and porch trellises, side by side with the wisteria and scarlet passion-vine. These gardens contain flowering plants of one or another kind throughout the year, and outside the immediate business district the streets are shaded with the slender, graceful eucalyptus and the æsthetic drooping pepper tree.

Los Angeles was founded September 7, 1781, by Don

Felipe de Neve, a Spanish Governor of California. Its name was originally *Pueblo de la Reina de los Angeles* (Town of the Queen of Angels), the present name affording another example in derivatives, the city of the Queen of Angels having become, by a simple contraction of the name, the property of the angels themselves. In 1822 the first Saxon was brought into the city, as prisoner of the Mexicans. He married into a Spanish family, and his example was frequently followed by American immigrants

RESIDENCE, LOS ANGELES.

in after years. Nine years later an overland outlet to the East was established in the Santa Fé Trail, and a large trade developed in consequence. In 1835 the city became the capital of California, and eleven years thereafter, on August 13, 1846, Commodore Stockton and Major Fremont raised here the American flag. In 1847 Fremont became Governor, and the house that served for his headquarters still stands at the corner of Aliso and Los Angeles streets. Don Pio Pico, the Mexican Governor succeeded by Fremont, is still alive at an advanced age, and is a voting citizen of Los Angeles.

In the last decade the population has increased about 40,000. The area of the city proper is thirty-six square miles, and there are numerous orchards and vineyards within its limits.

Los Angeles is chiefly modern, for its growth is recent, but there is much of Spanish atmosphere about it. In the suburbs Mexicans are numerous, and there is a Mexican quarter in the heart of the city, known as Sonora-town. One or two passable Mexican restaurants can be found, and those who have never ventured to taste " California chicken tamales " in the East, or tasting have repented, may find it worth while to patronize the street venders here, for the native mixture of green corn, chicken, olive, and chile, served hot in a corn-husk wrapper, is really a palatable morsel.

The population includes several thousand Chinese, who maintain their separate quarter in all the malodorous picturesqueness characteristic of American Chinatowns.

For educational institutions Los Angeles has the University of Southern California, with colleges of music, letters, and medicine; St. Vincent's (Catholic) College for boys; Los Angeles College for young women, and the Branch State Normal School, besides many private schools and the regular public city schools. There are some sixty churches, five hospitals, two orphan asylums, two theaters, eighteen banks, a Chamber of Commerce, and half a dozen parks.

THE KITE-SHAPED TRACK.— The main line of the Southern California Railway (Santa Fé Route) between Los Angeles and San Bernardino, that portion of the line south from Los Angeles as far as Orange, and the short line between Orange and San Bernardino, form a rough ellipse intersecting the principal settlements of the region. Eastward from San Bernardino another belt has been constructed, and the two together form a cross-belt not unlike a figure 8. Over this comprehensive circuit, known as the Kite-shaped Track, regular daily trains are run from

A LOS ANGELES HOME.

Los Angeles in both directions, each train following the outline of the figure and returning to Los Angeles without duplicating any of the journey except for the loop-crossing at San Bernardino. The Panorama Trains, as these are called, thus make a run of 160 miles through the fairest horticultural region of Southern California, for the accommodation of tourists.

The stations on the loop east of San Bernardino, a

circuit of twenty-five miles, are VICTORIA, DREW, GLA-
DYSTA, REDLANDS, EASTBERNE, MENTONE, APLIN, EAST
HIGHLANDS, BASE LINE, MOLINO, HIGHLAND, ASYLUM, DEL
ROSA, ARROWHEAD and HIGHLAND JUNCTION.

Redlands.—San Bernardino, nine miles. Altitude, 1,349 feet. Population, 1,904.

This is the largest of the towns named, and lies at the end of the upper Santa Ana Valley. Although only six years old, its assessed valuation is $2,000,000. The locality is particularly adapted to the culture of the orange and the raisin grape. Besides fruit growing and packing, the local industries include the manufacture of irrigating pipe, lumber, sashes and doors, and feed.

Arrowhead.—San Bernardino, four miles. Altitude, 1,226 feet.

Famed for the numerous hot mineral springs, already mentioned, which issue from the mountain side, at an elevation of 2,000 feet.

Carriages from Arrowhead Springs regularly meet trains at this station.

Asylum.—San Bernardino, seven miles. Altitude, 1,285 feet.

Named for the State Insane Asylum, which at this point overlooks the Santa Ana Valley from a mesa elevation.

Highland.—San Bernardino, eight miles. Altitude, 1,315 feet.

A young town whose natural advantages are similar to those of Redlands.

LOS ANGELES TO SANTA MONICA, REDONDO, AND SANTA CATALINA.

INTERMEDIATE STATIONS: Ballona Junction, Nadeau Park, Central Avenue, Slauson, Wildesin, Hyde Park, Centinela, Inglewood, Mesmer, Machado, South Santa Monica.

Santa Monica.—Los Angeles, 21 miles. Population, 1,580; township, 2,327.

An attractive beach resort. Frequent trains are run from Los Angeles daily, passing through a country scatteringly settled but nearly all under cultivation. The Southern California Railway branch to Santa Monica and Redondo diverges from the main line just outside of Los Angeles, on the south, at Ballona Junction.

Redondo Beach.—Los Angeles, 22 miles. Population, 603.

Another much frequented seaside resort ten miles beyond Inglewood, at which point the lines to Santa Monica and Redondo diverge, the latter through Wiseburn and Arena.

SANTA CATALINA ISLAND.—This island, one of the Channel group, lies about twenty miles off the coast, south of Redondo, between which point and Santa Catalina steamers ply three times a week, in summer, in connection with trains to and from Los Angeles. There is usually no regular steamer service in winter, but special trips are made for parties who desire the accommodation. Like the other channel islands, this is the portion of a mountain cap unsubmerged by the sea, above whose level its highest peaks rise more than 3,000 feet. Its shores are for the most part precipitous cliffs, which here and there give place to semicircular beaches. One of these, on the inner rim of a beautiful little crescent harbor, is called Avalon. This is the most populous of the summer pleasure resorts in Southern California, and although the throng of campers is not present in winter, it is only because that is not the period of vacation from shop and office.

It is an idyllic spot, more equable than any portion of the mainland, in consequence of the environment of the sea. The air is gentle by day and night throughout the year. It is a perfect spot for bathing, the shore of sand and pebble shelving gradually off into water so pellucid that through an incredible depth every weed and shell is clearly distinguishable upon the bottom, and brown and blood-red fishes may be seen swimming seventy-five feet below. In the summer season it is a famous fishery. Jewfish weighing 300 and 400 pounds are frequently taken with a hand-line, and are abundant. The capture of the

REDONDO BEACH.

jewfish is more exciting sport than tarpon fishing, if any can be, because of the prodigious weight and strength of the former. Boats are sometimes dragged for a long distance before the jewfish will surrender. The yellowtail ranks next as a game fish, and is highly valued for the table. It reaches a weight of fifty pounds, and the waters are at times churned into acres of foam by schools of yellowtail. Barracuda, which are a sort of cousin to the bluefish of the Atlantic, are also plentiful, besides Spanish mackerel and the usual smaller fry of ocean, some of which are peculiar to the Pacific. Flying fish are so common as to attract little notice after the novelty of first acquaintance. In crossing from Redondo to Avalon they shoot from under the bows of the steamer like startled birds from covert, and skim the surface of the water like swallows for a long distance. The flying fish does not ordinarily rise far above the water unless attracted by a light at night, when it can clear the hull of a small vessel, although it often falls on board. But it easily covers a horizontal distance of at least 500 yards at pleasure. Sharks and whales are also occasionally sighted between the island and the mainland.

In the interior of Santa Catalina, which is about thirty miles long and from a half-mile to nine miles broad, wild goats are numerous.

The island has few permanent residents, although as many as 3,000 visitors are congregated in summer. Its area is chiefly devoted to sheep grazing, the water supply being too small to encourage agriculture, even if its position at a distance from markets did not operate to disadvantage in that particular.

A point a dozen miles north of Avalon has been chosen by the proprietors for the site of a new watering place, whose development in the near future will shorten the journey from the mainland by just that distance.

Carrier-pigeon service between Avalon and the mainland has recently been instituted, for the convenience of men who desire to retain prompt business communication with the outside world while stopping on the island.

Los Angeles to San Diego.

Ballona Junction.— Two miles.

Point of divergence of trains from Los Angeles to Port Ballona, Redondo, and Santa Monica beaches.

INTERMEDIATE STATIONS: Bandini, Rivera, Los Nietos.

Santa Fe Springs.—Thirteen miles. Altitude, 159 feet.

A health resort. Whittier, the seat of a State Reform School, joins this town upon the east.

INTERMEDIATE STATIONS: Northam, Fullerton.

Anaheim.— Twenty-seven miles. Altitude, 164 feet. Population, 1,273; township, 2,917.

A prosperous German colony.

Orange.— Los Angeles, 31 miles; San Diego, 96 miles. Altitude, 178 feet. Population, 866; township, 2,721.

Junction with line from San Bernardino direct. A center of orange and grape culture.

Santa Ana.—Thirty-four miles. Altitude, 135 feet. Population, 3,628; township, 4,220.

Junction with the Santa Ana Railroad to Newport, on the coast.

INTERMEDIATE STATIONS: Irvine, Modjeska.

Modjeska was named for Madame Helen Modjeska, the actress, whose ranch is at the head of Santiago Cañon, some miles east of the station. In the vicinity of that cañon silver mines are operated.

El Toro.— Forty-seven miles. Altitude, 428 feet.

Point of departure by stage for Laguna and Arch Beach, seven miles. At Arch Beach the sandstone cliffs have been carved by the tide into arches and caverns, and large shells are abundant.

Capistrano.— Los Angeles, 56 miles; Chicago (short line), 2,277 miles; St. Louis, 2,137 miles; San Diego, 71 miles. Altitude, 138 feet. Population (San Juan Township), 801.

The gaunt ruins upon the left are those of the mission San Juan Capistrano, founded in 1776. In its original completeness it boasted a tower 120 feet high, which an earthquake toppled over in 1812, killing some thirty of the congregation which was assembled at the time. In 1818 a pirate named Bouchard landed on the coast three miles away and with his band terrorized the entire community for several days. While the inhabitants hid themselves in the coverts of the Rio Trabuco, Bouchard and his men caroused in the mission and despoiled it of most of its portable treasures, in which these establishments were, in their prime, very rich. A portion of the structure is still used by the resident Mexicans for a chapel.

Before the era of railroads, even after the decadence of the mission, San Juan Capistrano was a much more active town than it is now. A larger population was gathered here around the nucleus, and it was a halting place for the stages and all the vehicles of trade between Los Angeles and San Diego. But despite its forsaken air — perhaps the more because of it — it is an extremely interesting spot, and tourists not infrequently spend days and even weeks here pleasurably. There is a comfortable hotel, the Mendelson House, and apart from the powerful poetic charm of the ruins, reminiscent of a time when monks, soldiers, and Indians were the only inhabitants, and apart from incidental glimpses of the life of the Mexicans, who are descended from soldier and Indian, the little valley is full of natural beauties, and its fascination increases with familiarity. A few miles farther up the valley are still older ruins of the rudiments of the mission first designed for San Juan Capistrano, begun before the present site was determined upon.

A quarter-century back there were visible at Capistrano extensive ruins of covered masonry aqueducts, for the conveyance of water to be used for irrigation. The village is said to be honey-combed with them, although they are not now easily discoverable. The fact is mentioned as showing the greater comparative industrial activity of the town in a former time. Even so late as twenty-five years ago the population was probably four or five times greater. After the departure of the mission fathers the greater part of the appurtenant lands appear to have been acquired by an Englishman, Mr. John Forster, some of whose descendants still live here. For twenty miles beyond, on both sides of the railroad, his enormous ranch

SAN LUIS REY MISSION.

extended. It has, in recent years, been more or less subdivided.

San Juan.— Fifty-nine miles.

A favorite camping spot by the sea. One of the salients of the promontory upon the right is Dana's Point, referred to in the following extract from Richard Henry Dana's "Two Years Before the Mast":

Coasting along on the quiet shore of the Pacific, we came to anchor* in twenty fathoms water, almost out at sea, as it were, and directly abreast of a steep hill which overhung the water, and was twice as high as our royalmast-head. We had heard much of this place from the Lagoda's crew, who said it was the worst place in California. The shore is rocky, and directly exposed to the southeast, so that vessels are obliged to slip and run for their lives on the first sign of a gale; and, late as it was in the season, we got up our slip-rope and gear, though we meant to stay only twenty-four hours. We pulled the agent ashore and were ordered to wait for him while he took a circuitous way round the hill to the Mission, which was hidden behind it. We were glad of the opportunity to examine this singular place, and hauling the boat up, and making her well fast, took different directions up and down the beach, to explore it.

San Juan is the only romantic spot on the coast. The country here for several miles is high table-land, running boldly to the shore and breaking off in a steep cliff, at the foot of which the waters of the Pacific are constantly dashing. For several miles the water washes the very base of the hill, or breaks upon ledges and fragments of rocks which run out into the sea. Just where we landed was a small cove, or bight, which gave us, at high tide, a few square feet of sand-beach between the sea and bottom of the hill. This was the only landing-place. Directly before us rose the perpendicular height of four or five hundred feet. How we were to get hides down, or goods up, upon the table-land on which the Mission was situated, was more than we could tell. The agent had taken a long circuit, and yet had frequently to jump over breaks and climb steep places, in the ascent. No animal but a man or monkey could get up it. However, that was not our lookout; and, knowing that the agent would be gone an hour or more, we strolled about, picking up shells, and following the sea where it tumbled in, roaring and spouting, among the crevices of the great rocks. What a sight, thought I, must this be in a southeaster! The rocks were as large as those of Nahant or Newport, but, to my eye, more grand and broken. Besides, there was a grandeur in everything around which gave a solemnity to the scene, a silence and solitariness which affected every part! Not a human being but ourselves for miles, and no sound heard but the pulsations of the great Pacific! and the great steep hill rising like a wall and cutting us off from all the world but the

---
*May, 1835.

"world of waters"! I separated myself from the rest, and sat down on a rock, just where the sea ran in and formed a fine spouting horn. Compared with the plain, dull sand-beach of the rest of the coast, this grandeur was as refreshing as a great rock in a weary land. It was almost the first time that I had been positively alone — free from the sense that human beings were at my elbow, if not talking with me — since I had left home. My better nature returned strong upon me. Everything was in accordance with my state of feeling, and I experienced a glow of pleasure at finding that what of poetry and romance I ever had in me had not been entirely deadened by the laborious life, with its paltry, vulgar associations, which I had been leading. Nearly an hour did I sit, almost lost in the luxury of this entire new scene of the play in which I had been so long acting, when I was aroused by the distant shouts of my companions, and saw that they were collecting together, as the agent had made his appearance, on his way back to our boat.

We pulled aboard, and found the long-boat hoisted out, and nearly laden with goods; and, after dinner, we all went on shore in the quarter-boat, with the long-boat in tow. As we drew in, we descried an ox-cart and a couple of men standing directly on the brow of the hill, and having landed, the captain took his way round the hill, ordering me and one other to follow him. We followed, picking our way out, and jumping and scrambling up, walking over briers and prickly pears, until we came to the top. Here the country stretched out for miles, as far as the eye could reach, on a level, table surface, and the only habitation in sight was the small white Mission of San Juan Capistrano, with a few Indian huts about it, standing in a small hollow, about a mile from where we were. Reaching the brow of the hill, where the cart stood, we found several piles of hides, and Indians sitting around them. One or two other carts were coming slowly on from the Mission, and the captain told us to begin and throw the hides down. This, then, was the way they were to be got down, thrown down, one at a time, a distance of 400 feet! This was doing the business on a great scale. Standing on the edge of the hill, and looking down the perpendicular height, the sailors —

> "That walked upon the beach
> Appeared like mice; and our tall anchoring bark
> Diminished to her cock; her cock a buoy
> Almost too small for sight."

Down this height we pitched the hides, throwing them as far out into the air as we could; and as they were all large, stiff, and doubled, like the cover of a book, the wind took them, and they swayed out and eddied about, plunging and rising in the air, like a kite when it has broken its string. As it was now low tide there was no danger of their falling into the water; and, as fast as they came to ground, the men below picked them up, and taking them on their heads, walked off with them to the boat. It was really a picturesque sight; the great height, the scaling of the hides, and the continual walking to and fro of the men, who looked like mites on the beach. This was the romance of hide droghing!

Some of the hides lodged in cavities under the bank and out of our sight, being directly under us; but by pitching other hides in the same direction we succeeded in dislodging them. Had they remained there, the captain said he should have sent on board for a couple of pairs of long halyards, and got some one to go down for them. It was said that one of the crew of an English brig went down in the same way a few years before. We looked over and thought it would not be a welcome task, especially for a few paltry hides; but no one knows what he will do until he is called upon; for six months afterward I descended the same place by a pair of topgallant studding-sail halyards to save half a dozen hides which had lodged there.

INTERMEDIATE STATIONS: San Onofre, Las Flores, Los Angeles Junction.

Oceanside.— Los Angeles, 85 miles; Chicago (short line), 2,306 miles; St. Louis, 2,166 miles; San Diego, 42 miles. Altitude, 44 feet. Population, 427.

Situated upon a bluff by the seaside. Connection with branch lines to Escondido and De Luz.

OCEANSIDE TO ESCONDIDO.—This branch runs to the southeast, through the valleys of San Marcos and Escondido, old Mexican grants.

ESCONDIDO.— Twenty-two miles from Oceanside, 640 feet above sea-level. The township possesses a population of 1,200.

Raisins are the chief product of the valley. One of the colleges of the University of Southern California is located here.

INTERMEDIATE STATIONS: Escondido Junction, Loma Alta, Vista, Buena, San Marcos.

OCEANSIDE TO DE LUZ.—A portion of the original Temecula Cañon line from Oceanside to San Bernardino.

INTERMEDIATE STATIONS: Los Angeles Junction, Ysidora.

An example of the old-time Mexican life is offered the tourist in the great ranch-houses of the Santa Margarita Ranch, 230,000 acres in extent, near De Luz, which is thirteen miles distant from Oceanside, 147 feet above the sea.

INTERMEDIATE STATIONS: Escondido Junction, Carlsbad, La Costa, Leucadia, Encinitas, Del Mar, Sorrento, Linda Vista, Selwyn, Ladrillo, Morena.

There are noted mineral waters at Carlsbad. From Morena the bay of San Diego, the peninsula of Coronado and Point Loma may be seen.

Oldtown.— Three and one-half miles north of San Diego proper.

The first Spanish settlement in California was made here, this being the original site of San Diego, founded in 1769. It is located at the mouth of the San Diego River. Here are the foundations of the first mission church and the presidio, begun in the same year. The mission was in 1774 removed six miles up the valley of the San Diego River, known as Mission Valley, where its ruins still stand, near old olive trees and huge palms that were planted by the mission fathers. The old mission bells are lashed to a cross-bar behind the Catholic chapel, at Oldtown, where there is also an ancient burying-ground and many an adobe ruin of former dwellings. Here, also, stands the house which figures as the marriage-place of Ramona in Helen Hunt Jackson's well-known novel.

San Diego.— Los Angeles, 127 miles; Chicago (short line), 2,348 miles; St. Louis, 2,208 miles. Population, 16,159.

National City.— Five and one-half miles beyond San Diego. Population, 1,353. End of the Santa Fé Route on the south.

SAN BERNARDINO TO SAN DIEGO, VIA SHORT LINE

Colton.— San Bernardino, three miles. Altitude, 977 feet. Population, 1,315. Junction with Southern Pacific Railroad between Yuma and Los Angeles.

The location of one of the largest fruit-packing establishments in Southern California. Its other industries include the quarrying of marble and building-stone, lime-burning, and flour-milling.

East Riverside.— San Bernardino, six miles; Riverside, three miles. Altitude, 943 feet. Population, 330.

Junction with branch lines to San Jacinto and Temecula on the south.

EAST RIVERSIDE TO TEMECULA.—The line to Temecula extended through the remarkable cañon of that name to Oceanside until, in 1890, immense wash-outs carried away many miles of the road in and near the cañon, which portion has never been rebuilt.

INTERMEDIATE STATIONS: Box Springs, Alessandro, Perris, Elsinore, Wildomar, Murrieta, and Linda Rosa.

ELSINORE.— Altitude 1,281 feet.

Contains a lake that covers a dozen square miles, hot mineral springs, much resorted to by rheumatic invalids, and deposits of gold, silver, asbestos, tin, iron, coal, and fire-clay.

TEMECULA.— Altitude, 1,001 feet. Forty-five miles from East Riverside.

Is the site of an ancient Indian village at the mouth of the cañon.

EAST RIVERSIDE TO SAN JACINTO. The Temecula road is followed as far as Perris, eighteen miles, at which point a branch diverges to San Jacinto, thirty-eight miles from East Riverside. This is a trading and shipping point of considerable importance, with lumber manufactories and lime quarries. The Lake Hemet dam, under construction, is intended to supply water enough to irrigate 80,000 acres of land. Here also are hot springs. Mount San Jacinto, 10,894 feet high, is a magnificent mountain, and possesses a quasi-romantic interest for the numerous admirers of Alessandro and Ramona.

Strawberry Valley is a favorite summer resort, at an elevation of 6,000 feet. The altitude of San Jacinto is 1,535 feet. The population of the town is 661, and of the township 1,192.

Riverside.— Chicago, 2,214 miles; St. Louis, 2,074 miles; San Diego, 134 miles. Altitude, 875 feet. Population, 4,683.

In 1872 the site of this city was a sheep ranch. In 1892 its assessed valuation was more than $4,000,000. It lies within a small half-circle of foot-hills, in plain view of the San Bernardino Range, whose snow-draped summits

MAGNOLIA AVENUE, RIVERSIDE.

present in winter a remarkable contrast with the almost tropical splendor of its vegetation and fruitage. Its Magnolia Avenue is world-renowned — a magnificent double driveway beginning a short distance outside the business center and extending for seven miles in a straight line between rows of eucalyptus, pepper, and occasionally magnolia and palm trees. From this avenue private drives lead to adjacent mansion homes, in the midst of a wealth of golden fruit and ornamental shrubbery. There is not an idle acre of land. Orange groves or orchards of almond, peach, pear, apricot, fig, and walnut are everywhere to be seen. It has highly perfected systems of irrigation, comprising 200 miles of ditches and pipe-lines, with more in process of construction.

Riverside is the largest orange-shipping point in California, producing more than half a million boxes of oranges annually. In raisin-making it is second only to Fresno, and in addition raises large quantities of deciduous fruits and general farm products. Many establishments are required for handling its enormous product, packing oranges, curing lemons, and canning deciduous fruits, keeping in cold storage.

INTERMEDIATE STATIONS: Pachappa, Casa Blanca, Arlington, Alvord.

South Riverside.— Fifteen miles southwest of Riverside. Altitude, 603 feet. Population (precinct), 556.

The Circle Colony. Besides fruit raising, its industries include the manufacture of sewer-pipe, terra cotta, brick, and fertilizers; and porphyry and gypsum are quarried. The Temescal tin mines are situated seven miles east of South Riverside.

The road crosses the San Jacinto stream near South Riverside, and follows the course of the Santa Ana from Yorba to Olive.

INTERMEDIATE STATIONS: Rincon, Gypsum, Yorba, Olive.

Orange.— Chicago, 2,252 miles; St. Louis, 2,112 miles; Los Angeles, 31 miles; San Diego, 96 miles. Junction with main line between Los Angeles and San Diego.

For remainder of the journey to San Diego see page 217.

SAN DIEGO.— The bay of San Diego is twelve miles long, divided from the ocean by the low, slender, northward-extending peninsula of Coronado, and the bold headland of Point Loma, which overlaps it on the north, the narrow entrance to the bay lying between these two. It is as placid as a mill-pond, and as beautiful as an inlet of the Mediterranean. The city lies upon its eastern shore, covering the narrow level of its rim and climbing the slopes of a mesa that here forms a wall between the sea and the valley of the San Diego River. It will begin to be a great and wealthy city when the problem of extensive irrigation of the immediately surrounding country has been solved and the enormous areas of the county have been fairly directed toward general productiveness. The development of the resources of the soil is recognized as the essential preliminary to urban prosperity, and every succeeding year marks new development in agriculture and fruit raising upon the rich lands that form the surroundings of the city. In the meantime its chief interest to the tourist lies in its superb climate, its manifold and diverse beauties and attractions, and the examples of idyllic and prosperous rural life which its environs afford. California can boast no more magnificent or more profitable orchards and vineyards, in proportion to their size, than are found in its contiguous valleys, although their number is as yet too small for the maintenance of a great commercial center.

It is perfectly adapted for a sojourn. A good deal of business must necessarily be transacted in a city of 16,000 permanent inhabitants, but this fact will not obtrusively impress itself upon the casual visitor. It is quiet, restful, dreamy, picturable in a figure half-dozing amid the fragrant odor of flowers upon the shore of its blessed bay.

228   NEW GUIDE TO THE PACIFIC COAST.

Aside from the mere seduction of out-of-door wandering in such an idyllic spot, there are many special sights to be seen on the shore, in the valleys, and among the

UNITED STATES AND MEXICO BOUNDARY-LINE MONUMENT, NEAR SAN DIEGO.

hills. A drive to Oldtown and thence up the Mission Valley, returning over the mesa, will embrace the remains of the ancient régime. At Oldtown are the ruins of the first of the missions, founded July 16, 1769, with due ceremonial, and of the old presidio, or garrison, where a military force of seventy soldiers, with small arms and a few cannon, were quartered for the protection of the pueblo against Indian uprisings. One such uprising took place a few weeks after the beginning of work upon the mission, a boy being killed and a few men wounded on the side of the Spaniards, who, to the credit of their good judgment, and doubtless to their humanity, did not attempt to punish the Indians severely, but sought to subdue them without recourse to arms. For a full half-century after the settlement of San Diego nearly the entire population, except for those directly engaged in missionary labors, lived either within the presidio or close at hand. In 1800 its population numbered 167 soldiers and their families, and in 1821 there were only five houses in old San Diego. In 1837 the presidio was abandoned by the military. The chief business of the locality was the exportation of hides, and this was at one time the center of this traffic for the entire California coast.

Old paintings and statuary and the old mission bells are to be seen at the Catholic chapel, and at the foot of Presidio Hill stand two lofty and venerable palm trees, fenced about for their preservation, which are a legacy of the old era. In 1774 the mission was removed to a point six miles up the valley, where some seventy Indian *rancherias* were collected, the spot being known to them as Nipiguay. Three months after, these Indians, 1,000 strong, attacked and burned the mission, several of the Spaniards being killed and many seriously wounded in the battle. After two years the undaunted fathers began a new mission on the same site, which was completed in 1784. After its final abandonment in consequence of the act of secularization, the edifice rapidly fell into decay, and to-day only tottering fragments remain of a once imposing structure, by the side of which an Indian school has been erected. The orchard of olive trees, with a few intermingled palms and pomegranates, in the alluvial valley in front of the eminence on which the mission stood, has outlived the edifice itself. It is still in bearing, and is the stock from which a vast number of olive trees in California have been propagated. At the time the missions were broken up, this one of San Diego possessed some 28,000 cattle, horses, and sheep, and raised large quantities of wheat and barley, in addition to fruits and other farm crops. In 1846 a United States military post was established at this port, and the troops were quartered in the deserted mission for ten years.

Coronado is reached by ferry, and the beach lies at the end of a short ride by steam motor across the widest part of the peninsula. It is also connected with the mainland by railroad. Coronado Beach is a dozen miles in length, a wide, sweeping shore of white sand looking off to the horizon of the Pacific, which is unbroken save by the distant peaks of the Coronado Islands. In the space of half a dozen years what was originally a sterile waste, tangled with chaparral, has become one of the greatest of American seaside resorts. Numerous handsome residences have been built, grounds have been improved, thousands of tropical trees have been planted, avenues have been constructed and lined with palms and hedges of cypress and marguerites, parks and gardens have been created, and the peninsula has become a town by itself, populous and beautiful. The center of attraction is of course the Hotel del Coronado. There are actually in the world but few hostelries worthy of any comparison with it in point of magnificence, beauty, and attractiveness. It is built around an immense court, which is a tropical garden of rare shrubs and flowers, upon which the inner rooms of the hotel open by way of a broad encircling balcony. Toward the sea the galleries of each story are encased in glass, and are used as sunning-places by invalids and others who do not enjoy the ocean breeze. The entire structure, including the court, covers four and one-half acres, and accommodates 750 guests. The main dining-room has a floor area of 10,000 square feet, unsupported by a single pillar, and the ball-room a floor area of 11,000 feet. It is furnished throughout with the utmost magnificence. The Hotel del Coronado stands upon the edge of the beach, almost within reach of the waves, and commands charming views of ocean, bay, and coast, and mountain ranges across the Mexican border.

There is little difference here between summer and winter. The average number of rainy days in the year is thirty-four, and in the equable temperature much of the flora of both temperate and tropic zones is continually in bloom. There is a large conservatory where, under glass, the most delicate of rare tropical plants are reared in great profusion; a bath-house containing swimming tanks of warm salt water for those who do not care to indulge in surf bathing; a museum, an ostrich farm, a labyrinth, a race-track, and many other special devices for diversification of the pleasure of guests, and all the incidental attractions in and near San Diego are conveniently accessible.

Ocean Beach and Pacific Beach lie on the north, a short distance outside of San Diego, and Point Loma and its light-house are worth a visit, which may be made by carriage around the bay. La Jolla Park is a uniquely beautiful bit of coast thirteen miles from San Diego, reached by a pleasant carriage drive or by way of the San Diego & Pacific Beach Motor Railroad, and a short stage ride beyond.

Here the soft sandstone walls of a long bluff have been water-worn into numerous connecting caverns, which may be entered dry-shod only at very low tide. The erosion of the waves has wrought rock forms of striking appearance, and has sculptured the remaining faces of the cliff walls with delicately beautiful designs. Mosses, sea-anemones, crabs, and abalones are very plentiful. The water is exceedingly transparent, and the brilliant flashing of

LA JOLLA CAVES, NEAR SAN DIEGO.

golden fish that swim in schools near the shore adds to the novelty of the spot.

El Cajon Valley lies fifteen miles northeast from San Diego, and is reached over the San Diego, Cuymaca & Eastern Railway. It is one of the largest and richest valleys in the immediate vicinity of San Diego. The upper San Diego River flows through it, and the town of Lakeside stands near the river and by the side of a beautiful sheet of water known as Linda Lake. Allison, Cowles,

Riverview, and Foster's are other stations in this valley. One hundred and forty-five car-loads of raisins were shipped from El Cajon Valley in 1891, and besides the vineyards of raisin and table grapes, thousands of acres are covered with fruit trees. This has also been for many years a large wheat-producing region. The waters of the San Diego Flume Company pass through it.

National City is conveniently reached by railroad, or by a drive of four miles. Here are large olive orchards and manufactories of olive-oil. In the highly cultivated Paradise Valley, at National City, are many groves of orange and lemon, the quality of whose fruit is unsurpassed.

From San Diego the National City & Otay Railway extends through National City, Chula Vista, and Otay City to within a few hundred yards of the little Mexican village of Tia Juana, which lies just across the border, beyond the stream of the same name. A trip to Tia Juana is one of the popular excursions of tourists while in San Diego. The railroad ride is an enjoyable one of fifteen miles, after which comes a short walk or coach-ride, the latter being hardly worth the trouble of entering the vehicle, from the railway terminus to the village. Once arrived there is little to be seen besides a shop filled with Mexican curios and a few swart soldiers lounging about a custom house. It is better to take a few hours more time for the excursion and drive from Tia Juana to the seashore at Point of Rocks, where some really good scenery lies. The Boundary Monument also may be visited by a three-mile drive from Tia Juana. The return trip on the National City & Otay Railway includes a side-ride to Sweetwater Dam, which lies east of San Diego in a beautiful valley among the mesa lands. This is a reservoir covering 700 acres on the Sweetwater River, and contains six thousand million gallons of water.

The trip to Tia Juana and the Sweetwater Dam by railroad consumes the greater part of a day.

LOS ANGELES TO SANTA BARBARA.—Santa Barbara is reached over the Southern Pacific Railroad from Los Angeles, its main line being followed as far as Saugus, thirty-two miles, altitude 1,159 feet, at which point a branch line to the great seaside resort strikes off westward. South of Saugus there is little of interest by the way, except the long tunnel (altitude, 1,401 feet) just below Newhall (altitude, 1,265 feet). But the branch line speedily enters the fertile and most attractive valley of the Santa Clara River. This valley, named for its river, must not be confounded with the Santa Clara Valley which is most commonly spoken of in connection with California. The latter lies only a few miles southeast of San Francisco, the city of San Jose in its midst. The one now under consideration lies along the way for half the distance from Saugus to Santa Barbara, and is about forty miles long. Camulos, forty-seven miles from Los Angeles, is the first point of interest. Camulos Ranch, at this point, has become quasi-historic as the original home of Ramona. Orchards of orange and olive surround the buildings and screen them with foliage.

Santa Paula.—Sixty-six miles from Los Angeles. Population, 1,047.

Rich in most of the characteristic Southern California fruits.

Saticoy.—Seventy-three miles. Population, 218.
Ventura.—Eighty-three miles. Population, 2,820.

Ventura is a contraction of San Buenaventura, the name of the old mission town, whose church is still in a fair state of preservation. This is an oil-center, besides exporting very large quantities of grain, lima beans, potatoes, flour, wool, butter, hides, asphaltum, etc. It is a seaport.

Fifteen miles north of Ventura lies the village of Nordhoff, population, 244, in the Ojai Valley, which was made famous by the writings of Charles Nordhoff. The Nordhoff Hotel stages meet trains at Ventura. This beautiful valley is snugly nestled among the mountains, and is much in favor with tourists as a sojourning place, because of its fruitfulness, its diverse scenery, the Matilija Springs, and the gentle climate.

From Ventura the road closely follows the shore-line, on the edge of a narrow terrace between mountain and sea.

Carpinteria.— One hundred miles.
Montecito.— One hundred and seven miles.
Santa Barbara.— One hundred and ten miles. Population, 5,864.

Facing southward toward the sea, the city rises to the foot of the Santa Inez Mountains, which form a protecting back-wall from three to five thousand feet high, whose nearest pass on the west is the picturesque chasm of the Gaviota thirty-six miles distant. Facing thus, and sheltered thus, Santa Barbara knows but a slight change of temperature, the mean monthly figures for a period of thirteen years ranging between 55° and 71°, and the temperature of its sea-water varying only half a dozen degrees in the twelve months.

It is equally a resort of the invalid and the pleasure-seeker. Surf-bathing in California is not much practiced in winter, although the temperature of the sea is then much higher than at some of the Atlantic watering-places in summer, but at Santa Barbara there is hardly a day in the year when some enthusiast may not be seen taking a dip in the surf. The beach is smooth and firm, and is bordered by a boulevard, both much frequented by carriages and equestrians. There are also bold cliff points, like Sentinel Rock, overlooking the beach and the brine, where idlers love to lounge and fishermen angle for surf-fish. There are innumerable attractive drives, and saddle-horses are much in request. A lofty mesa, covered with live oaks, overlooks the town, and the side streets and avenues are densely shaded with ornamental trees. Cottages are buried in foliage and covered with clambering vines in bloom. In the profusion of blossoms the rose is conspicuous, one private garden alone containing more than 200 choice varieties of this flower. In April of every year a flower carnival is held, whose climax is a unique procession of all sorts of fanciful equipages elaborately decked with flowers and filled with joyous men, women, and children in gala attire. While Eastern cities are yet ice-bound, the streets of Santa Barbara are strewn with exquisite cultivated flowers, which are held so cheaply that they are not considered worth the trouble of picking up. Ten thousand fine roses have been used on these occasions to decorate a single vehicle.

The Santa Barbara Mission, situated in the northern part of the city, nearly two miles from the beach, has been preserved with care, and is regularly used for religious service. This is naturally one of the most noted objects of interest to the newcomer, but there are scores of other specific attractions, among which may be mentioned La Piedra Pintada, or the Painted Rock, a singular relic of aboriginal art, situated four miles from town, between the head of Montecito Valley and La Cañada de los Alisos. Whether these hieroglyphs were intended for a serious record of events, or were mere idle conceits of the barbaric artist, is not known.

Montecito, three miles from Santa Barbara, is a collection of superb homes, thought by many to outrival even Pasadena in beauty.

A favorite drive is westward to the Hollister and Cooper ranches, enormous cultivated tracts devoted to multifarious fruits and ornamental vegetation.

From twenty to thirty miles off the coast, southward from Santa Barbara, are four islands. Anacapa, the most easterly, is waterless. Formerly this was a favorite resort for sea-otters, and is still a sunning-place for numerous sea-lions. It has a peak over 900 feet above the sea.

Santa Cruz is the largest of the group, being twenty-one miles long and about four miles in average width. It reaches a height of 1,700 feet. Wood and water are plentiful on parts of this island.

Santa Rosa is fifteen miles long by ten miles broad. It attains an elevation of over 1,100 feet, and has numerous springs.

San Miguel, the most western of the group, is 7½ miles long and 2½ miles wide. This is the island on which the dead body of Cabrillo, the Spanish navigator, is supposed to have been buried, in January, 1543.

The chief value of these islands is for grazing, many thousands of sheep finding subsistence there, and contributing very substantially to the annual export of wool from California. They abound in picturesque localities, and are rich in archæological relics. No special facilities have been provided to enable the tourist to visit them, but once or twice a week fishing-boats leave Santa Barbara to fish in the waters among the Channel Islands, and passage can be secured on them for a reasonable consideration.

LOS ANGELES TO SAN FRANCISCO.—As far as Saugus the route is the same as that to Santa Barbara (see p. 234). At Saugus the railroad makes a sharp angle and runs a little north of east between the San Gabriel Range and the Sierra Peluna, and then turns northward to Mojave. The greater part of the region traversed is arid, and in the neighborhood of Mojave distinctly desert. Here the watermirage is frequently seen, a perfect illusion of a placid lake that would be bitter mockery to a caravan athirst.

INTERMEDIATE STATIONS: Tropico, West Glendale, Sepulveda, Burbank, Tejunga, Pacoima, Fernando, Tunnel, Newhall, Saugus, Lang, Ravenna, Acton, Vincent, Harold, Palmdale, Lancaster, Rosamond.

Mojave.— Los Angeles, 100 miles; Chicago, 2,195 miles; St. Louis, 2,055 miles; San Francisco, 382 miles. Dining station.

From this point the route is identical with that followed by the traveler to San Francisco, who was temporarily abandoned on page 201. The direction is generally northwestward for about eighty miles, after which it sweeps farther toward the north. The desert is soon left behind.

INTERMEDIATE STATION: Cameron.

Tehachapi.—Chicago, 2,215 miles; St. Louis, 2,075 miles; Los Angeles, 120 miles; San Francisco, 362 miles. Altitude, 4,025 feet. Population, 255.

The descent of the pass of the Tehachapi Mountain is full of beauty, and was accomplished for the Southern Pacific Railroad with no little ingenuity.

THE LOOP.— Ten miles beyond Tehachapi. Altitude, 3,050 feet. Here a complete loop is made in the railroad. The length of the loop is 3,795 feet; the altitude at the crossing over the tunnel, 3,034 feet; and the altitude of the tunnel, 2,956 feet, a local advantage of seventy-eight feet in elevation being thus gained. The grade is heavy and continues for many miles — through Keene, 2,705 feet; Bealville, 1,793 feet; Caliente, 1,290 feet; Pampa, 672 feet; Wade, 567 feet, and then we have fairly entered the San Joaquin Valley.

Bakersfield.—Chicago, 2,263 miles; St. Louis, 2,123 miles; Los Angeles, 168 miles; San Francisco, 314 miles. Altitude, 415 feet. Population, 2,626. Dining station.

County-seat of Kern County, on the Kern River, which supplies the greater part of the water used on the extensive irrigated lands of this county, 650 miles of ditches being fed by it. This region was desert, too, until water

TEHACHAPI PASS.

was supplied, and now it is one of the most productive portions of the valley. Fields of alfalfa and grain, and vineyards and orchards abound where a short time ago only a few tenacious shrubs relieved the monotony of the plain.

The county contains an artesian belt, with many flowing wells, likewise used for irrigating purposes. Salt, lime, petroleum, and asphaltum are among the natural products of Kern County, and its mines have yielded a total value of nearly one and a half millions. Apples, walnuts, almonds, apricots, peaches, figs, grapes, sugar-cane, tobacco, cotton, hops, and the cereals are successfully grown.

INTERMEDIATE STATIONS: Glenburn, Lerdo, Kimberlena.

Poso.— Twenty miles beyond Bakersfield. Junction with a side line through Portersville to the main line again at Fresno. Altitude, 414 feet.

INTERMEDIATE STATIONS: Delano, Alila, Pixley, Tipton, Tokay.

Tulare.— Chicago, 2,326 miles; St. Louis, 2,186 miles; Los Angeles, 231 miles; San Francisco, 251 miles. Altitude, 282 feet. Population, 2,697.

Junction with branch line to Visalia. Tulare Lake, a few miles distant on the west, is a large body of water, surrounded by marshes, and covering several townships.

INTERMEDIATE STATION: Tagus.

Goshen Junction.— Ten miles beyond Tulare. Altitude, 286 feet.

Junction with side line to Visalia on the east, and on the west with line through Hanford, thence northwestward to Tracy.

Visalia is the county-seat of Tulare County, with a population of 2,885. Mount Whitney, the highest point in the United States outside of Alaska, stands upon the eastern border of this county, and within its limits, in the Sierras, the Kern, King's, Kaweah, Tule, and White rivers take rise. There are 800,000 acres contained within six irrigation districts in this county, there being more than 500 miles of main canals, besides a large mileage of lateral ditches. Here, also, is an artesian belt, from whose wells an almost incredible amount of water steadily flows. One well alone is said to give 35,000,000 gallons per day. Grain and

THE DEAD GIANT.

stock raising have been the chief industries in the past, but orchards and vineyards have recently found favor, and large areas have been planted with trees and vines. The county contains a single raisin vineyard of 960 acres, and there are large orchards of the deciduous fruits.

INTERMEDIATE STATIONS: Cross Creek, Traver, Kingsburg, Selma, Fowler, Malaga.

Fresno.—Chicago, 2,370 miles; St. Louis, 2,230 miles; Los Angeles, 275 miles; San Francisco, 207 miles. Altitude, 293 feet. Population, 10,818. Dining station.

Junction with side line from Poso and with new line to Tracy, west of the main line.

County-seat of Fresno County, a modern metropolitan city, and center of the wool, raisin, wine, and fruit trade industries of the San Joaquin Valley. The farm-lands of this county are irrigated by the San Joaquin and King's rivers. Here, also, deciduous fruits, and cotton, tobacco, etc., are profitably cultivated, but the soil and climate are particularly adapted to the culture and preparation of the raisin-grape. At least half the raisin crop of the State is produced in this county, the yield in 1891 being 1,200,000 boxes. There is one vineyard of 600 acres. Two and sometimes three crops of raisin-grapes are gathered in the year.

The manufacture of lumber is also an important industry in Fresno County, the mountains being covered with a dense growth of cedar, redwood, and pine. The precious metals, also, have been produced in considerable quantity.

Fresno city is well worth a leisurely visit.

FRESNO TO TRACY VIA BERENDA AND LATHROP.

INTERMEDIATE STATIONS: Muscatel, Herndon, Irrigosa, Borden.

THE THREE BROTHERS, YOSEMITE.

Madera.—Twenty-two miles beyond Fresno. Population, 950. Altitude, 278 feet.

The location of the John Brown colony.

Berenda.—Chicago, 2,399 miles; St. Louis, 2,259 miles; Los Angeles, 304 miles; San Francisco, 178 miles. Altitude, 256 feet.

Junction with branch line to Raymond on the east, where connection is made by stage for the Yosemite Valley and the Mariposa Big Trees.

THE YOSEMITE AND THE MARIPOSA GROVE.— This remarkable valley of the Sierras lies in Mariposa County, at an elevation of 4,060 feet, 4,000 feet below the crests of the inclosing mountains. The valley proper is seven miles long, and its greatest width is 2½ miles, although it is for the most part from one-half to three-quarters of a mile wide. The Merced River, a tributary of the San Joaquin, flows through its gorges and between banks decked with flowers or shaded with cedars, silver pines, and oaks. The walls of the Yosemite are of granite, and stupendous in magnificence. On the northern side stands El Capitan, a mass of bare granite 3,300 feet high; the Three Brothers, Yosemite Point, the Royal Arches, Washington Tower, and the North Dome. On the southern side are Inspiration Point, Cathedral Rocks, Cathedral Spires, Sentinel Rock and Dome, Glacier Point, and the wall of the Tululawiak Cañon. At the eastern end are Grizzly Peak and Half (or South) Dome, the latter rising to a height of over 4,000 feet above its base and crowned with a summit whose area is ten acres. There are nine principal waterfalls: Bridal Veil, a slender, swaying column of spray 900 feet high; Ribbon, Sentinel, Yosemite, which falls 2,600 feet in three sections, one of which is a vertical plunge of 1,500 feet; Royal Arch, Tululawiak, Vernal, Nevada, and Cascade.

THE BIG TREES.

Although the area of the entire Yosemite Valley proper is very small as compared with the titanic chasm of the Grand Cañon of the Colorado River, it touches sublimity of beauty. Another valley, the Hetch-Hetchy, is included in the Yosemite National Park. This is similar in character, but less frequently visited because of the difficulties that intervene.

The word Yosemite is Indian, and signifies Great Grizzly Bear. The original Indian name was Ahwahnee.

The railroad branch from Berenda to Raymond (not to be confounded with Raymond near Los Angeles) is twenty-one miles in length. Beyond Raymond the distance to the Yosemite is about sixty miles, and is made by stage in a day and a half; the stop over night being made at Wawona. There are good hotel accommodations in the valley. On the return the stage leaves Yosemite in the morning and reaches Wawona at noon, where the remainder of the day is allowed for visiting the Mariposa Big Trees. In this grove of giant Sequoias there are 427 trees, the largest of which is thirty-four feet in diameter, the height ranging from 150 to 300 feet. A cut has been made through the standing trunk of one of them, large enough to permit the passage of the stage-coach with its load of passengers.

INTERMEDIATE STATIONS: Califa, Minturn, Athlone, Lingard.

Merced.—Twenty-six miles beyond Berenda. Altitude, 171 feet. Population, 2,000. Junction with side line, on the east of main line to Stockton.

County-seat of Merced County. The soil and climate are adapted to fruits and cereals.

INTERMEDIATE STATIONS: Atwater, Arena, Livingston, Turlock, Ceres.

Modesto.—Thirty-eight miles beyond Merced. Population, 2,402. Altitude, 91 feet.

County-seat of Stanislaus County. All the principal California fruits, nuts, vegetables, and grains are raised in this locality.

INTERMEDIATE STATIONS: Salida, Ripon.

Lathrop.—Chicago, 2,483 miles; St. Louis, 2,343 miles; Los Angeles, 388 miles; San Francisco, 94 miles. Altitude, 26 feet. Population, 577. Dining station. Junction with line running northward through Stockton and San Francisco.

INTERMEDIATE STATION: Banta.

Tracy.—Chicago, 2,494 miles; St. Louis, 2,354 miles; Los Angeles, 399 miles; San Francisco, 83 miles. Altitude, 64 feet. Junction with new line from Fresno via Collis, and with line through Niles to San Jose and Oakland.

FRESNO TO TRACY, VIA COLLIS.

Collis.—Fifteen miles from Fresno. Altitude, 219 feet.
Mendota.—Thirty-four miles from Fresno. Altitude, 178 feet.
Los Baños.—Sixty-eight miles from Fresno. Altitude, 121 feet.
Newman.—Eighty-nine miles from Fresno. Altitude, 92 feet.
Tracy.—One hundred and twenty-six miles from Fresno.

TRACY TO SAN FRANCISCO, VIA PORT COSTA.—Beyond Bethany, Byron, and Brentwood, in the vicinity of Antioch, twenty-eight miles from Tracy, the road swings westward by the side of the confluent San Joaquin and Sacramento rivers, through Avon and Martinez, on Suisun Bay, and Port Costa and Vallejo Junction, at the head of San Pablo Bay; thence by the shore of that bay, and southward along the bay of San Francisco to the city of Oakland. Most of this interval lies in Contra Costa County, in the center of which Mount Diablo rises 3,860 feet directly from the level of the sea. From the summit of Mount Diablo a territory as large as that of the entire State of New York, embracing thirty cities and villages that include one-half the population of California, may be surveyed.

The principal smelters of the Pacific Coast are located at Vallejo Junction. The anchorage of Port Costa is fresh-water, and of sufficient depth to accommodate the largest ships, as is also the case as far back as Antioch, on the San Joaquin. At Port Costa north-bound trains are ferried across. At a number of points along this water-front are immense docks and warehouses.

The distance between San Francisco and the most important stations along this last stage is as follows: Antioch, 55 miles; Martinez, 36 miles; Port Costa, 32 miles; Vallejo Junction, 29 miles.

Oakland.—Chicago, 2,573 miles; St. Louis, 2,433 miles; Los Angeles, 478 miles; San Francisco, 4 miles. Population, 48,682. Altitude (pier), 14 feet.

The first stopping of the train is at Sixteenth Street, and the second and last is at Oakland Pier, two miles beyond, where passengers leave the train and take the ferry across the bay to San Francisco.

Oakland is the county-seat of Alameda County. It contains, in addition to a large number of public city schools, many seminaries, academies, etc., a medical college, and Chabot Observatory.

It stands upon a peninsula that extends into the bay from the Contra Costra Range, from whose elevation the bay, the Golden Gate, and the cities of Oakland and San Francisco are seen as in a panorama. Oakland is an exceedingly attractive city, besides being a great manufacturing and commercial center.

Alameda, a city of 11,165 inhabitants, neighbors it upon the south, with separate ferries to San Francisco.

Directly west of Oakland, against the northern shores of San Francisco, lies the Golden Gate, ahead and a little to the right of the course of the ferryboat. It is the only tideway between the bay and the ocean, a passage $3\frac{1}{2}$ miles long and one mile wide, separating two embracing peninsulas.

San Francisco.— Chicago, 2,577 miles; St. Louis, 2,437 miles; Los Angeles, 482 miles. Population, 298,997. Altitude, from sea-level to 938 feet above. Altitude at Market Street Ferry, 12 feet.

Like most cities of the upper Pacific Coast, San Francisco is built upon many hills, some of which, like Mission Peaks and Russian, Telegraph, Rincon, and Reservoir hills, are abrupt and lofty. It occupies an entire county, which bears the same name, covering the northern extremity of the southernmost of the two peninsulas which separate San Francisco Bay from the Pacific Ocean. This bay is sixty-five miles long, and has an average width of eight miles. Upon the ocean front, at Point Lobos, a good sand-beach, the Seal Rocks, and the surmounting bluff of Sutro Heights form an attractive resort. On the Golden Gate frontage, at Fort Point, is the Presidio Reservation, a military station with the largest garrison on the Pacific Coast. Fort Point is furnished with heavy cannon, and commands the narrowest part of the Golden Gate. Alcatraz Island and Angel Island are likewise fortified.

San Francisco was founded in 1850 as a city, although since 1776 there has been a settlement here in consequence of the erection and maintenance of the Mission Dolores. The principal thoroughfare is Market Street, which begins at the ferry slips on the bay. The finest residences are located principally on California Street and **Van Ness Avenue.** Only of late has San Francisco ventured upon the construction of tall and substantial business buildings, because of the supposition that earthquakes would destroy them. For this reason the city is less imposing architecturally than many centers of a smaller population in other parts of the country; but the immunity enjoyed by the first experiments in many-

CHINESE RESTAURANT.

storied structures of brick and stone has given confidence in that direction, and every year many handsome edifices arise. The residences, however, are chiefly frame buildings, although many are very costly.

Oakland, Alameda, Berkeley, San Rafael, Menlo Park, etc., are used by many San Francisco business men for suburban homes. It is also claimed that a greater number of permanent residents live in this city, in hotels and boarding-houses, than is the case in any other city of the United States. Of hotels there are more than a hundred, and an extraordinary number of family boarding-houses, lodging-houses, and restaurants, among which last the visitor who enjoys knocking about may learn, by judicious inquiry, of two or three places, externally unpretentious, which for excellence of food and service can hardly be surpassed.

There are nine public libraries and many large private book collections, 114 churches and eighty-nine graded public schools. The city hall and the United States Mint are the noblest buildings. There are many public parks of various size, the largest of which is Golden Gate Park — the site of the Midwinter Fair of 1894 — an exquisite garden of 1,013 acres reached by a short ride on the street-cars.

The Mission Dolores stands on the corner of Dolores and Sixteenth streets.

SAN FRANCISCO'S CHINATOWN.— The abode of the Celestials covers about ten blocks in the heart of the city. They number more than 20,000, and follow the vocations of laborer, laundryman, and merchant for outside patrons, and are engaged in every conceivable industry and trade among themselves, dwelling in and on the houses, and underground in a labyrinth of dark passages and closet-like compartments. The Flowery Kingdom itself can hardly be more typically Chinese, for the quarter is entirely given up to them. Endowed with a fair ability to endure disagreeable odors, and to confront many sights that are not congenial to a highly civilized taste, the visitor to Chinatown will find much of absorbing interest. While the Chinese stores are frequented by day, for the purpose of making purchases, the conventional trip is made at night, in charge of a guide, who can be secured at short notice on application to the clerk at any of the leading hotels. Almost every night in the year tourists are thus conducted through Chinatown, and the solitary traveler who desires the experience can usually arrange to join a party, the cost of employing the guide being divided on a per capita basis. About three hours are consumed in making the customary round, which is so planned as to give the visitor a fair notion of the life of this quaint community. Shops of merchants, butchers, apothecaries, and artisans, and restaurants, joss-houses, theaters, gambling quarters, and opium dens are features of the programme.

The joss-houses, or temples, are very richly furnished and contain a number of hideous images of Chinese gods. The air is pungent with the fumes of burning joss-sticks and sandal-wood, and the worshipful attendants will interrogate Fate on behalf of the inquisitive for a consideration.

In the restaurants excellent tea and many palatable dainties are served. They are very neat and quiet, and in some instances the furniture is elaborate and costly.

In the theater will be found much that is grotesque and entertaining, aside from the purport of the play, which will be mainly unintelligible to the average Caucasian visitor. The stage is very deep, and on it are gathered actors, musicians, supernumeraries, and itinerant sightseers. The actors fairly elbow their way to and from the clear center of the stage; visitors and stage-hands smoke and walk about at will; the orchestra in the rear, made up of heavy cymbals or gongs and shrill-stringed instruments, hammers and squeals to give emotional stress to the passages of the play, and the actors deliver their parts in a forced artificial voice, half-singing in monotonous cadences. Only the most rudimentary suggestion of scenery is used, and only men are permitted to impersonate, as on the English stage up to a comparatively recent date. Youths, beautifully costumed, and made up for the part, bear the female rôles, and speak in falsetto tones. Some of these impersonators are celebrated actors among their race, and draw crowded houses, like the famous actresses of other nations. The plays are long-drawn out, and many of them require several evenings for a complete performance, although there are dramas that can be given entire between the hours of 5 P. M. and midnight. Many current Chinese plays are classics, having held the boards for many centuries with undiminished popularity. Of the Chinese theater-goers, the men sit in the pit with their hats on, and the women in the galleries. There is no applause, beyond the tribute of strained silence in the tragic passages and laughter in the comedy portions, which, in the case of the female rôles, are often rendered in a manner so mischievous and sparkling, and so full of feminine grace, as to call for a high artistic ability in the performance.

In regard to opium smoking, it should be stated that among the better class of Chinese, who are usually worthy of respect and confidence, the practice is deprecated and avoided, as any degraded habit is frowned upon by the refined among other nationalities. There are many Chinamen who smoke opium, but there are as many or more who do not. The opium pipe is a long-stemmed affair, with a thick round head which is nearly flat on top and solid except for a small aperture in the center. With this and a small lamp, tray, and implements for the manipulation of the drug at his side, the smoker, curled up on a broad bench or bunk, takes a small quantity of prepared opium on the end of a needle-like implement and holds it in the flame of the lamp, turning it over and over. The opium swells and undergoes a process of partial roasting while it is alternately held in the flame and rolled into a ball on the top of the pipe. When it has been brought to the proper condition it is pressed upon the aperture of the pipe, perforated by the needle, and held to the flame again while the smoker inhales the fumes through the pipe-stem. Two or three puffs exhaust the opium, and the process is repeated until the smoker is satisfied or stupefied. There are haggard and wasted old men in Chinatown who are said to subsist almost wholly upon the smoke of opium.

The Society of Highbinders is a perversion of an organization originally instituted in China by a band of patriots, and corrupted before its importation into this country. Blackmail, illicit traffic, and personal and party feuds were pursued under this organization in San Francisco until the audacity of its deeds of violence and its defiance of law became a scandal, and public opinion demanded its suppression. Foremost in the movement for its destruction were the women of the Chinese missions, whose sympathy was excited for the female slaves imported from China by members of the society and landed by the aid of corrupt American lawyers who were fertile in expedients for evading the law. A descent upon the strongholds of the Highbinders was made by the police, and many were captured, some of whom were executed and others imprisoned for their crimes. The society was not absolutely destroyed, but only at long intervals during the past two years has any outbreak occurred that could be charged to it.

SOUTHWARD FROM SAN FRANCISCO, THROUGH THE SANTA CLARA VALLEY.

SANTA CLARA VALLEY.— Southeastward from San Francisco, west of the bay, the Coast Division (Third and Townsend Streets Station) of the Southern Pacific Railroad extends, continuing on through the spacious valley of Santa Clara, which is hemmed by hills and mountains. This lovely valley, which constitutes the horticultural region of Santa Clara County, has a larger acreage of orchards and vineyards than any other county in the State. The largest seed-farms in the world and one-half of all the prune trees in the United States are here, and one-half the total annual crop of strawberries in the United States is raised here. The largest horse-breeding establishment in the United States and the largest herds of Jersey cattle are also in Santa Clara County, and its list of superlatives further includes the Lick Observatory, with the largest telescope in the world, and the Stanford University.

The visitor to Palo Alto, San Jose, Santa Cruz, and Monterey will pass through this valley.

Palo Alto.— Thirty-three miles from San Francisco. Altitude, 57 feet.

Location of the Leland Stanford Junior University and of the Stanford stables, which can also be reached from Menlo Park, the station one mile above Palo Alto. Public carriages are in waiting on arrival of trains.

The university, a memorial of the only son of the late Senator Stanford, is situated in a campus of 8,000 acres, which contains the mausoleum of the Stanfords — a small Greek temple of marble — and a great variety of trees and shrubs. The entire estate which ultimately is to accrue comprises 85,000 acres. The architecture of the buildings is Romanesque, after the type of the old missions — twelve oblong one-story structures of buff sandstone connected by a continuous arcade around an immense inner court containing three and a quarter acres, paved with asphalt and ornamented with beds of tropical flowers. All this is to be inclosed in another quadrangle whose buildings will be two stories high; and six smaller quadrangles outside the great quadrangle are included in the plan of future extension. The dormitories are taller buildings, with elevators, electric lights, hot and cold water, steam heat, etc. There are also cottages used by the president and the professors for homes, and a noble museum building. The scope of the university is broad. Students are encouraged to choose their future calling, and their course of study is shaped accordingly. It is open to both sexes.

The Stanford stables are full of entertainment and instruction for those who take an interest in race-horses and their training. The establishment includes stables, paddocks, "kindergartens" in which colts are taught from a tender age what is expected of them upon a track, and race-courses for the older horses.

San Jose. — Fifty miles from San Francisco. Altitude, 86 feet. Population, 18,060.

Connected with San Francisco by two other railroad lines, which run east of the bay. This city, together with its immediate neighbor Santa Clara, ships enormous quantities of green, dried, and canned fruits, berries, wine, brandy, and miscellaneous products. It is a wealthy modern city, with broad macadamized streets, excellent business blocks, attractive residences, many churches and schools, half a dozen banks, and first-rate hotels.

From San Jose a stage makes daily the round trip to Lick Observatory, only thirteen miles distant in an air line, but twenty-six miles by the road, which overcomes the mountain slopes by regular gradients involving 367 turns. The observatory is situated on the summit of Mount Hamilton, whose altitude is 4,443 feet. It was a bequest of the late James Lick, a millionaire of San Jose, and cost $750,000. The glass of the great telescope, thirty-six inches in diameter, consumed three years' labor in making, and cost $55,000. This is the glass through which the fifth satellite of Jupiter was discovered by Professor Barnard in 1892. On Saturday night in every week, between the hours of 7 and 10 o'clock, visitors are permitted to gaze through the great Lick telescope, and on that night the stage returns to San Jose at a late hour for the accommodation of those who desire to avail themselves of this privilege. On other days, however, all visitors are courteously shown through the observatory, and allowed to look through a twelve-inch telescope, which is powerful enough to magnify Venus to apparently half the size of the moon, and render it visible at brightest midday.

Monterey.— One hundred and twenty-five miles from San Francisco. Altitude (at station), 5 feet. Population, 1,662.

Named by Viscaino in 1602, in honor of the patron of his expedition, Gaspar de Zuniga, Count of Monte Rey. *Monte* means either "mountain" or "forest" in the Spanish tongue, but, in the case of Count Zuniga, *Monte Rey* signified "Mountain King," and that, therefore, is the proper translation of the name of this old town. In the case of the Hotel del Monte, however, the word *monte* means "forest," and *del monte* means "of the forest." This noble hotel, whose fame is inseparable from that of Monterey, stands among live-oaks and pines of great size and age, in a wonderful garden of 126 acres, whose bloom is most gorgeous in time of winter — rose, pansy, calla, heliotrope, narcissus, tulip, and crocus fraternizing with rare flowering plants from regions south of the equator. Every provision for enjoyment has been made for guests, both indoors and out. There are row-boats on a lake of fifteen acres extent within the grounds, tennis courts, croquet grounds, swings, mazes, delightful shady walks along which benches are scattered, and perfectly-kept macadamized drives leading to natural attractions of hill, valley, and shore.

The town of Monterey is a mile distant from the hotel, at the southern end of the bay. Here, first in California, a cross was planted, an altar erected, and a mass celebrated, by Viscaino, in 1602. In 1770 Serra founded here, by the sea, the mission San Carlos de Monterey, which in the following year was removed to Carmelo Valley, five miles back from the coast, and renamed San Carlos de Carmelo. The old stone church still stands, the remains of Serra buried beneath its sanctuary. Here took place the first Indian baptism in California, and the first European woman to emigrate to these shores arrived at Monterey in 1783.

Two miles beyond the town is Pacific Grove. A few years ago this was merely an annual camping-ground for the Conference of the Methodist Episcopal church. It has grown to a pretty town which numbers 5,000 inhabitants in the height of the season. Various religious and temperance organizations hold conventions here from year to year. Bathing, sailing, and fishing are to be had.

Half a mile beyond Pacific Grove is Point Pinos, upon which stands an old granite light-house, still in service, and beyond that lies Moss Beach.

From the Hotel del Monte a roadway leads through Monterey across the peninsula, and past Pescadero Beach, Chinese Cove, Pebble Beach, Cypress Point, Seal Rocks, Moss Beach, and through Pacific Grove back to the hotel. This is "the seventeen-mile drive," and includes most of the points of interest at Monterey.

Santa Cruz.— One hundred and twenty-one miles from San Francisco. Altitude, 18 feet. Population, 5,596.

Reached either by way of the Monterey line (Coast Division) as far as Pajaro, thence via the Santa Cruz line, or all the way by the Santa Cruz Division, leaving San Francisco by the Alameda ferry at the foot of Market Street, and from Alameda coasting the eastern shore of the bay and passing through San Jose and Pajaro.

Before the building of the Hotel del Monte at Monterey, and the Hotel del Coronado at Coronado, Santa Cruz

BIG TREES NEAR SANTA CRUZ.

was the most fashionable seaside resort in the State, and it is still very popular. It lies opposite Monterey, on the north, upon the same bay. Its location and surroundings are highly picturesque and full of interest, and the climate is only less delightful than at Monterey. There is a bathing beach of fine white sand, and there are many enjoyable drives; the light-house, Natural Bridge, Laguna Falls, Ben Lomond Road, Pebbly Beach, Magnetic Spring,

Loma Prieta, and the Big Tree Grove being a few of the attractions. This grove of mammoth redwoods (*Sequoia sempervirens*) is one of the sights of California, and not at all to be despised by the traveler who has seen the *Sequoia gigantea*, and is very easily visited, being only five miles distant by rail from Santa Cruz. It covers twenty acres, and numbers scores of trees from ten to twenty feet in diameter, the largest being 300 feet high and 21 feet through at the base. In 1847 Fremont camped in the hollow of one of these redwoods, which bears his name.

San Luis Obispo.—Two hundred and forty-six miles from San Francisco. Population, 2,995.

This poetic town lies ten miles beyond the end of the Coast Division, connected with the railroad at Santa Margarita by stage.

It can also be reached from Santa Barbara by stage to Los Olivos, forty-five miles, and thence via the Pacific Coast Railway, sixty-six miles.

Here this guide-book properly comes to a close. There are numerous points of interest in California upon the north and east of San Francisco, but their description can not be undertaken herein. The reader will find below, however, a brief memorandum locating and individualizing half a dozen cities whose names are most familiar.

Berkeley.—Population, 5,101. A short distance north of Oakland, reached by electric and steam roads, the seat of the University of California, and a suburb of San Francisco.

Stockton.—Ninety-two miles from San Francisco, via Niles and Tracy. One hundred and three miles via Port Costa and Tracy. Population, 14,424.

A manufacturing center, in a prosperous agricultural region.

Sacramento.— Ninety miles from San Francisco, via Port Costa and Benicia. One hundred and forty miles via Niles, Tracy, and Stockton. Also reached by river steamers from San Francisco. Altitude, 30 feet. Population, 26,386.

The capital of the State. A center of railroads, manufacture, and trade. Situated at the junction of the Ogden Route and the Shasta Route of the Southern Pacific Company. It is a well-built city, containing many features of interest, among which the capitol and the Crocker Art Gallery with a very valuable collection of paintings are conspicuous.

Marysville.— One hundred and twenty-five miles from San Francisco via Davis and Woodland; 142 miles via Port Costa, Benicia, and Sacramento. Altitude, 66 feet. Population, 3,991.

A wholesale trade center.

Napa.— Forty-six miles from San Francisco via Vallejo Junction. Population, 4,395.

Location of the Napa Soda Springs.

Santa Rosa.— Seventy-five miles from San Francisco via Vallejo Junction. Population, 5,220.

In Sonoma County, which is famous for fruits. Fruit-canning and wine-making are the chief industries.

VOCABULARY OF SPANISH AND INDIAN NAMES.

NOTE.— Except for the purpose of determining the syllabic accent of Spanish words, the reader who may chance to be unfamiliar with the Spanish tongue will have little need of a pronouncing dictionary if he will take note of the following easily remembered rules governing the sound of vowels and the exceptional consonants:

A never has the sound of *a* in *fate*, but is sounded as in *father*. *E* is like *a* in *fate*, and sometimes short, as in *met*. *I* is like *ee* in *feet*, and sometimes short, as in *bit*. *O* is nearly as sonorous as in the English word *bone*. (The clipped enunciation of the vowels *oa* in *road*, *coat*, etc., which one occasionally hears, is a more exact equivalent.) *U* is never like *u* in *acute*, nor quite like *oo* in *noon;* but like *u* in *full*. *Y* is sounded like the Spanish *i*.

Mexicans do not lisp *z* and soft *c*, as do Castilians, but give them the harshest sibilance of the letter *s*. *H* is not sounded at all, except when combined with *c* (when the two form a distinct consonant, which is invariably sounded as in *church*). *G* (when soft) and *j* are sounded almost precisely like *ch* in the German word *Ich*. It is almost impossible to acquire the exact sound except by imitation. It is a guttural, lying somewhere between the letter *k* and a forcibly aspirated *h*. For all practical purposes the latter will suffice. *Ll* is a separate letter of the alphabet, and in Spain has the sound of *lli* in *million*, but the Spanish-speaking peoples of America universally give it only the sound of an initial *y*, or of long *e*, as in *Cerrillo* (a little hill), which is pronounced ser-*re*-yo. *Ñ* (*n* with the tilde) is a distinct letter and is sounded like *ny* in *canyon*.

An English phonetic equivalent for the sound of foreign words, without the use of special marks, is not always practicable. One reason, among others, is that the equivalent offered will frequently be found to take on the form of an English word, by whose proper pronunciation the reader is liable to be misled. An example in point is the Spanish syllable *los*, whose pronunciation can not be communicated on a printed page by letters alone, for the natural phonetic equivalent would be spelled *lose*, and this is a word which happens to be pronounced quite unlike that whose sound is sought to be conveyed. In the following pages, therefore, where will be found a list of the most prominent Spanish names mentioned in the present volume as likely to be encountered on the journey, together with their pronunciation and their signification, unless they have been corrupted beyond identification with the original word, a few of the marks commonly used in dictionaries will be availed of to indicate the sound of vowels, namely, ä as in *father*, ā as in *fate*, ĕ as in *feet*, ĕ as in *met*, ī as in *bite*, ĭ as in *bit*, ō as in *bone*, ŏ as in *short*, ü as in *full*.

Acequia (Ä-sā'-kē-ä). Irrigating ditch.
Acequia Madre (Ä-sā'-kē-ä Mä'-drĕ). Parent (mother), or main ditch.
Acoma [Indian] (Ä'-cō-mä). A pueblo of the Quéres in New Mexico.
Adobe (Ä-dō'-bĕ). Sun-dried brick made of earth, mixed with chopped straw. Also a kind of soil whose character corresponds with that suitable for making adobe.
Agua Caliente (Ä'-wä Cäl-yĕn'-tĕ). Hot water.
Agua Fria (Ä'-wä Frē'-yä). Cold water.
Alameda (Ä-lä-mā'-dä). A grove of poplars: a shaded walk.
Alcatraz (Äl-cä-träs'). Pelican.
Albuquerque (Äl-bü-kĕr'-kĕ). Family name. Possibly a corruption of *albaricoque*, apricot.
Algodones (Äl-gō-dō'-nĕs). Cottons; cotton lands.
Aliso (Ä-lē'-sō). Alder-bush.
Almaden (Äl-mä-dĕn'). A place of mineral deposits.
Amargosa (Ä-mär-gō'-sä). Bitter.
Anacapa (Ä-nä-cä'-pä). One of the channel islands off Santa Barbara.
Arena (Ä-rā'-nä). Sand.
Arroyo (Är-rō'-yō). A wash made by water; an intermittent water-channel; less than a cañon.
Arroyo Seco (Sā'-cō). A dry *arroyo*.
Azusa (Ä-sü'-sä). Provocation; annoyance.
Baño (Bän'-yō). Bath.
Belen (Bā-lĕn'). The name is associated with a famous siege in Spain.

Bernal (Bĕr-näl'). Proper name.
Bernalillo (Bĕr-nä-lē'-yō). Little Bernal.
Buenaventura (B'wä'-nä-vĕn-tü'-rä). Good luck.
Buena Vista (B'wä'-nä Vēs'-tä). Unobstructed view.
Cabeza de Vaca (Cä-bä'-sä dĕ Vä'-cä). Cow's head; a Spanish explorer.
Cabrillo, Juan Rodriguez (Cä-brēl'-yō, H'wän Rō-drē'-ghĕs). A Spanish navigator.
Cajon (Cä-hōn'). Box.
Cajon Pass. Box pass.
Calaveras (Cä-lä-vä'-räs). Skulls.
Califa (Cä-lē'-fä). Caliph.
Cañada (Cän-yä'-dä). Glen; dale.
Cañada de los Alisos (Ä-lē'-sōs). Alder-glen.
Cañon (Cän-yōn'), but commonly accented on the first syllable. A ravine; a deep fissure.
Cañon de Chelly (Shä). A cañon in New Mexico.
Cañon Diablo (Dē-ä'-blō). Devil Cañon.
Carpinteria (Cär-pĭn-tĕr-ē'-ä). Carpenter shop.
Carrizo (Cär-rē'-sō). A kind of reed grass.
Casa Blanca (Cä-sä Blän'-cä). White house.
Casa Grande (Grän'-dĕ). Big house.
Centinela (Sĕn-tĭ-nĕl'-ä). Sentinel.
Cerrillos (Sĕr-rē'-yōs). Small round hills. Diminutive plural of *cerro*.
Cerro Gordo (Sĕr-rō Gŏr'-dō). A thick ridge.
Chaves (Chä'-vĕs). A family name.
Chico (Chē'-cō). Little.
Chino (Chē'-nō). Chinaman.
Cholla (Chŏ'-yä). A variety of cactus.
Cimarron (Sĭm-är-rōn'). Wild; unruly; a mountain sheep.
Cochití [Indian] (Cō-chĭ-tē'). Name of a pueblo.
Colorado (Cō-lō-rä'-dō). Red; ruddy.
Contra Costa (Cōn'-trä-Cōs'-tä). Coast opposite another.
Coronado (Cō-rō-nä'-dō). Family name; crowned.
Corral (Cŏr-räl'). Pen; out-of-door inclosure.
Cosnino (Cōs-nē'-nō).
Cubero (Cü-bä'-rō). Cooper.
Cucamonga (Cü-cä-mŏn'-gü).
Culebra (Cü-lä'-brü). Snake.

De Luz (Dĕ Lüs'). Of light.
Del Mar (Dĕl Mär'). Of, or by, the sea.
Del Norte (Nŏr'-tĕ). Of the north.
Dolores (Dō-lō'-rĕs). Pains; a woman's name.
El Capitan (El Cä-pī-tän'). The captain.
El Dorado (El Dō-rä'-dō). The golden; the gilded.
El Molino (Mō-lē'-nō). The mill.
El Monte (Mŏn'-tĕ). The forest; the mountain.
Elota (Ā-lō'-tä).
El Paso (Pä'-sō). The pass.
El Rito (Rē'-tō). The ceremony.
El Toro (Tō'-rō). The bull.
Encinitas (En-sī-nē'-täs). Little oaks.
Fresno (Frĕs'-nō). Ash tree.
Gallinas (Gä-yē'näs). Hens; turkeys.
Gaviota (Gäv-yō'-tä). Sea-gull.
Gila (Hē'-lä). Name of a river.
Glorieta (Glō-rī-ä'-tä). Summer-house; bower.
Goleta (Gō-lā'-tä). Schooner.
Hualpai [Indian] (H'wäl'-pī). Name of a tribe.
Indio (Ind'-yō). Indian.
Isleta (Is-lā'-tä). Little island. Diminutive of *isla*.
Jacal (Hä-cäl'). An Indian hut.
Jemez (Hā'-mĕs). Name of a Pueblo tribe.
Junipero Serra (Hü-nē'-pĕ-rō Sĕr'-rä). Founder of the California missions.
La Cañada (Lä Cän-yä'-dä). The glen.
La Costa (Cōs'-tä). The coast.
Ladrillo (Lä-drē'-yō). Brick.
Laguna (Lä-gü'-nä). Lake.
La Jolla (Lä Hō'-yä). An eroded cliff near San Diego.
La Joya (Lä Hō'-yä). The jewel.
La Junta (Lä Hün'-tä). The junction.
Las Animas (Lä-sä'-nī-mäs). (Pronounced like one word.) The souls.
Las Cruces (Läs Crü'-sĕs). The crosses.
Las Flores (Läs Flō'-rĕs). The flowers.
Las Vegas (Läs Vā'-gäs). The meadows.
Lerdo (Lĕr'-dō). Slow.
Linda (Lĭn'-dä). Pretty.
Loma (Lō'-mä). Slope; rising ground.

Los Angeles (pronounced like one word, Lō-sän'-hĕ-lĕs, but commonly Lō-sän'-ghĕ-lĕs. The name of this city has locally two or three pronunciations, all corrupt). The angels. (Contracted from *Pueblo de la Reina de los Angeles* — Town of the Queen of the Angels.)
Los Baños (Bän'-yōs). The baths.
Los Gatos (Gä'-tōs). The cats.
Los Nietos (Nē-ā'-tōs). The grandchildren.
Luna (Lü'-nä). Moon.
Machado (Mä-chä'-dō). Hatchet.
Madera (Mä-dā'-rä). Wood.
Madron (Mä-drōn'), Madrono (Mä-drō'-nō). A kind of tree.
Malpais (properly Mäl-pīs', but corrupted to Mäl'-pī). Bad country. Applied to small bowlders of volcanic rock, which are thickly scattered over some parts of the West.
Manitou [Indian] (Män'-ĭ-tü). Great Spirit.
Manuelito (Män-wĕl-ē'-tō). Little Emanuel. Diminutive of Manuel.
Manzanita (Män-sä-nē'-tä). Little apple; a California shrub.
Marcos de Niza (Mär'-cōs dē Nē'-sä). Mark of Nice; a Spanish monk and explorer.
Mariposa (Mä-rĭ-pō'-sä). Butterfly.
Mendocino (Mĕn-dō-sē'-nō). A little liar.
Merced (Mĕr-sĕd'). Mercy.
Mesa (Mā'-sä). A flat-topped hill; diminutive *mesilla*.
Mesa Encantada (En-cän-tä'-dä). Haunted hill.
Mesquit (Mĕs-kēt'). A shrub of the acacia family.
Modesto (Mō-dĕs'-tō). Modest.
Mogollon (Mō-gō-yōn'). Parasite.
Mojave (Mō-hä'-vĕ). Name of an Indian tribe.
Montecito (Mŏn-tĕ-sē'-tō). Little mountain, or forest.
Monterey (Mŏn-tĕ-rā'). Forest King.
Moqui (Mō'-kī). Name of a Pueblo tribe.
Morena (Mō-rā'-nä). Brown.
Nambé (Näm-bā'). Name of an Indian pueblo.
Navajo (Nä'-vä-hō). An Indian tribe. (The Spanish word, accented on the second syllable, signifies a level piece of ground.)
Navidad (Nä-vĭ-däd'). Nativity.
Olla (O'-yä). A round earthen pot.
Oro Grande (O-rō Grän'-dĕ). Much gold.

Pajaro (Pä'-hä-rō). Bird.
Pala (Pä'-lä). Wooden shovel.
Palo Alto (Pä'-lō Äl'-tō). Tall timber.
Pasadena (Pä-sä-dä'-nä). Of imputed Indian origin, signifying Crown of the Valley; or possibly a corruption of the Spanish *Paso de Eden* (Pä'-sō-dä-děn'), Gateway of Eden.
Patio (Pät'-yō). Court.
Pecos (Pā'-cōs). Freckles (supposed to be a corruption of *pecas*).
Penitentes, Los Hermanos (Lōs Ěr-män'-ōs Pěn-ĭ-těn-těs). The Penitent Brotherhood.
Pescadero (Pěs-cä-dä'-rō). Fishmonger.
Picacho (Pĭ-cä'-chō). Summit.
Piedra Pintada (Pē-ā'-drä Pĭn-tä'-dä). Painted rock.
Pima (Pē'-mä). Name of an Indian tribe.
Piñon (Pĭn-yōn') A species of nut-bearing pine.
Pinos (Pē'-nōs). Pines.
Placer (Plä-sěr'). Sand or gravel deposit in which free gold is found.
Plaza (Plä'-sä). Public square.
Poso (Pō'-sō). Rest.
Presidio (Prě-sĭd'-yō). Garrison.
Pueblo (P'wěb'-lō). Village; populace. Applied to the sedentary tribes of New Mexico and Arizona, and also to their habitations.
Puerco (P'wěr'-cō). Pig; dirty; foul.
Purisima (Pü-rĭs'-ĭ-mä). Purest; applied to the Virgin.
Quéres [Indian] (Cā'-rěs). Name of a Pueblo tribe.
Raton (Rä-tōn'). Mouse.
Rayado (Rä-yä'-dō). Streaked; variegated.
Redondo (Rě-dōn'-dō). Round.
Rincon (Rĭn-cōn'). An inside corner.
Rio, Rio Vista, Rio Grande, etc. (Rē'-ō, Vē'-stä, Grän'-dě). River, river view, big river.
Rosario (Rō-sä'-rē-ō). Rosary.
Rubio (Rüb'-yō). Red.
Saguache [Indian] (Sä-wäsh'). Name of a mountain range.
Salida (Sä-lē'-dä). Departure.
Salinas (Sä-lē'-näs). Salt mines.
San Andreas (Sän Än-drās'). St. Andrew.
San Bernardino (Běr-när-dē'-nō). St. Bernard.
San Carlos (Cär'-lōs). St. Charles.

San Diego (Dē-ä'-gō). St. James; diminutive *Dieguito*.
San Dimas (Dĭ-mäs'). St. Demas.
San Francisco. St. Francis.
San Gabriel (Gä-brē-ĕl'). St. Gabriel.
Sangre de Cristo (Sän'-grĕ dĕ Crĭs'-tō). Blood of Christ.
San Jacinto (Hä-sēn'-tō). St. Jacinth.
San Joaquin (H'wä-kēn'). St. Joachim.
San Jose (Hō-sä'). St. Joseph.
San Juan (H'wän — *Not* like *a* in *swan*). St. John.
San Juan Bautista (Bä-ü-tēs'-tä'). St. John Baptist.
San Juan Capistrano (Cä-pĭs-trä'-nō). Name of a sainted Italian monk.
San Luis Obispo (Sän Lü'-ĭs O-bĭs'-pō). St. Louis bishop.
San Luis Rey (Rā). St. Louis king.
San Mateo (Mä-tä'-ō). St. Matthew.
San Miguel (Mĭ-ghĕl'). St. Michael.
San Pascual (Päs-k'wäl'). Holy Easter.
San Pedro (Pä'-drō). St. Peter.
San Tomas (Tō-mäs'). St. Thomas.
Santa Ana (pronounced like one word, Sän-tän'-ä). St. Ann.
Santa Anita (pronounced like one word, Sän-tän-ē'-tä). Diminutive of Santa Ana.
Santa Catalina (Sän'-tä Cä-tä-lē'-nä). St. Catherine.
Santa Cruz (Crüs). Holy Cross.
Santa Fé (Fā). Holy Faith.
Santa Monica (Mŏn'-ĭ-cä). St. Monica.
Santa Paula (Sän-tä Pä'-ü-lä). St. Paulina.
Santa Ynez (pronounced like one word, Sän-tĭ-nĕs'). St. Inez.
Santiago (Sän-tĭ-ä'-gō). St. James; war-cry of the Spaniards.
Sierra (Sē-ĕr'-rä). Saw-tooth; range of mountains.
Sierra Madre (Mä'-drĕ). Mother (parent); range.
Sierra Nevada (Nĕ-vä'-dä). Snowy range.
Soledad (Sō-lĕ-däd'). Solitude.
Supai [Indian] (Sü'-pī). Name of a tribe.
Tahoe [Indian] (Tä'-ō). Name of a lake on the Nevada-California boundary.
Tamal (Tä-mäl'). An Indian tribe; a Mexican edible compound. Plural, *tamales*.
Tamalpais (Tä-mäl'-pîs, *but* the final *s* is not commonly sounded). Tamal country; a mountain near San Francisco.

Tehachapi [Indian] (Tĕ-hä'-chä-pī). Name of a mountain and pass.

Tehua [Indian] (Tā'-wä). Name of a Pueblo tribe.

Temecula (Tĕ-mĕc'-ü-lä). Name of a mountain pass.

Tesuque (Tĕ-sü'-kĕ). Name of an Indian pueblo.

Tia Juana (pronounced like one word, Tĕ-h'wä'-nä). Aunt Jane.

Tigua [Indian] (Tē'-wä). Name of a Pueblo tribe.

Tinaja (Tĭ-nä'-hä). A large earthen jar.

Trinidad (Trĭ-nĭ-däd', but commonly accented on the first syllable). The Trinity.

Tropico (Trō'-pĭ-cō). Tropical.

Tulare (Tü-lä'-rĕ). A place of rushes.

Ute [Indian] (Ūt). Name of a tribe.

Verde (Vĕr'-dĕ). Green.

Viscaino, Sebastian (Sĕ-bäs'-tĭ-än Vĭs-cä'-ī-nō). Biscayan; a Spanish navigator.

Yorba (Yŏr-bä). A family name.

Ynez (E-nĕs'). Inez.

Yosemite [Indian] (Yō-sĕm'-ĭ-tĕ). Big grizzly bear.

Zia (Sē'-ä). Name of an Indian pueblo.

Zuñi (Sün'yĭ). Name of a Pueblo tribe.

INDEX.

	PAGE		PAGE
Abbyville	33	ARIZONA.	
Acoma Pueblo	102	Historical	108
Acton	238	Descriptive	110
Agua Fria Valley	140	Industrial	113, 134
Alameda, N. M.	98	Arizona Climate	136, 145
Alameda, Cal.	248, 250	Arkansas River	32
Alameda County, Cal.	248	Arlington	226
Albuquerque	98	Arrowhead	213
Alden	33	Arrowhead Springs	203, 213
Alessandro	224	Ash Fork	134
Algodones	98	Ash Hill	198
Alila	240	Asylum	213
Allantown	114	Atherton	15
Allison	232	Athlone	246
Almond Culture	190	Atlantic & Pacific Junction	100
Alvord	226	Atwater	246
Amboy	198	Aubrey	156
Anacapa Island	237	Avalon	214
Anaheim	217	Avon	247
Ancona	13	Ayer	62
Angell	119	Aztec	114
Antioch	247, 248	Azul	83
Apache Cañon	91	Azusa	205
Aplin	213	Bagdad	198
Appleton	13	Bakersfield	239
Apricot Culture	192	Ballona Junction	213, 216
Arcadia	205	Bandini	217
Arch Beach	217	Banta	247
Arena, Cal.	214	Barclay	28
Arena, Cal.	246	Baring	14
Argentine	24	Barstow	201
Argyle	14	Barstow to San Bernardino	202

INDEX.

	PAGE
Base Line	213
Beal	196
Bealville	238
Bellefont	34
Bellemont	134
Bell's Cañon	138
Belpre	33
Bennett	29
Benton	62
Bent's Fort	39, 48
Berkeley	250, 260
Bernal	84
Bernalillo	98
Berenda	244
Berry	156
Bethany	247
Big Trees	244, 260
Billings	114
Bissell	201
Blake	198
Blanchard	84
Blodgett	12
Blossburg	79
Bluewater	105
Borden	242
Bosworth	15
Bottomless Pits	132
Box Cañon	139
Box Springs	224
Braddock	29
Brentwood	247
Bristol	198
Bucklin	15
Buena	222
Buena Vista	59
Buffalo Trails	33
Burbank	238
Burlingame	28
Burrton	30

	PAGE
Byrneville	12
Byron, Cal.	247
Byron, Col.	47
Cacti	111
Caddoa	47
Cadiz	198
Cajon	203
Cajon Pass	202
Caliente	238
Califa	246
CALIFORNIA.	
Historical	158
Descriptive	169
Climate	171, 231, 235
Industrial	180
Cama	14
Camden	15
Cameron, Cal.	238
Cameron, Ill.	13
Camulos	234
Cañoncito	92
Cañon de Chelly	107, 116
Cañon Diablo	118
Capistrano	217
Carbondale	28
Carlsbad	223
Carlton	47
Carmelo Mission	258
Carpinteria	235
Carrizo	114
Carrollton	15
Casa Blanca	226
Cascade Cañon	57
Castle Creek Hot Springs	140
Caton	13
Cave of the Winds	56
Cedar Grove	29
Cedar Junction	24
Centinela	213

INDEX.

	PAGE		PAGE
Central Avenue	213	Contra Costa County, Cal.	247
Ceres	246	Coolidge, Kan.	38
Chalcedony Park	114	Coolidge, N. M.	106
Challender	134	Coronado Beach	230
Channel Islands	237	Cosnino	119
Chapman	206	Cottonwood	202
Charleston	36	Cottonwood Valley	28
Chaves	105	Courtney	15
Cheyenne Cañon	51	Cowles	232
Chicago	10	Cripple Creek	58
Chicago to Kansas City	9	Crookton	155
Chillicothe	13	Cross Creek	242
Chinatown, San Francisco	251	Crozier	156
Chino	156	Cubero	102
Chino Valley	135	Cucamonga	204
Choteau	24	Daggett	198
Chula Vista	233	Dahinda	13
Cimarron, Kan.	36	Dallas	14
Cimarron, N. M.	82	Dana's Point	219
Cinder Pit	134	Danby	198
Claremont	205	Dartmouth	33
Clarendon	33	Davenport	134
Clements	29	Dean Lake	15
Cliff and Cave Dwellings	130	Death Valley	198
Coal City	13	Decorra	14
College Peaks	59	Deerfield	38
Collis	247	Defiance	107
Colmor	83	Delano	240
COLORADO.		Delhi	62
Historical	38	Del Mar	223
Descriptive	39	Del Rosa	213
Climate	42	De Luz	223
Industrial	46	Dennison	118
Colorado Resorts	50	Denver	61
Colorado River	157	Desert Plants	111
Colorado Springs	50	De Soto	24
Colton	224	Dillon	81
Continental Divide, Colo.	60	Dillwyn	33
Continental Divide, N. M.	71, 106	Dodge City	34

18

INDEX.

	PAGE		PAGE
Dolores Mission	249, 251	Fairview	134
Dorsey	81	Fenner	198
Dover	82	Fernando	238
Doyle	29	Fig Culture	191
Drake	157	Fisher's Peak	63
Drew	213	Flagstaff	119
Drummond	12	Florence	29
Duarte	205	Floyd	15
Dumas	14	Flying Fish	216
Dundee	33	Fort Defiance	107
Earl	62	Fort Leavenworth	19
Eastberne	213	Fort Madison	14
East Highlands	213	Fort Union	83
East Riverside	224	Fort Wingate	106
East Riverside to San Jacinto	224	Fossils	22
East Riverside to Temecula	224	Foster's	233
Edelstein	13	Fowler	242
Edson	198	Franconia	157
El Cajon Valley	232	Fresno	242
Ellinor	29	Fresno County, Cal.	242
Ellinwood	33	Fresno to Tracy, via Berenda and Lathrop	242
Elmdale	29		
Elmer	15	Fresno to Tracy, via Collis	247
Elota	98	Fruit Valley	33
El Rito	100	Fullerton	217
Elsinore	224	Fulton	84
El Toro	217	Galesburg	13
Emporia	28	Galisteo	96
Emporia Junction	28	Gallup	107
Encinitas	223	Garden City	36
Escondido	222	Garden of the Gods	55
Escondido Junction	222, 223	Garfield	33
Ethel	15	Garvanza	209
Etiwanda	204	Gary	12
Eudora	24	Gibbs	14
Evans	29	Gila Monster	112
Experimental Agricultural Station, Kansas	36	Gladysta	213
		Glenburn	240
Fair Oaks	207	Glendale	27

INDEX.

	PAGE		PAGE
Glendora	205	Hillside	79
Glen Eyrie	56	Hilton	47
Glenwood Springs	60	Hinckley	201
Glorieta	91	Hoehne's	62
Glorieta Pass	69, 91	Holbrook	114
Golden Gate	249	Holleys	47
Gorin	14	Holliday	24
Goshen Junction	240	Homer	198
Granada	47	Horners	29
Grand Cañon of the Colorado	120	Hot Springs Junction	140
Grand Caverns	56	Howell	36
Granite	135	Hualapai	156
Granite Cañon	59	Hurdland	14
Grant's	105	Hutchinson	31
Grape Culture	185	Hyde Park	213
Great Bend	33	Ibex	198
Green Mountain Falls	57	ILLINOIS	10
Grover	27	Ingalls	36
Gypsum	226	Inglewood	213
Hackberry	156	IOWA	14
Hagerman Pass	59	Iron Springs	62
Halstead	30	Irrigation	75, 77, 141
Hamburg	33	Irrigosa	242
Hancock	157	Irvine	217
Hanford	240	Irvington	203
Hardin	15	Isleta Pueblo	99
Hardy	115	Java	198
Harold	238	Jewfish	215
Harper	201	Joliet	12
Hart	15	KANSAS.	
Hartland	38	Historical	18
Haslett	198	Descriptive	20
Hebron	81	Climate	23
Herndon	242	Industrial	24
Hesperia	202	Kansas City	15
Hetch-Hetchy Valley	246	Kaster	157
Highland	213	Keenbrook	203
Highland Junction	203	Keene	238
Highland Park	209	Kendall	38

INDEX.

	PAGE		PAGE
Kent	31	Lathrop	247
Kenwood	14	Laura	13
Kernan	13	Lava Beds	71, 105, 132
Kern County, Cal.	239	Lavic	198
Kimberlena	240	Lawrence	25
Kingman	156	Leadville	59
Kingsburg	242	Lecompton	26
Kinsley	33	Leeds	13
Kinsman	13	Lemon Culture	184
Kirkland Valley	138	Lemont	12
Kite-shaped Track	211	Lerdo	240
Klinefelter	198	Leucadia	223
Knappa	12	Levy	83
Knox	13	Lewis	33
Koen	47	Lexington Junction	15
Kramer	201	Lick Observatory	256
Kroenig's	83	Lincoln Park	209
La Costa	223	Linda Rosa	224
Ladrillo	223	Linda Vista	223
Laguna, Cal.	217	Lingard	246
Laguna Pueblo, N. M.	101	Livingston	246
La Jolla Park	231	Lockport	12
La Junta	47, 62	Loma Alta	222
Lakeside	232	Lomax	14
Lake View	26	Lordsburg	205
Lakin	38	Lorenzo	13
Lamanda Park	206	Los Angeles	209
Lamar	47	Los Angeles Junction	222, 223
Lamy	92	Los Angeles to San Diego	216
Lancaster	238	Los Angeles to San Francisco	237
Lang, Cal.	238		
Lang, Kan.	28	Los Angeles to Santa Barbara	234
Lantry	38		
La Plata	15	Los Angeles to Santa Monica, Redondo, and Santa Catalina	213
Larned	33		
La Rose	13		
Las Animas	47	Los Baños	247
Las Flores	222	Los Cerrillos	97
Las Vegas	83	Los Nietos	217

INDEX.

	PAGE
Lucky Baldwin Ranch	205, 206
Ludlow	198
Luna	100
Lynn	79
Machado	213
Macksville	33
Macuta	14
Madera	244
Magnolia Avenue	225
Malaga	242
Manitou	52
Manitou Park	57
Mansfield	36
Manuelito	107
Marceline	15
Mariposa Grove	244
Martinez	247, 248
Marysville	261
Matilija Springs	235
Maxwell City	81
Maxwell Grant	79
Mayline	38
Mazon	13
McCarty's	105
McCook	12
McLellan	134
Media	14
Medill	14
Medway	38
Mellen	196
Mendon	15
Mendota	247
Menlo Park	250
Mennonites	30
Mentone	213
Merced	246
Merced County, Cal.	246
Mesa City	145
Mesa Encantada	103
Mesmer	213
Millsdale	12
Minturn	246
Mirage	238
Mission	30
Missions, California	162
Missions, New Mexico	66
Mississippi River Bridge	14
MISSOURI	14
Missouri River Bridge	15
Mistletoe	119
Mitchell	105
Modesto	247
Modjeska	217
Mojave	201, 238
Mojave Cañon	157
Mojave Desert	196
Mojave Indians	157, 196
Molino	213
Monica	13
Monrovia	205
Montecito	235, 236
Monterey	257
Moqui Snake Dance	116
Morena	223
Morgan	209
Morley	63
Morris	24
Morse	47
Murrieta	224
Muscatel	242
Nadeau Park	213
Nambé Pueblo	96
Napa	261
National City	223, 233
Navajo Reservation	116
Navajo Springs	114
Needles	157, 196
Nelson	156

	PAGE		PAGE
Nemo	13	Ontario	204
Neosho Valley	28	Orange	217, 226
Nettleton	33	Orange Culture	182
Newberry	198	Ormonde	14
New Boston	14	Oro Grande	202
Newcomb	15	Ortiz	96
Newhall	234, 238	Osage City	28
Newman	247	Ostrich Farming	192
NEW MEXICO.		Otay City	233
Historical	64	Otero	81
Descriptive	67	Pachappa	226
Climate	71	Pacific Beach	231
Industrial	75, 81	Pacoima	238
Newton	29	Painted Desert	133
Nickerson	33	Palemon	15
Nimrod	15	Palmdale	238
Niota	14	Palo Alto	255
Nolan	83	Pampa	238
Norborne	15	Partridge	33
Nordhoff	235	Pasadena	207
Northam	217	Pasadena Mountain Railway	207
North Cucamonga	204	Patterson	12
North Ontario	204	Pauline	28
North Pomona	205	Pawnee Rock	33
Oak Creek Cañon	132	Paxton	30
Oakland	248, 250	Peabody	29
Ocean Beach	231	Peach Springs	156
Oceanside	222	Pecos	91
Oceanside to Escondido	222	Pecos River and National Park	90
Oceanside to De Luz	223		
Offerle	34	Pecos Ruin (Mission and Pueblo)	87
Ojai Valley	235		
Old Camp Date Creek	138	Penitentes	85, 86
Oldtown	223	Perris	224
Olive	226	Peterton	28
Olive Culture	186	Phœnix	143
Oliver	15	Pierceville	36
Olivewood	207	Pike's Peak	53, 62
Onava	83	Pineveta	155

INDEX.

	PAGE
Pixley	240
Plevna	33
Plymouth	29
Point Loma	231
Point of Rocks, Ariz.	135
Point of Rocks, Cal.	202
Point of Rocks, Lower Cal.	233
Pomona	205
Ponemah	14
Pontoosuc	14
Port Costa	247, 248
Poso	240
Powell	157
Prairie Dog Towns	22
Prehistoric Ruins	147
Prescott	136
Prescott, Phœnix, and the Salt River Valley Region	134
Princeville	13
Prowers	47
Prune Culture	186
Pueblo	50
Pueblo Indians, 65, 71, 87, 96, 99, 101, 102, 106, 116.	
Putnam	115
Querino Cañon	114
Ransom	13
Raton	79
Raton Pass	63
Raton Tunnel	64
Ravenna	238
Rayado	83
Raymond, Cal.	209
Raymond, Cal.	246
Raymond, Kan.	33
Reading, Ill.	13
Reading, Kan.	28
Redlands	213
Red Mesa	156

	PAGE
Redondo Beach	214
Red Rock Cañon	60
Revere	14
Rhodes	134
Rialto	204
Rincon, Cal.	226
Rio de Chelly	107
Rio Grande del Norte	70
Rio Puerco	100
Riordan	134
Ripon	247
Rivera	217
Riverside	224
Riverview	233
Robinson	47
Rochester	204
Rogers	201
Romeo	13
Romero	84
Rosamond	238
Rosario	97
Rothville	15
Rowe	87
Rutledge	14
Sacramento	261
Saffordville	29
Salida	247
Salt River Valley	140
Salt Wells	31
San Antonio Cañon	205
San Bernardino	203
San Bernardino to Los Angeles	204
San Bernardino to San Diego, via Short Line	224
San Buenaventura Mission	234
Sanders	114
San Diego	223, 227
San Diego Mission	228

	PAGE		PAGE
San Dimas	205	Santiago Cañon	217
San Domingo Pueblo	97	Saticoy	234
Sands	84	Saugus	234, 238
San Francisco	249	Scranton	28
San Francisco Peaks	127	Seligman	155
San Gabriel Cañon	205	Selma	242
San Gabriel Mission	207	Selwyn	223
San Jacinto	224	Sepulveda	238
San Joaquin Valley	238	Seven Castles	60
San Jose, Cal.	256	Seven Falls	52
San Jose, N. M.	100	Sheffield	15
San Juan	219	Sherlock	38
San Juan Capistrano Mission	217	Sherman	33
San Luis Obispo	260	Shoemaker	83
San Marcos	222	Siberia	198
San Mateo Mountains	105	Sibley	15
San Miguel	84	Simpson's Rest	63
San Miguel Island	237	Skull Valley	137
San Onofre	222	Slauson	213
San Rafael	250	Smithshire	14
Santa Ana	217	Sorrento	223
Santa Anita	206	South Pasadena	207
Santa Barbara	235	South Riverside	226
Santa Barbara Mission	236	South Santa Monica	213
Santa Catalina Island	214	Spanish Peaks	62
Santa Clara Valley, Northern California	254	Speareville	34
		Spencer	27
Santa Clara Valley, Southern California	234	Springer	82
		Stafford	33
Santa Cruz	258	Standard Time	34
Santa Cruz Island	237	Stanislaus County, Cal.	247
Santa Fé	92	Starkville	63
Santa Fé Springs	217	Starvation Peak	84
Santa Fé Trail	19, 63	Sterling	33
Santa Margarita Ranch	223	Sterry	29
Santa Monica	214	St. John	33
Santa Paula	234	St. Joseph, Ariz.	115
Santa Rosa	261	Stockton	260
Santa Rosa Island	237	Streator	13

INDEX. 281

	PAGE		PAGE
Strong City	29	Turlock	246
Stronghurst	14	Turner	24
Sulzbacher	84	Tyrone	62
Summit, Cal.	202	Ute Park	57
Summit, N. M.	105	Ute Pass	52, 56, 57
Supai	134	Vallejo Junction	247, 248
Surrey	13	Ventura	234
Sweetwater Dam	233	Verona	13
Sylvia	33	Victor	202
Syracuse	38	Victoria	213
Tagus	240	Vincent	238
Taos Pueblo	82	Visalia	240
Tecumseh	27	Vista	222
Tedens	12	Volcanic Cones and Lava	
Tehachapi	238	Beds	132
Tehachapi Pass	238	Wade	238
Tejunga	238	Wagon Mound	83
Temecula	224	Wakarusa	28
Temecula Cañon	224	Waldo	97
Tempe	145	Wallace	97
Tesuque Pueblo	96	Walnut	119
Thatcher	62	Walnut Culture	190
Tia Juana	233	Walnut Grove	137
Timpas	62	Walton	29
Tipton, Cal.	240	Waterman	201
Tipton, N. M.	83	Watrous	83
Tokay	240	Wawona	246
Toluca	13	Wayne	15
Topeka	27	Weaver	24
Tracy	247	West Glendale	238
Tracy to San Francisco, via		Whipple Barracks	136
Port Costa	247	Wickenburg	139
Traver	242	Wilburn	13
Trinidad	62	Wilder	24
Tropico	238	Wildesin	213
Truxton	156	Wildomar	224
Tulare	240	Williams	134
Tulare County, Cal.	240	Williams Cañon	56
Tunnel	238	Williamsfield	13

	PAGE		PAGE
Willow Springs	12	Yampai	156
Wingate	106	Yorba	226
Winslow	115	Yosemite Valley	244
Wiseburn	214	Ysidora	223
Woodland Park	57	Yucca	157
Wooten	63	Yucca Brevifolia	202
Wright	34	Zenith	33
Wyaconda	14	Zuñi Pueblo	106

www.ingramcontent.com/pod-product-compliance
Lightning Source LLC
Chambersburg PA
CBHW032117230426
43672CB00009B/1766